Into the Mess and Other Jesus Stories

# Into the Mess and Other Jesus Stories

*—— Reflections on the Life of Christ ——*

Debie Thomas

CASCADE *Books* · Eugene, Oregon

INTO THE MESS AND OTHER JESUS STORIES
Reflections on the Life of Christ

Cascade Books
An Imprint of Wipf and Stock Publishers
199 W. 8th Ave., Suite 3
Eugene, OR 97401

www.wipfandstock.com

PAPERBACK ISBN: 978-1-6667-0622-2
HARDCOVER ISBN: 978-1-6667-0623-9
EBOOK ISBN: 978-1-6667-0624-6

*Cataloguing-in-Publication data:*

Names: Thomas, Debie, author.

Title: Into the mess and other Jesus stories : reflections on the life of Christ / by Debie Thomas.

Description: Eugene, OR : Cascade Books, 2022 | Includes bibliographical references.

Identifiers: ISBN 978-1-6667-0622-2 (paperback) | ISBN 978-1-6667-0623-9 (hardcover) | ISBN 978-1-6667-0624-6 (ebook)

Subjects: LCSH: Christian life. | Bible. New Testament. | Bible—Theology. | Jesus Christ.

Classification: BV4501.2 .T480 2022 (print) | BV4501.2 .T480 (ebook)

05/13/22

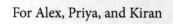

For Alex, Priya, and Kiran

"What you must realize, what you must even come to praise, is the fact that there is no *right way* that is going to become apparent to you once and for all. The most blinding illumination that strikes and perhaps radically changes your life will be so attenuated and obscured by doubts and dailiness that you may one day come to suspect the truth of that moment at all. The calling that seemed so clear will be lost in echoes of questionings and indecision; the church that seemed to save you will fester with egos, complacencies, banalities; the deepest love of your life will work itself like a thorn in your heart until all you can think of is plucking it out. Wisdom is accepting the truth of this. Courage is persisting with life in spite of it. And faith is finding yourself, in the deepest part of your soul, in the very heart of who you are, moved to praise it."

—CHRISTIAN WIMAN[1]

"I am a Christian," I concluded, "because the story of Jesus is still the story I'm willing to risk being wrong about."

—RACHEL HELD EVANS[2]

1. Wiman, *My Bright Abyss*, 29–30.
2. Evans, *Inspired*, 164.

# Contents

MYSTERIES

# Acknowledgments

My deepest gratitude to:

Dan Clendenin, and the Board and readers of *Journey with Jesus,* for supporting my writing and giving these essays their first home.

The staff and readers of *The Christian Century.* Thank you for welcoming my work in your pages.

The team at Cascade Books, in particular my editor, Charlie Collier. Thank you for making this dream a reality.

The beautiful people of St. Mark's Episcopal Church, Palo Alto, my spiritual home, for strengthening my faith with your kindness and generosity.

My priests of recent years: the Reverends Matthew McDermott, Salying Wong, Ricardo Avila, Lindy Bunch, and Nikky Wood, for your wisdom, honesty, patience, and trust. I have been shepherded so well.

My spiritual director, Liz Lawhead Stewart. Thank you for guiding this wanderer on her journey.

My fierce and brilliant "Committee"—Anne Turnbow-Raustol, Jennifer Seidel, Amy Olrick, Cheri Bowling, and Debby Prum. Where would I be without you, my sisters?

Erin McGraw, for the gift of your friendship and for mentoring me in life and on the page. You are everywhere in this book.

My parents, my extended family, and my ancestors, for introducing me to Jesus and giving me a rich heritage of faith to explore.

Alex, Priya, and Kiran, my dear ones. Thank you for putting up with my writing life and for loving me through joy and sorrow, faith and doubt. I'm so blessed to live the messiness with you.

# Introduction

I don't like messes, in life or in faith. I doubt I'm alone; no one chooses Christianity because they crave unruliness or disruption. In fact, many of us embrace religious faith for the opposite reason; we assume—and our churches encourage us to believe—that our spiritual commitments will keep life neat and orderly.

At the same time, many of us twenty-first-century believers are tired of religious language and imagery that skirt the messiness of our lived lives. We're weary of platitudes, easy answers, and quick "fixes" that fix nothing. We might want tidiness, but we also want a faith with hard edges—a robust and relevant faith that integrates the hard stuff of our days and still makes possible transcendence and joy. We desire honesty. Authenticity. Complexity. A faith, a language, and a practice that enable us to inhabit life on earth as it is, here and now. Poet and theologian Christian Wiman describes this as a craving for "speech that is true to the transcendent nature of grace yet adequate to the hard reality in which daily faith operates." Both "the poetry *and* the prose of knowing."[1]

For the past eight years, I've written reflections on the stories of Jesus. The stories he told, the stories he lived, the stories he encountered through the men and women he met along the way. What I have attempted in these reflective essays is integration, the honest and unapologetic "speech" Wiman describes. How can I bring the ancient stories of Jesus to bear on the messy circumstances of contemporary life? What grace, meaning, and challenge might the Gospel stories offer, as we inhabit our own narratives of love and loss, hope and fear?

Though I grew up in the church—a preacher's kid, a Bible nerd—I spent decades relating to Jesus from an abstracted distance. I prayed to him. I sang about him. I believed in him. But at a fundamental level, he remained

---

1. Wiman, *My Bright Abyss*, 4.

a stranger. Someone I embraced in theology, creed, and doctrine, but not in the fray, not in the messy business of real life.

I've written these reflections first and foremost for myself, hoping that my knowledge *about* Jesus, gleaned from years of Sunday School lessons, Bible studies, Sunday sermons, and religion classes, might evolve into something more intimate, more personal, and more nuanced. For as long as I can remember, I've written in order to figure out my life, especially my life with God. I don't write as an expert, but as a fellow traveler, hungry to explore the questions that matter, hungry to circle the pathways of my life until I see old things with new eyes. T. S. Eliot describes the journey as cyclical, but also startling: "We shall not cease from exploration, and the end of all our exploring will be to arrive where we started, and know the place for the first time."[2]

I've written these fifty essays to explore, to question, to push, to resist, and to surrender. Most of all, I've written in order to make discoveries about the Messiah I yearn to know and love as a friend. Who *was* Jesus, the charismatic rabbi who walked the earth two-thousand years ago, healing, storytelling, saving, and dying? And who *is* Jesus, the resurrected one we now call the Christ? What does he ask of us? What kind of story is he inviting us into? And why?

The essays are personal and "occasional," in the sense that they reflect the particulars of my life as a daughter, a wife, a mother, a post-evangelical Christian, a lay minister, and a South Asian American woman living in northern California in the early decades of the twenty-first century. But they also exceed these confines in the sense that they seek the eternal and universal Jesus of Scripture, history, liturgy, and tradition. They don't offer a full portrait—only glimpses of the Christ I continue to discover.

The process of writing has been a process of finding. What I've found is a Jesus who is much more comfortable with life's messes than I am. A Jesus who preferred the unwashed and unloved to the polished and perfect. A Jesus whose piety compelled him to break the Sabbath, feast with sinners, and wield a whip in God's house. A Jesus who experienced first-hand the plight of the refugee and the prisoner. A Jesus whose most loyal friends included bleeding women and despised tax collectors, and whose fiercest enemies included the religious elite and the politically powerful.

Jesus is not who I thought he was. His ways are not my ways. The life he offers is not the life of safety, immunity, and order I'd choose if I could. And this is *good* news.

2. Eliot, *Four Quartets*, 27.

I've divided the essays in this book into four sections. The divisions aren't perfect—several essays could meaningfully belong in more than one—but hopefully, the sections offer the collection a structure and a chronology.

The first section, "Encounters," focuses on the men and women Jesus crossed paths with—the family members, friends, followers, critics, and enemies who entered into his life and found themselves changed as a result. The section begins with the first people who found themselves caught up in Jesus's story—Mary, Joseph, and John the Baptist. An essay on Jesus's forty days in the wilderness reflects on Jesus's encounter with himself—his identity, his vocation, and his vulnerabilities as a human being facing the realities of evil. The section then opens out into myriad encounters. How did Jesus interact with the people of his time? With religious authorities? With women? With the poor, the rich, the forgotten, the powerful, and the oppressed? What drew people to him? Who embraced him? Who resisted?

The second section, "Wonders," looks at the Jesus stories we call "miraculous." I consider the Jesus who healed the sick, fed the hungry, calmed the storm, liberated the demon-possessed, and raised the dead. What are we to make of these amazing, baffling stories? How might we hold in productive tension the miracle stories of the Gospels and our contemporary experiences of pain, loss, and unanswered prayer? What might it look like for us to carry forward the sacred work of healing and liberation that Jesus modeled?

In the third section, "Teachings," I reflect on Jesus's parables and sermons. My intention in this section is not to reduce the richness of Christian teaching to something formulaic, but to hold Jesus's wisdom in its strangeness, challenge, and paradox. There's a reason he liked to tell stories; stories are layered and multifaceted. They resist summary and exceed interpretation. They invite our engagement and creativity and excite our imaginations. In exploring Jesus's teachings, I have learned not to seek answers, but to ask more and better questions.

The last section of the book, which I've entitled "Mysteries," focuses on the death, resurrection, and post-resurrection appearances of Jesus. I reflect on his last, tender days with his disciples; the scandal, agony, and beauty of the cross; and the slow dawning of new life that began with an empty tomb in a quiet garden on Easter morning. Holy Week holds within it our entire human story, all of the hope, tragedy, love, and joy that shapes our days. It shows us the horrors of evil and injustice. It reveals the depths of Christ's love. And it epitomizes the power of God to defeat injustice, conquer death, and renew all things. All of this is a mystery, and I don't presume to explain it. These essays seek only to gaze upon the mystery in ways that might change and enliven us.

Of course, to write about Jesus at all is to delve into mystery. He is the son of a carpenter and the son of humanity. He is a first-century Jewish rabbi and the second person of the Holy Trinity. He is a convicted criminal and he is God Incarnate. He is a wounded scar-bearer and he is the Great Physician. He is the Crucified One and he is Risen.

In other words, his is a story that takes us into complicated territory. Hard territory. Messy territory. To choose Jesus is to choose not a sanitized religion, not a tidy existence devoid of confusion and contradiction, but the possibilities that emerge when we embrace truth in all of its facets. Truth beyond piety. Truth beyond denial. Truth too rich and resonant for bumper-sticker theologies.

Jesus invites us "into the mess" because he knows how resurrection works. Loss precedes recovery. Grief precedes joy. Surrender precedes victory. Death precedes life.

The invitation embedded in the Gospels is ongoing; we will never exhaust, outrun, or deplete it, because the love at its heart is infinite. My hope for these essays is that they extend to you an invitation and a welcome. As you enter deeply into the stories of Jesus, may your own longings, hopes, and questions guide you. May you find meaning in the search, the yearning, the mess. May the Christ you seek find you, and in the finding, may you know joy.

# Encounters

"He never approached from on high, but always in
the midst, in the midst of people, in the midst of
real life and the questions that real life asks."

—FREDERICK BUECHNER[1]

1. Buechner, *The Magnificent Defeat*, 87.

# The God Bearer
## Luke 1:26–38

*In the sixth month the angel Gabriel was sent by God to a town in Galilee called Nazareth, to a virgin engaged to a man whose name was Joseph, of the house of David. The virgin's name was Mary. (Luke 1:26–27)*

I was seven years old when I graduated from the ranks of lambs and donkeys to play Mary in a church Christmas pageant. I remember feeling quite sophisticated the first time I donned her light blue gown and white head scarf. I practiced my lines for days and worked hard not to break character until Gabriel tripped over his enormous wings during dress rehearsal and fell flat on his face.

For all the chaos of those childhood performances, there was something straightforward back then about Mary. Kneeling on stage with my head demurely covered and my eyes glued on the baby doll in the manger, I didn't think much about what Mary's choices might have cost her. Her decision to say yes to God seemed unremarkable to me, her obedience easy.

How times have changed. At this stage in my faith journey, nothing about the mother of Jesus feels straightforward. Like so many others raised in the church, I have baggage around the mother of Jesus. Depending on what faith background we come from, the baggage looks different. I grew up in a tradition that poured its energies into minimizing Mary's role in Jesus's story. I was taught early on that Mary is *not* God and *not* an intermediary, and that I should *not* allow my curiosity about her to upstage the Son of God.

Some of us carry a different kind of baggage. We were given the "virgin mother" as an impossible ideal to measure ourselves against. We were taught to conflate sexual abstinence with spiritual purity, or told that heterosexual marriage and motherhood are the only appropriately feminine paths open to women. Some of us were led to believe that Mary's docility, submissiveness, and self-effacement are the aspects of faith God values most.

All of this is regrettable, because there is so much more to Mary's story than what we've inherited. At its heart, Mary's story is about what happens when a human being encounters the divine and decides of her own volition to lean into that encounter. The Gospel of Luke makes it abundantly clear that there is nothing straightforward about saying yes to God. Mary's yes is layered and complicated. Even as it blesses and elevates her, it also bewilders and pierces her. Her yes is costly. Her yes is dangerous. Her yes is lonely. But her yes is also what enables her to craft a coherent and joyful life.

In pondering Mary's yes, we are invited to consider what our own might look like. What can we anticipate if we give our consent to God? What will happen within and around us if we agree to bear God into the world? Who will we become, and who will God become, in the long aftermath of our consent?

As I reflect on the many meanings of Mary's yes in Luke's famous Annunciation story (Luke 1:26–38), five lines in the text stand out:

- Greetings, highly favored one.

- But she was much perplexed.

- You will bear.

- Here I am.

- Then the angel departed from her.

The first is the line Gabriel uses to begin the conversation: "Greetings, highly favored one!" I *love* this line, because it's more than a greeting; it's a naming ceremony. The angel begins by giving Mary a new name, a new identity, a new possibility of seeing herself in the light of how God sees her.

Specifically, the name Mary receives is a name bursting at the seams with God's delight. It's a name that says, "Mary, God sees you. God smiles upon you. God holds you in God's gaze with pleasure and tenderness. God rejoices, basks, *dances,* at the very thought of you."

I love that in this first moment of sacred encounter, the divine messenger's move is not to indict, instruct, convict, or diminish. It is to bestow favor. What would the church look like in the eyes of the world, I wonder, if we followed Gabriel's example and made God's delight our foundation?

Consider what this favoring of Mary reveals about God's character. Consider how it speaks to the vulnerability of God, who freely chooses limits, surrenders power, and entrusts a tiny, naked infant to fallible human beings like ourselves.

Consider what it reveals about the gynecology of God, who includes the most intimate spaces and capacities of a woman's body in the work of the Incarnation, as if to say: these spaces, these processes, these capacities—the very ones that are often devalued, policed, and shamed in human cultures—are precious. They constitute sacred ground. They, too, are temples for the holy.

Consider what it reveals about the priorities of God, who instructs the angel to rename Mary at the *beginning* of their encounter, indicating that Mary is God's highly favored one before she says or does anything to earn it. In her ignorance, in her lowliness, before anything else transpires in the story of her faith—she is favored already.

I know that Mary is often described as docile, but I see something remarkably bold in her willingness to receive and to rest in the delight of her Creator. Imagine the audacity of this young peasant girl, scandalously pregnant, peddling an angel story that no one will believe, living on the unremarkable outskirts of empire, to declare without shame or apology that she is highly favored of God. This is not the song of a spiritually timid human being. This is the song of a young woman who is passionately in love with a God who is passionately in love with her.

In contrast, I fear that many of us never allow ourselves to lean into God's delight. We shy away from our re-naming, not daring to entertain the possibility that God's gaze lingers on us in love. We wear ourselves out, trying to earn what God longs to lavish on us for free.

What would it be like to stop striving? What would it be like to allow divine joy, delight, and pleasure to become our bedrock?

The second line I appreciate in the Annunciation story describes Mary's confusion: "But she was much perplexed." We wrongly assume that Mary's inner life is a spiritual blank slate before the angel shows up at her door, but of course this is not true. Mary grows up in a faithful Jewish community. We know from the Magnificat that she is well-versed in the Hebrew Scriptures; she knows the spiritual history of her people. She recognizes her God as the God of Miriam, of Hannah, of Judith, and of Deborah—a compassionate God who delivers the oppressed out of slavery and secures a homeland for the exiled.

In other words, Mary already has a vibrant relationship with God before Gabriel shows up. It is not that the Annunciation leads her out of doubt and into faith; it is that her encounter with the angel leads her out of certainty and into holy bewilderment. Out of familiar spiritual territory and into a lifetime of pondering, wondering, questioning, and wrestling. *She was much perplexed.* Or, as she puts it to Gabriel: "How can this be?"

Like Mary, I was raised with a fairly precise and comprehensive picture of who God is and how God operates in the world. If anyone had asked me to describe God when I was fifteen, twenty, or thirty years old, I would have rattled off a list of divine attributes as readily as a kindergart-ner recites the alphabet: "God is omnipotent, omniscient, and omnipres-ent. God is Three and God is One. God is holy, perfect, loving, righteous, merciful, just, and sovereign."

In other words, I would have insisted that I had God and religion more or less down, and that whatever gaps remained in my knowledge would be filled in along the way—the point of the Christian life being to grow in absolute certainty about the sacred.

What an interesting shock reality has been. Who knew that my life with God would actually be one long goodbye? That to know God is to *unknow* God? To shed my neat conceptions of the divine like so many old snakeskins and emerge into the world bare, vulnerable, and new, again and again?

This, of course, is what Mary has to do in the aftermath of Gabriel's announcement. She has to consent to evolve. To wonder. To stretch. She has to learn that faith and doubt are not opposites—that beyond all the easy platitudes and pieties of religion, we serve a God who dwells in mystery. If we agree to embark on a journey with this God, we will face periods of bewilderment.

But this frightens us, so we compartmentalize our spiritual lives, trying to hold our relationships with God at a sanitized remove from our actual circumstances. We don't realize that such efforts leave us with a faith that's rigid, inflexible, and stale. In his wise and beautiful memoir, *My Bright Abyss,* poet Christian Wiman writes,

> Life is not an error, even when it is. That is to say, whatever faith
> you emerge with at the end of your life is going to be not simply
> affected by that life, but intimately dependent upon it, for faith
> in God is, in the deepest sense, faith in life—which means that
> even the staunchest life is a life of great change. It follows that
> if you believe at fifty what you believed at fifteen, then you have
> not lived—or have denied the reality of your life.[1]

In other words, it's when our inherited beliefs collide with the messy cir-cumstances of our lives that we go from a two-dimensional faith to one that is vibrant and textured.

The third line I want to call attention to is the hardest one of the five: "You will bear." The literal ending to that sentence is, "You will bear a son," which of course, Mary does. But as we know from the rest of her story, she bears a lot more than an infant, and her many "bearings" teach us more than we want to know about the life of faith. Here is a list, just for starters:

1. Wiman, *My Bright Abyss,* 7.

Mary bears the scandal of an unplanned pregnancy in a culture that shuns or stones women in her condition. She bears the suspicion and disappointment of her fiancé, Joseph, and then bears whatever scars his distrust leaves on their marriage over the long haul. She bears the pain of labor and delivery in threadbare circumstances, far from her home and kin. She bears the terror of all refugees who flee their homes and homelands to save the lives of their children. She bears the complicated guilt and relief of the survivor, whose own baby lives while countless others in Herod's realm die.

She bears the horror of all parents whose children go missing, and when she finally finds her twelve-year-old boy discussing theology in the temple, she bears the bewilderment of having a child who is already surpassing her, becoming a young man whom she can neither contain nor comprehend. She bears the financial risk of her firstborn leaving the stable vocation of carpentry to become an itinerant preacher and would-be Messiah. She bears a fierce mixture of pride and embarrassment when he returns to Nazareth with his band of ragtag disciples and appalls her extended family with his unconventional views on God, faith, and the temple.

As Jesus's ministry expands and begins to get sinister pushback, she bears the terrible fear that he is going too far, risking too much, and generating too much controversy for his own good. She bears the resentful whispers of her other children, who conclude that their big brother is insane. Maybe, in her secret heart, in her darkest moments, she bears the possibility that they are right.

When things come to a head on that Friday we now call Good, Mary, like so many mothers and fathers across history, stands under a lynching tree and bears the pain of watching her child die at the hands of unjust empire and complicit religion. Alongside that horror, she bears the public humiliation of having a supposed criminal for a son.

Finally, after the best of the best happens—after the tomb is emptied, death is destroyed, and every hope of her heart is realized—Mary casts her eyes upward forty days after Easter and bears one more letting go, as the child she carried in her own body ascends away from her.

*You will bear.* Or, to use the prophetic Simeon's chilling words, "A sword will pierce your own soul."

We so want this to be untrue. We want to say yes to God without saying yes to the sword. We want to be God-bearers without bearing what the vocation demands. But to say yes as Mary does *is* to say yes to the sword. Poet and Benedictine oblate, Kathleen Norris once wrote that "one of the most astonishing and precious things about motherhood is the brave way in which woman consent to give birth to creatures who will one day die."[2]

This is not a courage unique to mothers. To love anyone in this broken world takes tenacity and grit, long-suffering and great strength. Anybody who tells you otherwise—anyone who peddles ease as a go-to reward of Christianity—is lying. Mary's story testifies to the fact that, sometimes, we are called to bear, but not save. To accompany, but not cure. To hold, but not fix. To sow, but not reap.

The particularities of our own stories might differ from Mary's, but the weight and cost of "bearing" remain the same—and so does the grace. When we consent to bear the unbearable, we learn a new kind of hope. A hope set free from expectation and frenzy. A resurrected hope that doesn't need or want easy answers. A hope that accepts the grayness of things and leaves room for mystery.

When we consent to carry God's love out into the world, we learn how small and stingy our own resources are, and how inexhaustible God's resources are in comparison. We discover that we don't have to give birth to love all by ourselves; God's Spirit hovers over us when we're depleted, creating fresh wells of compassion, empathy, tenderness, and strength. In ways we might not recognize until years later, God comes and makes the work of bearing possible.

The fourth line I'm drawn to in the story is my favorite: "Mary said, 'Here I am.'" I know that the more theologically consequential line is the next one, the one where Mary officially gives Gabriel her consent: "Let it be with me according to your word." But for me, the "here I am" moment that precedes the yes is gorgeously significant, and I want to linger over it.

Often, we minimize the fact that God desires our wholeness, coherence, and integrity as human beings made in God's image. We jump too quickly to surrender, renunciation, and death-to-self. In our zeal to preach self-denial, we miss a crucial first step. We forget that before we can give ourselves away, we need to have coherent selves capable of that giving.

This is true for all of us, but it's especially true for people on the margins. People who've been historically silenced. People who have been told that their selfhood is expendable, worthless, or dangerous. People who have never been allowed to rest and revel in the *imago Dei* which is their birthright. People who have been shamed and traumatized for some integral aspect of who they are—their race, their ethnicity, their culture, their gender, their sexuality, their appearance, their faith.

---

2. Norris, *The Cloister Walk*, 24.

In a world that diminishes so many people, I'm grateful for the boldness of the girl-child, Mary, standing at the cusp of everything in the presence of God's own messenger and saying without inhibition, "Here I am. Here is all of me, coherent and whole, free and unfettered, ready and receptive, fearful and faithful. Exactly as you, oh God, have created me. Here I am."

I know that for us contemporary Christians, the "virgin mother" business feels like a stretch. I wonder if we might hold the paradox like this: Mary the virgin is one-in-herself, whole and free, unhindered and open, able to come before God with an absolute newness and freshness of heart. And it is *out* of that virginity, that essential and authentic wholeness, that she is able to become Mary the mother: a radically self-giving human being mature enough to provide a nurturing home for the Son of God.

To say yes to God is to say yes to the promise of wholeness, both for ourselves and for the world, and to stand firmly against all violations of that wholeness.

The last line I want to lift up is the closing line of the story: "Then the angel departed from her."

When I read Luke's account of the Annunciation, I can't help but wonder what might have happened if Gabriel stuck around after Mary's yes. How different her experience would have been if the angel had said, "You know what, Mary? The next nine months are going to be rough for you. Shoot, the next thirty years are going to be rough for you! I think I'll take a leave of absence from heaven, camp out down here, and stick by you for a while. If anyone has an issue with your pregnancy or with your child, you can refer them to me."

But that is not how the story unfolds. Mary doesn't get a shining side-kick after the Annunciation. The glow fades, the angel departs, and Mary is left to do the ongoing work of discernment and discipleship on her own.

I imagine there are days when she longs for Gabriel to come back and reassure her. When she pleads with God to give her critics some irrefutable proof that she isn't delusional, that the child growing in her body is in fact the Christ.

We know what this feels like, don't we? We've all been there. We've all experienced the moment when the epiphany ends, the vision recedes, the clarity fades. It's the moment after the yes, the moment when the glowing mountaintop experience dissolves into memory, and we are left to obey God in the muck of life down in the valley.

We have a choice in such moments. We can chase elusive mountain-tops, expending all of our energy in the pursuit of one spiritual high after another. Or we can choose what Mary chooses. We can offer God our creativity, our patience, our own active and robust participation in the work of bearing Jesus into the world. We can dare to trust that the God who chose the womb of a colonized peasant girl two-thousand years ago still chooses the ordinary, unexceptional stuff of our everyday lives to birth the Messiah into our midst. To say yes to God is to say yes to the silence *after* the divine announcement. It is to trust that even in the valley where nothing shimmers, nothing will be impossible with God.

Mary's story is a story about what happens when a human being encounters the divine and decides of her own volition to lean into that encounter. I hope that we, like the God-bearer herself, will lean in and say yes to the God who has said yes to us. As we do so, may the courage, faith, and joy of Mary be ours, and may the Holy Spirit who hovered over her body to quicken the life of her Son, quicken us to new life as well.

# Into the Mess
## Matthew 1:18–25

*Her husband Joseph, being a righteous man and unwilling to ex-*
*pose her to public disgrace, planned to dismiss her quietly. But just*
*when he had resolved to do this, an angel of the Lord appeared to*
*him in a dream and said, "Joseph, son of David, do not be afraid*
*to take Mary as your wife, for the child conceived in her is from the*
*Holy Spirit." (Matt 1:19–20)*

Who gives Joseph a thought once Christmas is over? The poor carpenter who dreams dreams; he's so easy to sideline. He barely speaks
in the Gospels, his pivotal narrative moments occur while he's asleep, and
he fades from sight soon after Jesus's infancy. According to the Gospel of
Matthew, though, Joseph's role in the Incarnation is pivotal. It is the humble
carpenter's willingness to abandon his notions of holiness and embrace the
scandalous that allows the miracle of Christ's arrival to unfold. As Matthew
makes clear, the Messiah must come from the house and lineage of David,
so it rests on Joseph to give Mary's child his name and legitimacy. The fulfillment of ancient prophecy rests on him.

Matthew describes Joseph as a "righteous man," which is to say, a
man devoted to God and concerned with ethical living. Though Matthew
doesn't elaborate, we can assume that Mary's fiancé is not a guy who likes
to make waves, call attention to himself, or venture close to controversy.
Like most of us, he wants an orderly life. He's honest and hardworking,
he follows the rules, and he expects to lead an uncomplicated life in exchange. Is that too much to ask?

Poor Joseph.

As Matthew tells the story, the God-fearing descendent of King David
wakes up one morning to find his world shattered. His betrothed is pregnant,
he knows that he is not the father, and suddenly, he has no good options to
choose from. If he calls attention to Mary's pregnancy, she might be stoned to
death, as Levitical law proscribes. If he divorces her quietly, she'll be reduced

11

to begging or prostitution to support herself and the child. If he marries her, *her* son will be Joseph's heir, and Joseph's biological offspring will not. Moreover, Joseph will be tainted by the scandal of Mary's illicit pregnancy and by her ridiculous claim that the baby's dad is somehow God.

Matthew doesn't go into much detail about Joseph's anguish. However, the *Protoevangelium of James,* an extracanonical text from the second century CE, gives us a fuller, harsher picture of the carpenter's pain.[1] When Joseph sees Mary's swollen belly, he throws himself on the ground, strikes his own face, and cries bitterly. He wonders long and hard how to respond and asks Mary why she has betrayed him so cruelly.

Though this text isn't in our canon, it's not hard to imagine a similar scene playing out between Joseph and Mary in real life. The fact is, Joseph doesn't believe Mary's story until Gabriel tells him to. Why would he? Why would anyone?

We make a mistake when we sanitize Joseph's consent. We distort his humanity if we assume that his acceptance of God's plan comes easily. In fact, what Joseph's pain shows me is that God's favor is not the shiny, anodyne thing I'd like to believe it is. It's not the God of the New Testament who promises us wealth, health, comfort, and ease. That's just me, getting it wrong.

In choosing Joseph to be Jesus's earthly father, God leads a righteous man with an impeccable reputation straight into doubt, shame, scandal, and controversy. God's call requires Joseph to reorder everything he thinks he knows about fairness, justice, goodness, and purity. It requires him to become the talk of the town—and not in a good way. It requires him to embrace a mess he has not created, to love a woman whose story he doesn't understand, to protect a baby he didn't father, to accept an heir who is not his son.

In other words, God's messy plan of salvation requires Joseph—a quiet, cautious, status quo kind of guy—to choose precisely what he fears and dreads the most. The fraught, the complicated, the suspicious, and the inexplicable. So much for living a well-ordered life.

Then again, Joseph's story gives me hope. I can't relate to a person who leaps headlong into obedience. I *can* relate, however, to a person who struggles, a person whose acceptance of God's will is cautious and ambivalent. I'm grateful that Joseph's choice is a hard one. I'm glad he struggles, because I struggle, too.

Interestingly, in the verses that immediately precede Joseph's story, Matthew gives us a genealogy of Jesus's ancestors. He mentions Abraham,

---

1. Vuong, *The Protoevangelium of James,* 1–116.

the patriarch who abandons his son, Ishmael, and twice endangers his wife's safety in order to save his own skin. He mentions Jacob, the trickster usurper who humiliates his older brother and his father-in-law. He mentions David, who sleeps with another man's wife and then orders that man's murder to protect his own reputation. He mentions Tamar, who pretends to be a sex worker, and Rahab, who is one. These are just a few representative samples.

Notice anything? Anything like messiness? Complication? Scandal? Imperfection? How interesting that God, who is free to choose any genealogy for the Christ, chooses a long line of broken, imperfect, dishonorable, and scandalous people. The perfect backdrop, I suppose, for God's relentless work of restoration, healing, and hope.

There is much to ponder in the Nativity story, much to consider about the surprising ways of God. What kind of God brings salvation to the world via a young woman whose story about her own sex life is not believed? Via a well-meaning man who has to let go of righteousness in order to follow God? Via a cultural system obsessed with male honor and female purity? Via the flimsiness of dreams? Via a helpless, illegitimate baby?

No wonder the angel Gabriel's first words to Joseph are, "Do not be afraid." If we want to enter into God's messy story, then perhaps these are the first words we need to hear, too. *Do not be afraid.* Do not be afraid when God's work in your life looks alarmingly different than you thought it would. Do not be afraid when God upends your cherished assumptions about piety and faithfulness. Do not be afraid when God asks you to stand alongside the scandalous, the defiled, the suspected, and the shamed. Do not be afraid when God asks you to love something or someone more than your spotless reputation. Do not be afraid when your role in the story feels minor, and the spotlight of fame and fortune doesn't land on you. Do not be afraid of the precarious, the fragile, the vulnerable, the impossible.

Do not be afraid of the mess. Embrace it. The mess is where God enters the world.

# What Kind of Story Is This?

## Matthew 11:2–11

*When John heard in prison what the Messiah was doing, he sent word by his disciples and said to him, "Are you the one who is to come, or are we to wait for another?" (Matt 11:2–3)*

"All sorrows can be borne," the Danish writer Isak Dinesan once said, "if you put them into a story."[1] I wonder if John the Baptist, the grizzled forerunner of Jesus, would agree. *Are* all sorrows bearable? *Can* all human griefs find redemption in stories?

Consider this example: a faithless king forsakes his own wife to marry his brother's. When a truth-telling prophet condemns the dishonorable marriage, the king's new wife seethes, and the king—ignoring his own conscience—imprisons the prophet. Soon afterwards, the king throws himself a birthday party, gets drunk, and invites his stepdaughter to dance for his guests. Her performance "pleases" him so much that he promises her anything she desires, even up to half of his kingdom. The girl (spurred on by her mother) demands the imprisoned prophet's death. Unwilling to lose face in front of his guests, the king reluctantly keeps his promise. Before the birthday party is over, the girl receives the prophet's head on a platter.

This is a story. Is it a bearable one?

Here's its prelude: One day, an angel of God appears to an elderly priest who is serving in the temple. The angel promises the priest and his long-barren wife a son, a special child who will become a messenger for the Messiah. Though the stunned priest doubts the angel's message, a baby boy arrives nine months later, and everyone who hears of his birth rejoices, wondering what the miraculous child will become.

With the sky-high expectations of his community ringing in his ears, the boy grows up, becomes a prophet, and takes to the wilderness. Eager to fulfill his vocation, he calls everyone he meets—even the king of the

---

1. Dinesan, quoted in Mohn, "Talk with Isak Dinesen."

land—to repentance, faithfulness, and justice. He prepares the way of the Lord, baptizes the Messiah with his own hands, and eagerly announces the arrival of God's kingdom.

But then? Then he lands in prison for speaking truth to power; suffers doubt and despair about the Messiah he staked his life on; experiences no dramatic rescue *from* that Messiah; and loses his life to appease a clueless girl, a cruel-hearted queen, and a cowardly king.

How's *that* for a bearable story?

To ponder John the Baptist's place in the arc of the Gospels is to ponder the "good news" of Jesus from a deeply complicated place. Christians are often trained to slap redemptive meaning on tragedies. "Nothing happens in this world unless God wills it," is one of the stories I grew up with. "The Lord never gives anyone more than they can bear," is another. "God has a plan," is still another, and so is, "For everything, there is a season. A time to be born and a time to die."

If we Christians have a unidirectional way of telling our conversion stories ("I journeyed from shadow to light, from ignorance to knowledge, from despair to joy"), then John's story should stop us in our tracks, because it is an *anti-conversion* story. By our stock logic, John's journey is a backwards one. From certitude to doubt. From boldness to hesitation. From knowing to unknowing.

What should we do with this disturbing trajectory? Should we call it a case of spiritual failure? Faithlessness? Backsliding? The fact is, most of the pious stories I've inherited as a Christian are not jagged enough for the locust-eating prophet who struggles with doubt and dies in prison. They're far too tepid and polite. Where is the Christian story that can handle horror? Where is the Christian story that will sit in the deepest shadows and testify that God is alive there, too?

What bothers me most about John the Baptist's story is its utter sense-lessness. John suffers at the whim of a thoughtless teenager. He languishes because of other people's moral cowardice. He dies for a dance.

In other words, John is one of those people—we all know them—who does everything right and suffers anyway. He dies disillusioned, unsure of his Messiah, and as far as we know, his death saves no one. As Teresa of Avila purportedly told God, "Lord, if this is how you treat your friends, no wonder you have so few!"[2]

I suppose if we try hard enough, we'll find a way to pummel John's story into something bearable. But is that what we're called to do? What if instead, "the point" of John's story is to prepare us for the way of Jesus, which is a

2. Teresa of Avila, *The Life of St. Teresa*, 548.

costly way? A narrow way? A risky way? What if the Gospels give us John's story so that we can ready ourselves for the Messiah who is coming—a Messiah who will indict all forms of transactional religion that promises comfort, prosperity, and blessing in exchange for our professions of faith? Maybe salvation isn't about immunity, however much it offends our sensibilities to admit it. Maybe the point is that we don't need to slap meaning on every human experience in order to prove that we are pious and God is good. Maybe some things are just plain horrible. Period.

It's tempting to read a story like John the Baptist's and tell ourselves that it's anachronistic, that it comes from a rougher, cruder, more barbaric time. But the opposite is true. We still live in a world where infidelity and betrayal are accepted norms. We still live in a world where the innocent are detained, imprisoned, tormented, and killed. We still live in a world of sudden and random violence. We still live in a world where young girls fall prey to powerful men. We still live in a world where speaking truth to power is a radical and sometimes lethal act.

Closer to home, I still live in a world where I distance myself from people who tell me truths I'd rather not hear. I still live in a world where I worry more about sounding foolish or losing face than I do about practicing discretion, admitting my mistakes, and humbling myself in front of people I'm desperate to impress. I still live in a world where people within my reach live lonely lives and die meaningless deaths—and I barely notice.

Maybe what I cherish about John's story is his utter honesty in the face of pain. He doesn't hold back; he voices his doubt in all of its terrifying fullness: "Are you the one who is to come, or are we to wait for another?" (Luke 7:19). In other words: "Lord, I've staked my entire life on you. Has it all been for nothing?"

Jesus doesn't chastise John for his honesty. Instead, he responds to his cousin's pained question with composure, gentleness, and calm. "Go and tell John what you hear and see," Jesus tells the disciples who bring him the prophet's question. Tell him that "the blind receive their sight, the lame walk, the lepers are cleansed, the deaf hear, the dead are raised, and the poor have good news brought to them. Blessed is anyone who takes no offense at me" (Luke 7:22).

In other words, Jesus says: go back to John and tell him your *stories*. Tell him what your eyes have seen and your ears have heard. Tell him what only the stories—quiet, scattered, and questionable as they are—will reveal.

Why? Because Jesus is not a pronouncement. He is not a sermon, a slogan, or a billboard. He is far more elusive, mysterious, and impossible-to-pin-down than we can imagine. He emerges in the lives of the plain, poor, ordinary people all around us. We glimpse him in shadows. We hear him in whispers. He comes to us by stealth, with subtlety, over long, layered stretches of time.

What version of Jesus would emerge if we gave our stories of doubt and disillusionment their due? How much divine richness have we squandered by mistaking certainty for faith?

According to Matthew's Gospel, when Jesus hears of John's death, "he leaves in a boat to a remote area to be alone" (Matt 14:13). He doesn't preach. He doesn't turn the horror of his cousin's story into a morality tale. He doesn't numb himself to his loss by plunging straight back into ministry.

Instead, he withdraws. He lingers over his pain and creates space for it to spend itself. And then? Then he feeds people. The story of the feeding of the five thousand directly follows the story of John's death. Jesus returns from mourning, asks a crowd to sit down, gathers whatever scraps of nourishment he can find, and multiplies the scraps into a feast for all.

The platitudes of religion notwithstanding, some things are too terrible for words. Some hurts can't be salvaged with a story. To hold silence in the face of the world's horrors is a holy response, one that creates space for mystery, meaninglessness, and grief. It's right to mourn freely when the unbearable descends upon us. It's enough to feed the people around us with whatever we have at our disposal. Somehow, in the generous economy of God, our scraps will be enough, even if we can't explain how or why.

The story isn't what we thought it was going to be; John's haunting question from a jail cell testifies to this dissonance. But the Messiah still feeds us and calls us to feed others in return. In the asking, feeding, and listening, we make our sorrows bearable.

# Tempted

## Mark 1:9–15

*And the Spirit immediately drove him out into the wilderness. He was in the wilderness forty days, tempted by Satan; and he was with the wild beasts; and the angels waited on him. (Mark 1:12–13)*

All three Synoptic Gospels describe Jesus's temptation in the desert. Unlike Matthew and Luke, however, Mark gives us the short version of the story. He doesn't tell us how Satan tests Jesus, or how Jesus responds to the testing. But there are powerful details in Mark's version, details that can help us navigate our own experiences of brokenness and healing.

What I notice first in Mark's version is the oddness of the scene at a big-picture level. Consider who and what populates the wilderness that Mark describes. We have the Holy Spirit. We have Jesus. We have Satan. We have wild beasts. And we have angels. All together in one place at one time, co-existing.

I start with this image because it offers a necessary corrective to our visions of the Christian life. I tend to divide my spiritual landscape into neat, inviolable sections. Shadow and light. Secular and religious. Profane and holy. I assume that if I'm in a healthy spiritual place, evil will stay far away. I imagine that angels don't share space with wild predators. I believe that God's Spirit never leads us into wastelands.

But no. Spirit, Jesus, Satan, beasts, angels, and wilderness. *Together.* Not for an hour, an afternoon, or a day, but forty days. Which is the Bible's handy way of saying, "A very, very, *very* long time."

It's worth holding onto this image of Mark's crowded desert because the austere and complicated landscape he describes, the bizarre menagerie of despair and solace, isolation and accompaniment, is where we live. This is the realm where God's work of holy repair begins.

Three details stand out to me in this text. First, Jesus doesn't choose the wilderness. Mark tells us that the Spirit of God drives him there. The verb in the Greek is *ekballei*—literally, "to throw out." As in, the Spirit throws or casts or hurls Jesus out into the desert. It's the same verb Mark later uses to describe the casting out of demons and the flinging of corrupt moneychangers out of the temple.

In other words, what we have here is not a first-century version of Jesus giving up chocolate as a spiritual discipline or making a retreat of silence at a beautiful monastery. What we have is the Spirit of God grabbing Jesus by the scruff of the neck and throwing him headlong into a place he doesn't want to go. A place of isolation, deprivation, danger, and testing.

To be clear, this is not how I first heard the story, growing up. I learned about Jesus's temptation in Sunday School. I still remember my teacher, a grandmotherly woman in a hairnet and beige panty hose, stretching the Judean wilderness across a flannelgraph board in front of my first-grade class. At the far left of the fuzzy felt landscape, an innocuous-looking devil—scrawny, fork-tailed, and ridiculous—stooped in the sand and reached for a loaf-shaped stone. To his right, a supremely undisturbed Jesus towered over the landscape in a pristine white robe, his finger pointed devastatingly at his tempter.

Looking back now, I give my teacher credit for doing the best she could with a bunch of wiggly six-year-olds. But I regret the version of Jesus that I carried away from those Sunday school lessons, because it was a version that did me harm. The Jesus I absorbed as a young person was a muscular superhero who wielded perfect control over his environment and his choices. His temptation wasn't real, because *he* wasn't real. His experience in the desert had no sting, no suspense, no edge. Jesus was pretending, putting on a performance of temptation to set me an example. In this performance, Satan was an inept clown, doomed to fail, and Jesus's triumph over him was so painless and predictable, it cost the Son of God nothing.

At no point in my childhood or young adulthood did I hear that Jesus actually *struggled* in the wilderness. That he feared and resisted the movement of the Spirit in his life. That he craved what the evil one offered. That he hurt, wept, wrestled, and suffered.

The corollary to this belief in a divine superhero was a terrible misunderstanding about the wilderness itself. If I found myself stuck in a desolate spiritual place for any length of time, I assumed it was my fault. After all, Jesus aced his temptations without breaking a sweat, so what was wrong with me? Surely, I was failing as a Christian. Harboring some secret sin, or giving way to doubt, or praying too sporadically. It couldn't be the case that God *wanted* me to be out there in the desert, wandering and lost. Could it?

In Mark's story, the Spirit of God *drives* Jesus into the wilderness. The same gentle Spirit who descends on him as a dove, the same delighted God who tears the heavens open to assure Jesus that he is precious—that same

God hurls Jesus into what feels like oblivion. Not because Jesus is sinful or faithless, but because he is dearly loved.

I want to pause here and make sure I'm being clear. I am *not* saying that God wills terrible things to happen to us, or that suffering in and of itself is life-giving. The church has historically done great harm in ennobling pain, and it's important that we name and repent of that lie. There are many forms of suffering in this world that should only ever be addressed, healed, resisted, or rejected outright. The suffering that results from abuse, trauma, racial and economic injustice, misogyny, homophobia, mental or physical illness—we are *not* called to passively accept these forms of suffering as God's will.

Rather, what I'm saying is that sometimes, even in the midst of circumstances that don't originate with God, the Spirit chooses the wilderness for us so that God can deepen and purify our comprehension of our belovedness. At his baptism, Jesus hears the absolute truth about who he is. He experiences God's love and pleasure so intensely, the skies split open. That's the easy part. The much harder part comes in the desert, when he has to face down every vicious assault on his identity as God's treasured child.

As the divine voice from heaven fades, as the cunning words of the tempter grow louder in his ears, as the isolation of the wilderness plays tricks on his heart and mind, Jesus has to learn a kind of love that is independent of external circumstances. He knows what God's love feels like in the baptismal font, in the gathered community, in the sacred realm of bells and smells. Now he has to learn the shape and color of God's love in the barren places. In the emptiness. In the lonely shadows.

Parker Palmer, a Quaker theologian and writer, talks about this process as a "pressing down onto ground on which it is safe to stand."[1] In a 2021 interview he gave about his experience with clinical depression, Palmer says that for many years, he lived his spiritual life at "great elevation." He visualized faith as an "up, up, and away" mountain climb, in which he'd attain greater and greater heights until finally, he would touch the hand of God.

What he learned in the throes of depression is that deep spiritual growth actually happens in the opposite direction. The danger of living at high elevation, he says, is that every time you fall, you have to fall a long distance, a distance that will make impact brutal. Every landing, if it doesn't kill you outright, will shatter bones. But if you allow the Spirit of God to press you down onto ground on which it is safe to stand, then you can fall all day long, and that secure, steady ground beneath your body— the ground of God's own being—will hold you.

1. Palmer, "The Soul in Depression."

Jesus doesn't choose the wilderness, but he consents to stay there. He consents to learn what only the desert—not his family, not the temple, not his traditions, not even the Scriptures themselves—can teach.

If you are in a wilderness you haven't chosen, consider the possibility that you are on holy ground. Consider that the Spirit who has driven you there knows what she's doing. Consider that it's divine mercy, not divine condemnation, that brings you down from the heights and teaches you to cherish the low ground. Because the unnerving truth is this: we can be loved and uncomfortable at the same time. We can be loved and bereft at the same time. In the wilderness, the love that survives is hardcore. It is flinty, not soft. Salvific, not sentimental. We don't learn to trust it quickly. It takes forty days. Forty years. *Lifetimes.*

The second detail I want to highlight is this one: Jesus stays with the wild beasts. That's all Mark gives us, just this one intriguing line: "He was with the wild beasts." The noun in the Greek emphasizes that these animals are dangerous. Not cuddly mice and timid deer, but vipers, scorpions, jackals. Possibly even Asian lions, wild boars, and bears.

Mark doesn't tell us that Jesus traps, fights, or kills these animals. He doesn't tell us that Jesus tames them. He just says that Jesus is "with" them.

I love this image of Jesus keeping company with the wild beasts, because I think it speaks eloquently to an important aspect of holy repair. Sometimes, we use faith, religious doctrine, prayer, or even the church itself to fend off anything in our lives that feels untamed, unsettled, undomesticated, or unpredictable. We assume that Christian maturity is all about borders and boxes, clean lines and carefully delineated belief systems. We fear wild things and we flee from them.

I grew up in a very tight-knit Christian community. I was a preacher's kid, so I probably spent more hours inside of church buildings than I did in my childhood home. I was steeped in Scripture, theology, prayer, and worship from my earliest years, and I was loved well by many good and generous people who practiced their faith as fervently as my family did.

Because my parents were first-generation immigrants from India, our faith community was also inextricably tied to our ethnic and cultural identity; there was no separating of the two. From as early on as I can remember, I was taught that our way of being Christian was the only true way, the only way that honors God.

I know that some people who grow up in immersive, cloistered faith environments resent it, but that was not the case for me. I *loved* it. I loved all of it. The music, the worship, the teaching, the community. Most of all, I loved the security of my own belonging, my crystal-clear sense that I knew exactly where the boundaries were between right and wrong, Christian and non-Christian, us and them. As long as I stayed within the bounds of my sanctified community, I would know who to be and how to be. My spiritual life was a walled-off garden, and I had no desire to leave it.

And then? Then the wild beasts showed up.

For me, they showed up in the form of questions I wasn't supposed to ask: Why can't women preach or lead worship? What's so threatening about evolution, psychology, social justice, and feminism? Why is it wrong to be gay? How is it that we keep reading the Bible literally when the book begs for a more varied approach? Why do we make heroes of men who lust after power? Why are stories of abuse and neglect in our midst swept under the rug? Why do we consider depression and anxiety spiritual failures? Where is God's grace in our honor-shame culture? Why does God have to be male?

The questions didn't emerge all at once. They came slowly as my world expanded and I met faithful people whose Christianity looked different than mine. Over time, I began to sense a growing impatience, restlessness, *wildness* within my own heart.

Needless to say, my questions were met in all the predictable ways: "You're losing your faith. You're reading dangerous books. You're becoming undisciplined. You're idolizing your intellect. You're breaking God's heart."

Wanting to be loved and accepted, I ignored the questions, and spent many more years pretending to be fine. Pretending that if I just tried harder, my doubts would disappear. Pretending that I was perfectly content in my manicured garden.

The wild beasts didn't disappear. They stalked and bellowed and roared and clawed. They demanded my attention until I had to make a choice. Either I would leave the version of faith I loved, or my soul would wither.

There was *no joy* in leaving. No relief, no freedom, no consolation. All of those beautiful things came later. What came first was death. Death, sorrow, guilt, and raw fear. Because it wasn't just that I didn't know how to be a Christian anymore. It was that I didn't know how to be a *person* anymore. What would my identity be? Who would love me? How would I find a path in the midst of so much confusion and loss?

Somehow, even in the midst of that terrible grief, I had a dim sense that choosing wildness—choosing a way of faith that honored the questions, respected the mysteries, and left space for the unconventional and the undomesticated—was the right choice. It felt lonely. It felt precarious. It felt sad beyond language. But it also felt like God.

In Mark's story, Jesus consents to stay with the wild beasts. He learns how to be with them, and he learns how to let them be. During those forty days in the desert, he grows within himself the capacity to sit with all that is rough and unpolished. He learns how to respond to wildness with serenity, patience, and gentleness, not rushing to tame or tamp down, but to let the feral flourish.

We know that this is true both literally and metaphorically, because Jesus emerges from the desert to become something of a "wild beast" himself. Until his crucifixion, he spends his days provoking, disrupting, and upending the religious conventions of his time. Not to destroy them, but to repair and reinvigorate them. He refuses to be tamed by the people who insist they have the divine figured out. He refuses to squeeze the God he loves into a box of abstract certainties.

Instead, breaking all taboo, and collapsing all tribalism, he embraces the lepers and befriends the bleeding women and eats with the tax collectors and heals on the Sabbath. Having learned the wild wisdom of the desert, he becomes a "thin space" himself, a sacred place where men and women can encounter the untamable divine for themselves.

It takes an exhausting amount of energy to resist the wildness of God. If your resistance is wearing you out, then consider the possibility that God is inviting you to stay with the wild beasts for a while. Consider that a bigger, wilder, and far more expansive God than you've yet known is calling for you, hungering after you, and longing to bless your wildness with God's own.

The last detail I want to highlight is this one: there are angels in the wilderness. Mark writes that the angels wait on Jesus. Just as a shepherd tends his sheep or a nursing mother tends her infant, these angels keep vigil and sustain Jesus through his forty days of suffering and struggle.

I draw attention to this detail because it's an easy one to miss when we're wandering in broken places. In the midst of the wilderness, our eyes are often fixated on our pain, and if we bother to look for angels at all, we look only for them to rescue us.

This is understandable; Jesus himself struggles with a misapprehension regarding angels. In Matthew's and Luke's versions of the wilderness story, Satan tempts Jesus to jump from the pinnacle of the temple, promising him that God's angels will prevent him from getting hurt. The implication is that if God loves us, God's angels will keep us safe.

It's such an enticing lie—one that targets our deepest fears about surviving in a chaotic world. But the angels in Mark's Gospel don't medi-vac Jesus out of the wilderness. They *tend* to him. They accompany him. They stick with him and help him bear what he must bear.

As I think about the loneliness of the desert, I wonder if the angels who help Jesus arrive in forms very different from what we imagine. *Maybe* they manifest as celestial creatures with powerful wings and blinding faces. But maybe they show up as cool breezes across the sun-scorched hills. As trickles of water for Jesus's parched throat. As shade on a blazing afternoon.

As the sweetness of bird song. As a brilliant display of wildflowers or the swirl of constellations on a clear, cloudless night.

If the earth and everything in it is God's, then God might very well send us angels in guises we take for granted. Our challenge is to remember that even in the land of shadow and starvation, even in the places where the wild beasts roam, God's agents of love and care abide. We might not recognize them as angelic until years later. But they abide.

In my own life, God's angels have come in a thousand different guises, and I'm still learning how to recognize them. They've come in the form of wise friends, mentors, priests, and teachers. They've offered themselves up in the beautiful language of poetry, liturgy, song, and story. They've welcomed me as a fellow parishioner in the church I now consider my spiritual home. They've called to me in the old redwood trees, the pounding surf, and the winding hiking trails I have the privilege to enjoy here in northern California.

Sometimes, they've arrived as strangers who show up for a moment and speak the words I most need to hear exactly when I most need to hear them. I want to share the story of one such angel, because I think her message speaks to the heart of what grace in the wilderness looks like.

Several years ago, when my daughter was in middle school, she went through a period of intense struggle and developed anorexia. My husband and I feared for her life, and during the worst of her illness, we hospitalized her for her own safety.

I don't know quite how to describe the abyss we fell into after we made that decision. It was an abyss of terror and anguish and anger and failure. For my part, I was filled with shame, because I felt as though I'd failed at job no. 1 of motherhood, the job of keeping my child well-fed and healthy. I was toxically angry at the culture we live in for its sick obsession with thinness. What I felt towards God was a poisonous combination of rage, bewilderment, and heartbreak, because I was praying nonstop, and as far as I could tell, God was doing *nothing*.

On the morning after the admission, after the doctors explained that we wouldn't be able to see our daughter for several days, I stumbled out of the hospital, got into my car, and started driving without aim or purpose.

I ended up in some part of town I wasn't familiar with, in the parking lot of a Catholic bookshop I'd never seen before. Without knowing what I was doing, or why, I walked in and wandered the aisles until a woman—a Catholic sister who worked at the shop—came up to me. All she said was, "Can I help you find anything?" I burst into tears.

For at least three or four minutes, I cried so hard, I couldn't speak. She took my hands in hers and let me cry. When I could breathe again, she said,

"Wait here." She disappeared for a minute and returned with a small, velvet box. Inside it was a silver crucifix on a chain, Jesus's broken body clearly outlined against the beams of the tiny cross.

At that point in my life, I was a stranger to crucifixes. The church I attended displayed empty crosses—crosses that celebrate resurrection. But the woman pressed the crucifix into my hands, looked into my eyes, and said, "Keep this. Hang onto it. Only a suffering God can help."

I didn't know at the time that she was quoting Dietrich Bonhoeffer, who penned this line in a Nazi prison not long before his execution. All I knew was that the God I was busy hating was sending me an angel, someone to tend me, someone to bear the unbearable with me, someone to show me precisely where God was in the pain, because I was busy looking in another direction and could not find that God on my own. The holy repair I needed in that moment was a capacity to see God as God really is. Not a wizard God, but a God who accompanies. A God who dwells in mystery, but never abandons me to face the mystery alone.

There are angels in the wilderness. They don't always come with cures. They don't hand us the control we crave. But they come as messengers of unfailing love. They come because the God who knows that we are dust, the God who drove Jesus into the wilderness so that for all of eternity our Messiah would understand human pain from the inside—keeps sending them.

The Spirit drives Jesus into the wilderness. He remains with the wild beasts. And the angels wait on him. *All this,* so that when Jesus finally emerges from the desert to proclaim good news, that good news will be unassailable. Rock solid. Tested in the barren places, brought to its knees, and proven true.

This, of course, is precisely the kind of good news the world needs so desperately right now. Good news that is credible, authentic, and resilient enough to survive the ravages of the desert. God mends our broken places not simply for our own benefit, but so that our stories of mending can bless, inspire, heal, and challenge the world.

As we encounter the wilderness in our own lives, may we experience the companionship of the Christ who knows the barren places better than we do. May our long stints amidst the wild beasts teach us who we really are—the precious, beautiful, and wholly liberated children of God. And when the angels in all their sweet and secret guises whisper the good news into our ears, may we listen and believe them.

# Come and See

## John 1:43–51

*Philip found Nathanael and said to him, "We have found him about whom Moses in the law and also the prophets wrote, Jesus son of Joseph from Nazareth." Nathanael said to him, "Can anything good come out of Nazareth?" Philip said to him, "Come and see." (John 1:45–46)*

"What would Jesus do?"

I was in college when the question became a slogan. I'd walk into Christian bookstores and see entire shelves dedicated to the phrase. Teenagers came to church with the acronym emblazoned on bracelets, T-shirts, caps, and hoodies: "WWJD?" Pastors used the question to title sermons, and youth group leaders chose it as an organizing theme for summer camps and vacation Bible schools. Goldmine industry though it became, the goal of the paraphernalia was to encourage kids to orient their lives around Jesus. If he were here now, facing the situation we're facing, what would he do?

As I reflect on Jesus's first encounters with his disciples, I wonder if we might shift the WWJD question a bit, from "What would Jesus do?" to "What would Jesus *see?*" After all, the Jesus of the Gospels spends a lot of time looking, noticing, and discerning. Perhaps we should begin where Jesus begins. If he were here right now, looking at what we're looking at, what would he see?

In this Scripture from John's Gospel, a skeptic named Nathanael journeys from doubt to faith. He experiences an epiphany, discovering for himself that Jesus of Nazareth is in fact the Son of God, the light that has come into the world.

But the story at its core is not about what Nathanael sees; it's about what Jesus sees. It's a story about Jesus's way of looking and seeing, and about what becomes possible when we dare to experience his gaze. In this story, what makes salvation possible is not what Nathanael sees in Jesus, but what Jesus sees in Nathanael.

The encounter begins with Jesus going to Galilee, finding Philip, and inviting him to "follow me" (John 1:43). Philip accepts the call and immediately runs off to find his friend Nathanael. He finds him sitting under a fig tree. "We have found him about whom Moses in the law and the prophets wrote, Jesus son of Joseph from Nazareth!" Philip tells Nathanael. But his friend isn't impressed. "Can anything good come out of Nazareth?" he asks skeptically. Instead of arguing, Philip simply tells his doubtful friend to "come and see" (vv. 45–46).

When Nathanael does so, he receives the surprise of his life. As soon as Jesus lays eyes on him, he sees right into Nathaniel's core and names what he sees: "Here is truly an Israelite in whom there is no deceit!" (v. 47).

Seeing is always selective. We have choices when it comes to what we see, what we prioritize, what we name, and what we call out in each other. The selves we present to the world are layered and messy, and it takes both love and patience to sift through those layers and find what lies at the center of who we are. But there is great power in that sifting, too. Something happens to us when we are deeply seen, known, named, and accepted.

Jesus has a choice when it comes to seeing Nathanael. I wonder what would have happened if instead of calling out Nathanael's purity of heart, Jesus said, "Here is a cynic who is stunted by doubt," or, "Here is a man who is governed by prejudice," or, "Here is a man who is careless in his speech," or, "Here is a man who sits around, passive and noncommittal, waiting for life to happen to him."

Any one of those things might be true of Nathanael. But Jesus looks past them all to see an honesty, a guilelessness, a purity of thought and intention that makes up the true core of Nathanael's character. Maybe the other qualities are there as well, but would Nathanael's heart melt in wonder and joy if Jesus saw and named those first? Or would Nathanael withdraw in shame? Jesus names the quality he wants to bless and cultivate in his would-be follower, the quality that makes Nathanael an image-bearer of God.

What would happen if we routinely saw as Jesus sees? If beneath the anger, we saw a passion for justice? If beneath the shyness, we saw a hunger for connection? If beneath the bossiness, we saw a great capacity for leadership? If beneath the loudmouthed banter, we saw prophetic truth-telling? If beneath the quietness, we saw a gift for reflection? If beneath the recklessness, we saw courage?

In *Just Mercy*, a powerful book on the blight of mass incarceration in the United States, lawyer and author Bryan Stevenson insists that "each of us is more than the worst thing we've ever done."[1] Each of us, in other

1. Stevenson, *Just Mercy*, 21.

words, benefits from a second look—and a third and a fourth. To offer that second look, that deeper, kinder, and more penetrating look, is grace. It is the gracious vision of Jesus, and it is the vision we are called to practice in a world that too often leads with judgment and condemnation. Is there anything that feels lonelier than the experience of being unseen and dismissed? Is there anything more life-giving than being seen for who we really are, deep down beneath our fragile defenses?

The invitation to "come and see" is an invitation to leave our comfortable vantage points and dare to believe that, maybe, we have erred in our original certainties about each other, God, and the world. To come and see is to approach all of life with a grace-filled curiosity, to believe that we are holy mysteries to each other, worthy of further exploration. To come and see is to enter into the joy of being deeply seen and deeply known, and to have the very best that lies hidden within us called out and called forth.

Epiphanies are funny things, hard to explain outside the context of our own lives. I wonder how, in later years, Nathanael tells his friends about his first meeting with Jesus. I wonder how they react. "No, no, you don't get it! He *saw* me! Don't you understand? He really saw me! And then I just knew!"

But he is telling the truth. Whether anyone else understands or not, it's because Jesus sees who Nathanael is that Nathanael is able to see who Jesus is: "Rabbi, you are the Son of God!" (v. 49). In other words, it is when we have been seen in a profoundly personal and compassionate way that we find ourselves able to see others. It is when we have been loved right down to the core of who we are that we find the capacity to love other people as God loves us.

What would Jesus see? Come and see likewise.

# A House Divided

## Mark 3:20–35

*Then his mother and his brothers came; and standing outside, they sent to him and called him. A crowd was sitting around him; and they said to him, "Your mother and your brothers and sisters are outside, asking for you." And he replied, "Who are my mother and my brothers?" (Mark 3:31–33)*

I'll be honest: this Gospel story hurts. It cuts close to home and raises questions I don't know how to answer.

A bit of my own story will explain why. My parents left their native India when I was two months old and raised me in an immigrant community in the United States. Like many "second generation" Americans, I have spent most of my life agonizing over my identity. Who am I? *What* am I? American or Indian? Who are my people? To whom do I belong? Where should my cultural loyalties lie?

It's from this background that I come to Mark's story of Jesus's blunt encounter with his hometown and his family. Let's get the obvious over with first: if you need Jesus to be soft and cuddly, this story is not for you. If you need Jesus to make your life decisions comfortable and scandal-free, this story is *definitely* not for you.

The setting is Nazareth. Jesus has returned home after inaugurating his ministry, and it's clear from the size and frenzy of the crowds pressing against him that his reputation precedes him. After all, much has happened since he first left home. The heavens have opened at his baptism. He has survived a forty-day fast in the wilderness. He has driven out unclean spirits, healed the sick, eaten with sinners, chosen his disciples, and declared himself the Lord of the Sabbath.

Through these and other acts, he has mesmerized every crowd he's come into contact with, stirring up such hope, excitement, and yearning in people's hearts that they can't leave him alone. They follow him to Nazareth and pour into the house where he's staying, pressing in so tight that Jesus can't even lift his hand to his mouth to feed himself.

This state of affairs is more than enough to alarm both his family and the religious authorities. Jesus's mother and siblings arrive on the scene first, intending to stage an intervention. Mortified by neighborhood rumors that Jesus has lost his mind, Mary and her other children stand outside the jam-packed house and call for Jesus, hoping to restrain him so that they can salvage their reputation and keep him safe.

The scribes show up shortly thereafter (having come down from Jerusalem to investigate this new teacher) and declare that Jesus is evil and a threat, not a benign healer empowered by God, but a fiend possessed by Beelzebub, "the ruler of the demons" (Matt 12:22–30).

It's easy for us, having the benefit of hindsight, to write off these people who accuse Jesus of insanity and demon possession. As if discernment is a neat and tidy process for us contemporary human beings. As if we never mistake evil for good, or better for best, or bravery for insanity. The fact is, neither Jesus's family nor the scribes from Jerusalem are evil or ill-intentioned. They are earnest people dedicated to maintaining stability in a fraught time and place. Jesus's family desires order and peace in the domestic sphere, and the scribes desire order and peace in the religious sphere. Don't we all? They're not out to thwart God; they just want to keep things respectable.

Which is why, I think, I find Jesus's behavior in this story so upsetting. The Jesus of Mark's Nazareth encounter is harsh, austere, and impatient. Instead of responding compassionately to the scribes, he shreds their arguments with clever parables and accuses them of blasphemy against the Holy Spirit—an "unforgivable" sin. Instead of going out to greet and reassure his mother and siblings, he rejects their interventions, renounces their claims on his life, and trades them in for a new family of his own making.

What is Jesus doing? And why does he do it so impolitely?

I wonder if he's navigating the same terrain I described vis-à-vis my childhood. Asking the same questions I've asked as a daughter of immigrants in a bifurcated world: Who am I? Who are my people? To whom do I belong? Where should my loyalties lie?

Redefining one's identity, whether in a family or in a religious institution, is a provocative act, and it almost always comes at a price. Some of the most searing and traumatic encounters I've had with my family have been around cultural and religious identity, around my longing to share with them the fullness of who I am—both American and Indian, both Christian and progressive, both feminine and feminist.

In this story, Jesus proves himself even more provocative and pays a higher price than I can imagine. Picture the scene. Outside the house stand the insiders—the family, the religious folk, the pious, the careful. They think they have God pinned down. They know what the Holy Spirit is supposed to look like, and Jesus doesn't fit the bill.

Inside the house sit the outsiders—the misfits, the rejects, the tax collectors, the sex workers. They're not interested in dogma or piety; they just need love and they seem to have found it in a man who heals the sick and feeds the hungry. And in the midst of them? Smack in the center of the sick, the deviant, the hungry, the unorthodox, and the unwashed? There sits Jesus. Saying, "*This.* This is my family."

If we're not shaken, we're not paying attention. Jesus isn't calling for surface change here; he's dividing the house. He's going for the deep, the institutional, and the systemic. He's burning things down. Outside is in, and inside is out, and the people least likely to get it are the ones who consider themselves the most knowledgeable, the most "churchy," the most spiritually stable. I don't know about you, but when I think about who the blasphemers are in this story, I tremble. It is entirely possible (who knew?) to look God's wild, disturbing, unpredictable Spirit in the eye and call that loving Spirit insane or demon-possessed. Let's be careful at all times with our certainties.

Again, I find this Gospel reading difficult. When I think of Mary standing outside, waiting for her son without comprehending who he has become, my heart breaks. I think of my own mother and of the many times I have kept her waiting. I think of my son, and of how devastated I would feel if he renounced me.

It helps to imagine that this moment of breakage and rupture costs Jesus something dear. He knows he is Mary's son. He knows the agony of letting her go. But he knows that he's God's Son first, and that his divine identity supersedes all others. Still. I hope that it's with a secret lump in his throat that he bids his family goodbye.

At the same time, I can't help but imagine what it must have felt like to be *inside* the house with Jesus that day. I know the hunger to belong, to have someone safe and loving to belong to. Regardless of our circumstances, we all know what it's like to yearn for someone who can hold all of who we are, and love us still, without flinching. That's exactly what Jesus does for the crowds that day. He invites them in, he asks them to stay, and he makes them family.

Yes, Jesus divides the house, and division hurts. But he doesn't divide to make us homeless; he divides to rebuild. To make the house more spacious, more welcoming, and more beautiful. The fact that his work of rupture and restoration costs him in tangible ways—deeply familial and communal ways—only makes it more precious for all of us who yearn to come home.

# In a Nutshell
### John 3:1–17

*For God so loved the world that he gave his only Son, so that ev-
eryone who believes in him may not perish but may have eternal
life. (John 3:16)*

J ohn 3:16 was the first Bible verse I memorized as a child. In Sunday
School, I learned that it's a simple formula for faith, a handy evangelism
tool, and a perfect summary of the good news. Over the years, I've seen the
verse displayed on billboards, T-shirts, coffee mugs, and cross-stitch sam-
plers. I've heard it described as Christianity 101.

And so it is. When we read about Jesus's nighttime encounter with
Nicodemus, John 3:16 jumps out of the long dialogue for its efficiency and
pithiness. In just twenty-seven words, the verse describes a loving God, a
cherished world, a self-giving Son, a universal invitation, a deliverance from
death, and a promise of eternal life. Christianity in a nutshell, right?

Maybe not. The problem is not the verse itself, but what the church
so often does with it. In our well-intentioned efforts to make the gospel
message accessible, we reduce salvation to a soundbite, forgetting that when
Jesus originally speaks these words to Nicodemus—a Pharisee, a member
of the Sanhedrin, one of the more erudite men of his day—his listener finds
Jesus's words incomprehensible.

"How can these things be?" Nicodemus asks in astonishment when
Jesus speaks to him in the obscure and metaphorical language of birth,
flesh, water, and spirit. Jesus, unfazed by the Pharisee's confusion, refuses
to simplify his explanation. If he intends to "save" Nicodemus quickly and
easily that night, he fails. What the seeker experiences is not salvation; it's
bewilderment.

If Jesus's conversation with Nicodemus is representative of God's
preferred "evangelism style," then I have to wonder: What does my more
formulaic approach to Christianity leave out? Am I so invested in keeping

faith efficient and palatable that I minimize its weirdness? Its otherness? Its offensiveness?

Jesus has no problem leaving Nicodemus confused and muddled. He's in no hurry to get the Pharisee to sign on a dotted line. The Spirit "blows where it chooses," Jesus says (John 3:8). The Spirit cannot be caged or contained. Which means the journey of faith and the workings of salvation can't be caged or contained, either. When we speak of God's kingdom, we are in a realm of mystery. It's okay to be surprised. It's okay to be stricken.

What Jesus offers Nicodemus is not a tune-up; it's a *brand new life*. A down to the foundations beginning. What newborn enters the world without birth pangs, shock, disorientation, or pain? Downright bewilderment isn't the exception in a birth story; it's the rule. If we don't find Christianity at least a little bit confusing, then perhaps it's not Christianity we're practicing.

As I sit with Nicodemus's baffled reaction to Jesus, I wonder what my glib reading of John 3:16 prevents me from seeing about God, Christ, faith, sin, and salvation. Do I lean too hard on the importance of individual belief and forget the stunning truth that God loves and longs for all of creation to experience new life? Do I treat Jesus's words as a litmus test, using it not to communicate God's all-encompassing compassion and mercy, but to threaten unbelievers with God's judgment? Do I allow my interpretation to flatten and distort the meaning of "belief," reducing its nuance and complexity to mere intellectual assent? What does it mean, after all, to say, "I *believe* in Jesus?" Why is "belief," of all things, so important to God?

Growing up, I was taught that being a Christian means affirming the right truths. To accept Jesus into my heart, to be "born again," was to agree to a set of doctrines about who Jesus is and what he accomplished through his death and resurrection. To enter into orthodox faith was to believe that certain theological statements about God, Jesus, the Holy Spirit, the human condition, the Bible, and the church, were true. When we spoke of "growing in the faith," what we meant was that we were honing our doctrinal commitments. To be a mature Christian was to have one's theological ducks in a row.

This honing, moreover, was a serious business. As a teenager, I watched congregations split up over the legitimacy of infant baptism over "believer's" baptism. I knew Christians who considered speaking in tongues a firewall for authentic faith. I heard pastors fight over whether the communion table should be open to all or restricted to baptized members only.

For the earnest people involved, these questions were neither silly nor peripheral; they cut to the heart of what it means to be Christian. Getting the theological particulars right was paramount. After all, what else could faith entail?

I fear that I fall into the same trap when I speak glibly of John 3:16 as "Christianity in a nutshell." The verse sounds so gorgeously precise, so deceptively simple. But does all of Christianity really come down to my accepting certain propositions about Jesus as factual?

For me, this way of believing, this way of defining faith as an intellectual assent to precisely codified doctrines, has fallen apart. Not because I can't assent, but because my assenting, in and of itself, hasn't fostered the relationship I desire to have with God. If anything, my intellectual assent has functioned as a smokescreen. A distraction. A substitute.

In her 2013 book, *Christianity after Religion*, historian Diana Butler Bass points out that the English word "believe" comes from *belieben*, the German word for love.[1] To believe is not to hold an opinion. To believe is to treasure. To deem something precious and invaluable. To give my heart over to it without reservation.

This is true in the ancient languages of the Bible, as well. When the writers of the Hebrew Bible and the New Testament wrote of faithfulness, they were not advocating intellectual assent. They were making a case for trust, fidelity, dependence, and love. To believe in God was to place their *loving confidence* in God. To entrust their hearts, minds, and bodies into God's hands.

I can't think of any significant human relationship in which doctrine matters more than love. Why should my relationship with God be any different?

What does it mean to believe in Jesus? To hold onto him? To trust him with my life? For Nicodemus, it means starting anew, letting go of all he thinks he understands about the life of faith. It means becoming a newborn: vulnerable, hungry, and ready to receive reality in a fresh way. It means coming out of the shadows and risking the light. None of this can be reduced to an altar call or a litmus test.

In other words, the work of trusting Jesus is mind-bending, soul-altering work. It is hard, it takes time, and it involves setbacks, fears, and disappointments. No wonder Nicodemus walks away baffled that night. Jesus is calling him to so much more than a rote recitation of the sinner's prayer; he is calling him to fall in love and stay in love. Why is belief important to God? Because *love* is important to God. To believe is to be-love.

"Christianity in a nutshell" sounds catchy, but in the end, I don't think it exists. Yes, John 3:16 is a beautiful passage of Scripture, and we are right to recite it, memorize it, and cherish it. But the way of faith it points to is as vast and mysterious as all the workings of a human heart reaching

---

1. Bass, *Christianity after Religion*, 116.

out for God's. That's why we can trust it; its challenge corresponds to reality. No love as rich, demanding, costly, and free as God's love for us can ever be reduced to a formula.

# The Woman at the Well

## John 4:5–26

*The woman said to him, "I know that the Messiah is coming" (who is called Christ). "When he comes, he will proclaim all things to us." Jesus said to her, "I am he, the one who is speaking to you."* (John 4:25–26)

I t's only in recent years that I've learned to appreciate the Samaritan woman at the well, because her story wasn't one of my favorites growing up. The problem wasn't with the narrative itself; it was with the way preachers often mistreated its central character. Long before I was old enough to read John's Gospel for myself, I "knew" that the woman at the well was promiscuous and immoral. In the version I learned, the good news of the story resided in Jesus's shocking condescension: "God *even* forgives the sins of *such a woman!*"

The fact is, nowhere in the narrative is the Samaritan woman described as promiscuous. Nowhere does Jesus call her a sinner (sexual or otherwise), or tell her (as he tells so many others) to "go and sin no more." This is not a story about morality. It is not a story about Jesus liberating a woman from her own sex life. It is a story about Jesus revealing himself as the Messiah to a fellow human being in whom he sees genuine spiritual hunger, a learned and engaged mind, and a tremendous gift for preaching, evangelism, and apostleship.

Let's begin with what the story actually is. For starters, Jesus's dialogue with the woman at the well is his longest recorded conversation in the New Testament. He talks to the Samaritan woman longer than he talks to his twelve disciples, his critics, or even his own family members. Moreover, she is the first person (and the first ethnic and religious outsider) to whom Jesus reveals his identity in John's Gospel. And—this might be the most significant fact of all—she is the first believer in any of the Gospels to become an evangelist and bring her entire city to a saving experience of Jesus. So much for fallen women! How I wish I'd heard these bits of the story amplified when I was a little girl.

As I rethink the encounter now and allow its richness and nuance to wash over me, I'm noticing grace in very different places than I used to. In particular, I'm finding good news I can carry forward into my own life. Here are some examples of what I see:

*Jesus breaks religious and cultural rules to make the encounter possible.* By the time Jesus meets the woman at the well, the enmity between Jews and Samaritans is ancient, entrenched, and bitter. The two groups disagree about everything that matters: how to honor God, how to interpret sacred texts, and how and where to worship. They practice their faith in separate temples, read different versions of the Torah, and avoid social contact with each other whenever possible.

Moreover, the Samaritan is a woman, and it is not customary or appropriate for Jesus—a Jewish man—to converse alone with a Samaritan woman, much less to ask her for a drink of water. That sort of thing is not done.

To put this in more contemporary language, the Samaritan woman is the Other. The alien, the outsider, the heretic, the stranger. She represents all the boundaries that must not be transgressed in the religious life, all the spiritual taboos that must not be broken. But Jesus breaks them, anyway.

Is there anything we can do in our contemporary lives to recover the scandal at the heart of this story? Because its heart *is* a scandal. Not a sexual scandal, but a spiritual one. The enmity between the Jews and the Samaritans in Jesus's day is not theoretical; it's embodied and real. The differences between them are not easily negotiated; each is fully convinced that the other is wrong. What Jesus does when he enters into conversation with a Samaritan woman is radical and risky; it stuns his own disciples, because it asks them to dream of a different kind of social and religious order. A different kind of kingdom.

Jesus's willingness to break the rules compels us, his followers, to live into the truth that people are more than the sum of their political, racial, cultural, and economic identities. Jesus calls us to put aside the stereotypes we carry, the prejudices we nurse, the social and cultural lines we draw. He invites us to look at the Samaritan woman and see a sister and an apostle, not a harlot, a heretic, a foreigner, or a threat.

Where might God be calling you to break a rule? Transgress a boundary? Embrace a stranger? What lines has Jesus crossed in order to find you?

*Jesus leads with vulnerability.* As John describes the scene, Jesus is sitting by a well in the desert heat at high noon. He's "tired out" from his long journey, and he's all by himself. Along comes a woman with a water jar, and the first thing Jesus says to her is, "Give me a drink" (John 4:7).

I had to sit with this moment in the story for a long while before its irony and strangeness really struck me. The Son of God is thirsty at the mouth of a well, and it's the outcast whom no one else wants to interact with who provides the water he needs. How long, I wonder, does Jesus sit there with his parched throat and dry lips, longing for water? The wilderness at noon is no joke; people die of thirst out there. Do any echoes of his temptation in the wilderness come back to him as he leans over the well and smells the fresh coolness far below? (Matt 4:3: "If you are the Son of God, tell these stones to become bread.") Surely if the Messiah wants to, he can access the water himself. But he waits. He waits so that when the woman appears, she can recognize the incarnate Messiah in his vulnerability, his humanity, his need.

It's a remarkable moment. How often, in contrast, do we plunge into ministry with a sense of complete self-sufficiency? How hard do we work to hide our needs and our weaknesses, as if what's most human and authentic about us must be walled off for the sake of a more impressive "witness"? How stubbornly do we insist that we have everything to offer others, without recognizing how much they have to offer us?

Jesus wins the woman's trust by humbling himself. By naming his own thirst. By asking for something she can give. There is no triumphalism in his approach, no smugness, no arrogance. He's thirsty and he says so. Of course, we know that as Jesus's story plays out, he will once again thirst in a lonely place at noon, and once again ask for water. On that terrible day, he will receive only the mockery of vinegar from the foot of his cross. On *this* day by the well, however, Jesus's disarming honesty opens the door for a spiritual seeker to find new life and then share that new life with her entire city.

*Jesus tells the truth without shaming.* The conversation between Jesus and the woman pivots when he tells her what he knows about her life: "You are right in saying, 'I have no husband,' for you have had five husbands, and the one you have now is not your husband. What you have said is true!" (John 4:17–18).

This is the "sordid" revelation commentators often point to when they try to make a case for the woman's sexual wantonness. But there are any number of reasons why the Samaritan woman might have the past she has. Perhaps she was married off as a child bride, then widowed and passed along among her dead husband's brothers, as per the "Levirate marriage" practice of the day. Maybe her various husbands abandon her because she's ill, disabled, or infertile. Maybe she's a victim of abuse. Whatever the case, we know that in first century Palestine, women don't have the legal power to end their own marriages—the authority to file for divorce rests with men alone.

There's a great deal we can't know about the woman's history. What we can infer is that she prefers to be invisible. For whatever reason, she doesn't expect the other women in town to accept her, so she heads to the well in the scorching heat of the day instead of in the cool of the morning. She hopes to come and go, undetected, carrying around in isolation whatever trauma, wound, sin, fear, or desperation her complicated history has left her with.

But then Jesus comes along and sees her. He sees the whole of her. The past. The present. The future. Who she has been. What she yearns for. How she hurts. All that she might become. And he names it all.

But he names it all without shaming, castigating, or condemning her. He sees and names the woman in a way that makes her feel not judged, but loved. Not exposed, but shielded. Not diminished, but restored. He doesn't shy away from the painful, ugly, broken stuff in her life. Instead, he allows the truth of who she is to rise to the surface. "Let's name what's real," he tells her. "Let's confess what *is*. No more games. No more smokescreens. No more posturing. I see you for who you are, and I love you. Now see who I am. The Messiah. The one in whom you can find freedom, love, healing, and transformation. Spirit and Truth. Eternal life. Living Water. Drink of me, and live."

Just as he does for the Samaritan woman, Jesus invites us to see ourselves and each other through eyes of love, not judgment. Can we, like Jesus, become soft landing places for people who are all alone, carrying stories of humiliation too heavy to bear? Can we see and name the world's brokenness without shaming? Can we tell the truth and honor each other's dignity at the same time?

*Jesus endorses the woman's proclamation.* When Jesus tells the Samaritan woman who he is, she leaves her water jar at the well, runs back to her city, and says, "Come and see a man who told me everything I have ever done! He cannot be the Messiah, can he?" (John 4:29).

There's so much to love about this moment. I love that in her excitement, the woman forgets all about her water jar. I love that her need to share her sacred experience overwhelms her desire to remain anonymous and invisible. I love that her history—once the source of such pain and secrecy—becomes the evidence she uses to proclaim Jesus's identity. I love that she says, "Come and see," recognizing that Jesus can't be reduced to secondhand summary. I love that she shares her experience of Jesus even though her faith is still young and in process. ("He cannot be the Messiah, can he?") Even her questions become a part of her truth-telling. Even her curiosity becomes a tool that arouses the curiosity of others.

Most of all, I love that Jesus honors, blesses, and validates the woman's proclamation. John writes that Jesus stays in the woman's city for two days, so that everyone who hears her testimony can meet him directly and see that the woman is a reliable witness. She, like John the Baptist, like the Apostles, like Mary Magdalene, like Paul, "prepares the way of the Lord," and Jesus encourages her to do so. "Many Samaritans from that city," the Gospel writer tells us, "believed in him because of the woman's testimony" (John 4:39).

Who is speaking good news into your life? How are you receiving their testimony? In the most unlikely places, through the most unexpected voices, from the minds and bodies of the disempowered and the overlooked, God speaks, and living water flows. May we have ears to hear, hearts to receive, and courage to share what we are given.

# What the Body Knows
## Luke 7:36—8:3

*Then turning toward the woman, he said to Simon, "Do you see this woman?" (Luke 7:44)*

A few years ago, a Harvard professor of divinity announced the discovery of an ancient Coptic papyrus fragment in which Jesus purportedly mentions his wife. The announcement led to widespread controversy and debate, not only among academics, but within the church. What intrigued me at the time was not the possible authenticity of the fragment (scholars eventually proved it a fake), but the vehemence with which many Christians responded to its existence.

"Jesus wasn't married!" was the answer I routinely got when I mentioned the announcement. "He *couldn't* have been married! He was divine!" In other words, Jesus was human, but, well, not *that* human. He couldn't be *that* human and still be holy, antiseptic, immaculate. Heaven forbid that the Son of God might have been so embodied. So sensual.

In her book, *An Altar in the World*, Barbara Brown Taylor tells a related story about visiting a beautiful old church in Alabama.[1] Having arrived for the service too early, she stood for a while in front of the altar, admiring a mural of Jesus emerging from his tomb. Though the painting was impressive, Taylor felt that something was off. After gazing at the mural for several seconds, she realized what was missing: Jesus had no body hair. Without thinking, she shared her realization with a parishioner, a polite, well-put-together woman with expensive clothes and a flawless manicure. "He has the arms of a six year old. His chest is as smooth as a peach." The parishioner's smile froze, and she stared at Taylor in abject horror. "I can't believe you're saying this to me," she said without moving her red lips. "I just can't believe you're saying this to me."

1. Taylor, *An Altar in the World*, 36–37.

Christians, Taylor concludes, often find themselves "in the peculiar position of being followers of the Word Made Flesh who neglect our own flesh or worse—who treat our bodies with shame and scorn." Or again: "Here we sit," says Taylor, "with our souls tucked away in this marvelous luggage, mostly insensible to the ways in which every spiritual practice begins with the body."[2]

The story of Jesus's encounter with the woman in Simon's house confronts our shame head-on. No matter how hard we try to theologize or intellectualize it away, the story is naked-making. It exposes, it confronts, it directs our gaze. It's a story about the body. What the body is. What the body knows.

Feet. Tears. Perfume. Hair. All four Gospels tell it, the scandalous story of a woman who dares to love Jesus in the flesh—to love his spirit and his body with her own. Each writer frames the story differently to suit his own thematic and theological concerns, but that hardly matters; the story at its core remains the most sensual and shocking one in the New Testament.

In Luke's version, the story is set early in Jesus's ministry at the home of a Pharisee named Simon. No doubt curious about the young rabbi garnering both praise and outrage in the surrounding villages, Simon invites Jesus to a dinner party. After all, why *not* check out the would-be prophet from Nazareth? Perhaps he'll have some fascinating things to say about religion. Maybe he'll impress the other dinner guests with a nifty miracle or two—wouldn't that be a credit to Simon? If nothing else, Jesus's presence might make for some interesting chit-chat around the table and some delicious gossip afterwards.

So the invitation is extended and accepted. The guests arrive on the appointed evening, and as they recline around an impressively laden table, Simon settles in for a few hours of good food and lively conversation.

Enter the woman with the alabaster jar. In Luke's account, the woman is unnamed and unwelcome: "a woman in the city, who was a sinner" (Luke 7:37). How exactly she crashes the party, we don't know, but she manages to get in the door, approach the table, kneel quietly behind Jesus, and let down her hair.

Then, while God-knows-what transpires between the dinner guests, the woman bends over Jesus and begins to cry. She soaks Jesus's feet with her tears, caresses them with her hair, bends to kiss his soles, his toes, and his ankles, and finally breaks open her alabaster jar to anoint his salty skin with a costly perfume. As far as we know, Jesus doesn't say a word. Neither does the woman. But they communicate volumes.

2. Taylor, *An Altar in the World*, 40–41.

Can you imagine the scene? I wonder if the conversation around the table falters as the woman begins to cry. I wonder if the temperature rises a few significant degrees, and everyone in the room reaches simultaneously for the water jug. I wonder where the men look—or don't look—as the woman wraps Jesus's feet in her lustrous hair. I wonder if Jesus (never one to make things easy for the etiquette-obsessed) captures Simon's gaze and holds it, extending the discomfort, forcing his host to endure every searing kiss that grazes Jesus's skin.

The temptation here is to deflect. To minimize: "Perhaps it wasn't such a big deal in the first century. I'm sure people in that culture were more demonstrative than we are today. Showing affection like that was probably normal back then."

No. No, it wasn't. The Gospel writer takes pains to describe just how scandalous and unseemly the woman's behavior is in Jesus's own time and place. Simon is nothing less than disgusted, not only with the woman, but with Jesus, who tolerates her. Specifically, it's the woman's touch that makes Simon squirm with indignation: "If this man were a prophet, he would have known who and what kind of woman this is who is *touching* him—that she is a sinner" (v. 39).

Luke sets the woman's story in the theological context of sin and forgiveness. Those who are forgiven little, Jesus says, love little, but those who are forgiven much, love lavishly. Simon's love is thin in this story because he doesn't recognize his need for grace. The woman, in contrast, knows the extent of her sin and the wide embrace of Jesus's forgiveness, so her love is boundless. This is an important lesson, and Jesus teaches it beautifully.

But what interests me more about this story is how much it conveys *without* language. What happens between Jesus and the weeping woman happens skin to skin. The woman never says, "I need you," or "Thank you so much," or "I love you." Her contrition, her worship, her yearning, and her love are enacted wholly through her body, and Jesus receives them into his own body with gratitude, love, tenderness, and pleasure. The holy sacraments here are skin, salt, sweat, and tears. The instruments of worship are perfumed feet and ardent kisses. This is not a polite piety of the mind; this is physical extravagance. What writer Mary Gordon calls, "A Sabbath of the skin."[3]

Meanwhile Simon, the religious expert? Simon misses the encounter entirely. Unable to recognize what only the body can know, Simon fails to see the sacred transformation happening at his own table. Notice what Jesus asks him: "Simon, do you see this woman?" (v. 44). It's a lacerating

3. Gordon, *Reading Jesus*, 37.

question. Because no, Simon doesn't see her. He doesn't see her humanity, her generosity, her capacity for deep and embodied love. Neither, in fact, does he see *Jesus's* humanity—his dusty feet in need of cool water, the sun-baked skin in need of fragrant ointment, the ever-giving, ever-sacrificing Messiah in need of reciprocity, affection, and loving touch. Though he accuses Jesus of ignorance, Simon is the one who is both blind and ignorant in this story. In his eyes, Jesus needs to remain a curiosity, an idea, an abstraction—and one can't love an abstraction.

In fact, Simon needs Jesus to remain "a prophet," and the woman to remain "a sinner." His own identity depends on every other identity at his table remaining fixed. But this is exactly what the woman unhinges when her body enters the room. With her hair, her tears, and her touch, she forces each guest back into his own skin. With her more perfect, more radical, and more offensive hospitality—a hospitality that breaks through cultural barriers, a hospitality attentive to mind, soul, and body—she confronts everyone in the room with their common humanity. *Do you see this woman?* The weeper? The washer? The anointer? She's the one who sees and knows. She's a prophet, too.

There is a cost to seeing. A cost to seeing Jesus's body. A cost to seeing my own. I, too, inhabit a culture that treats bodies with scorn. Most of the time, I see my body as something to shrink, starve, conquer, or tame. I see its flaws more clearly than I see its God-ordained dignity and beauty. Rarely do I see it as a vehicle for worship, love, hospitality, and grace. But if I can't see my own body as God's temple, if I won't embrace it as pleasing and delightful to its Creator, how will I ever see or embrace yours?

We are people of the Incarnation, called to look, to see, to break bread, share wine, and wash feet. Can we learn to see our embodied lives, our sensory lives, as fully implicated in our lives with God? Can we move past contempt, squeamishness, and fear, and offer God the Sabbath of our skin?

# Vain Worship

## Mark 7:1–8

*So the Pharisees and the scribes asked him, "Why do your disciples not live according to the tradition of the elders, but eat with defiled hands?" (Mark 7:5)*

I grew up in a faith community that didn't allow churchgoers to wear jewelry. No one wore engagement rings, wedding bands, necklaces, or bracelets. Even play jewelry—the pink plastic rings I'd pull out of cereal boxes, or the bead bracelets I'd make at a friend's birthday party—was banned. Anyone who showed up on a Sunday morning sporting "ornaments" could be denied communion.

As a child, I had no idea why God hated jewelry. I was told that my bare ears and unadorned wrists were visible signs of my wholehearted devotion to Jesus. I was told that storing up treasure in heaven is more important than wearing silver, gold, or diamonds on earth. I wasn't bold enough to argue with my elders, but in secret, I knew they were wrong. I knew that there was no correlation between bare wrists and deeper piety, because the rules didn't make me love God more; they made me respect God less. Why, after all, did Jesus want me to feel weird and excluded at school? Why did he care more about my outsides than he did about my insides? What was the point of parading my unadorned ears and wrists in church every Sunday morning, while my hidden heart seethed?

I only learned the whole story years later. Apparently, when my great-grandparents had been newlyweds, a large-scale charismatic revival had swept through South India, winning many converts from the ornate mainline churches of my forebears. Many young adults had embraced the simple faith the revivalists encouraged in those days, and decided—often at great personal and social cost—to change their lifestyles for the sake of the gospel.

One of the lifestyle changes centered around jewelry. At a time when gold was social capital in India, when even Christian families judged each other's worth by the weight of the jewelry their women wore, and girls whose fathers couldn't produce enough jewelry for their dowries had to remain unmarried, the decision to forsake "ornaments" in the name of Jesus was a radical one. It spoke to the equalizing power of the gospel. No longer would my great-grandparents and their peers participate in the snobbery of their time and place; they would live counter-culturally and practice what Jesus preached, even if it meant losing their social standing and family honor. At great cost, they would embrace humility, simplicity, and equality as testimonies of Christ's non-discriminating love.

That was the history behind my church's "no ornament" rule. It was a noble history, but the problem was, its nobility had frozen in time. Our context had changed, and so had the cultural and social meanings behind wearing jewelry. What began as an earnest attempt to bring the sacred into everyday life had hardened into a loveless legalism. What started out as a gesture of radical welcome had become a tool of exclusion, self-righteousness, and rigidity.

The Gospel of Mark records an encounter between Jesus and a group of Pharisees who accuse Jesus's disciples of disregarding "the tradition of the elders" (Mark 7:1–8). Specifically, the Pharisees ask why some of Jesus's followers eat their meals with "defiled hands." That is, why they eat without performing the ritual hand washing expected of observant Jewish people.

To our modern ears, the accusation sounds trivial. But in fact, the Pharisees are asking a legitimate question, a question that still has relevance for us today. Consider the context: the first-century Jewish people among whom Jesus ministered were an oppressed minority living in an occupied land. How were they supposed to keep their faith pure and vibrant against the backdrop of colonization? In the midst of profound religious and cultural diversity, how were they to maintain their identity? Their integrity? Their heritage?

In Mark's story, the Pharisees' solution to the problem is to contain and codify the sacred. How can God's people show their faith among pagans? They can practice the ancient rituals of their elders down to the last letter. They can wash their hands before every meal; refuse table fellowship with tax collectors, sex workers, and other morally compromised sinners; and set themselves apart in everyday life as God's righteous people.

I can't speak to the Pharisees' intentions. But Jesus can—and he does. Quoting the prophet Isaiah, Jesus rebukes the Pharisees, saying, "This people honor me with their lips, but their hearts are far from me; in vain do they worship me, teaching human precepts as doctrines" (vv. 6–7).

Ouch. But aren't the Pharisees just trying, like the people at my childhood church, to honor and protect the sacred? Aren't they making a noble attempt to serve God in a public, visible way?

It's important to note that Jesus doesn't condemn ritual handwashing in his response to the Pharisees. He doesn't argue that all religious traditions are evil. What he indicts is the legalism, self-righteousness, and exclusivism that keeps the Pharisees from freely loving God and loving their neighbors in ways that are relevant to their time and place. What he challenges is their unwillingness to evolve and mature for the sake of God's kingdom. What he grieves is the Pharisees' compulsive need to police the boundaries—to decide who is "in" and who is "out" based on their own narrow definitions of purity and piety.

Again, it's easy for us to look down on the Pharisees, but honestly, are we any different? Don't we often behave as if we're finished products, with nothing new to discover about the Holy Spirit's movements in the world? Don't we cling to spiritual traditions and practices that long ago ceased to be life-giving, simply because we can't bear to change "the way we've always done things"? Don't we set up religious litmus tests for each other and decide who's in and who's out based on conditions that have nothing to do with Jesus's open-hearted love and hospitality? Don't we fixate on the forms of piety we can put on display for others to applaud, instead of cultivating the secret and hidden life of God within our souls?

It doesn't matter what specific forms our legalism takes. In some churches, it centers around jewelry and clothing. In others, it comes down to deifying one worship style over another. In still others, it means policing the political affiliations and allegiances of parishioners. The guises vary, but in the end, legalism in any guise deadens us towards God and towards our neighbors. It freezes us in time, making us irrelevant to the generations that come after us. It makes us stingy and small-minded, cowardly and anxious. It strips away our joy and robs us of peace. It causes us, in Jesus's chilling words, to "honor God with our lips" but to "worship him in vain."

What can we do instead? How can we discern whether a tradition is life-giving or not? Jesus gives his listeners this advice: notice what comes out of you. Notice what *fruit* your adherence to tradition bears. Does your version of holiness lead to hospitality? To inclusion? To freedom? Does it cause your heart to open wide with compassion? Does it lead other people to feel loved and welcomed at God's table? Does it make you brave? Does it ready your mind and body for a God who is always doing something fresh and new? Does it facilitate another step forward in your spiritual evolution?

Like everything else Jesus offers us, his encounter with the Pharisees is an invitation. An invitation to consider what is truly inviolable in our spiritual lives. An invitation to go deeper—past lip service, past tradition, past piety—and practice a religion that liberates. Not a "safe" religion. Or an easy one. But a religion of the whole heart, more valuable than gold.

# Only One Thing

## Luke 10:38–42

*But the Lord answered her, "Martha, Martha, you are worried and distracted by many things; there is need of only one thing. Mary has chosen the better part, which will not be taken away from her." (Luke 10:41–42)*

What do our domestic lives reveal about our relationships with God? What priorities, preoccupations, and anxieties do we lay bare in the way we conduct ourselves in our homes? In this Gospel story, Jesus's good friend, Martha, welcomes Jesus into her house. As soon as he arrives, Martha busies herself with the practical work of hospitality, cleaning, organizing, cooking, and serving. Meanwhile, her sister, Mary, sits at Jesus's feet and listens to his teaching, paying no attention to her harried sister.

It's a simple scene, its dramas small and subtle, but I cherish it for that very reason. I know this world—the world of quiet resentments that play out between close family members, the secret yearnings we harbor as we move through our daily chores and responsibilities, the martyr complexes we give into even as we attempt to be generous. This is a world I can relate to. Apparently, so can Jesus.

Luke's account doesn't tell us how long Martha holds her tongue after Jesus and his disciples arrive. I imagine she spends a good hour or so in the kitchen, banging pots and slamming drawers, hoping to catch someone's attention. Eventually her frustration boils over, and hospitality gives way to confrontation: "Lord, do you not care that my sister has left me to do all the work by myself? Tell her then to help me" (Luke 10:40).

It's quite the accusation. *"Lord, do you not care?"* Ouch. This isn't just frustration; it's a sense of abandonment. Of betrayal.

If I were in Jesus's place, I think I would give Mary a nudge into the kitchen, at the very least to keep the peace and ward off further conflict between the sisters. But Jesus redirects Martha instead: "You are worried and

48

distracted by many things. There is need of only one thing. Mary has chosen the better part, and it will not be taken away from her."

I'll confess at the start that Jesus's response leaves me feeling conflicted. Here are some of the reasons why:

I grew up in a traditional South Asian community that placed a high value on hospitality. I also grew up in an ethnic and religious context where "women's work" carried little spiritual value. Some of my earliest and most vivid memories involve sari-clad women (my mother, my aunts, and dozens of other "church ladies") hovering over tables laden with fragrant dishes, refilling a cup of juice here, offering a third helping of rice and chicken curry there, mopping up a coffee spill somewhere else—while the men talked, studied, debated, relaxed, and feasted.

Whether the occasion was a weekday home Bible study, a Sunday evening potluck, or the all-church Christmas party, the women prepped, cooked, served, and cleaned to make the gathering festive and fun. They did so with a strong sense of dignity and pride; after all, this was the work they had been raised to do. It was the work that marked their identities as "good women of God." But it didn't take me long as a kid to figure out that what counted as "real" spiritual work was the work the men did. The work of preaching, teaching, and leading worship.

To be fair, I don't think this was because the men were bad people. I think it was because the patriarchal culture that raised them made sure they never experienced the inside of a kitchen, a pantry, a clothes dryer, or a bottle of Pine Sol. They never saw the work that makes hospitality possible.

This is some of the baggage I bring to Martha's story, so when I read Jesus's response to her, my first response is disappointment. Yes, Jesus elevates the status of women by affirming Mary's right to discipleship. (Traditionally, only male disciples sat at a rabbi's feet to study the Torah.) This gender reversal is significant, and I don't take it for granted.

And yet. I want Jesus to do more. I want him to round up his (male) disciples, usher them into the kitchen, and direct them to bake the bread, fry the fish, and chop the vegetables—ideally, while Martha takes a much-needed nap. I want him to say, "Peter, please wash the dishes. James and John, put away the leftovers. Judas, get the beds made. Andrew, you're on mopping duty, and the rest of you: go ask the women what else they need done. Oh, and in case you're wondering: this work isn't a prelude to the sacred. This work *is* the sacred."

I wrestle with this story precisely because the implications are significant: if Jesus had taken a more radical stance in Martha's house, would his followers have wasted the next two-thousand years arguing over "a woman's rightful place" in the home and in the church? Would countless women today feel so self-conscious, judged, and shamed over how well they do or don't juggle the competing demands of their domestic, professional, and religious lives? Maybe. But maybe not.

I do believe that Jesus championed women in some essential ways during his lifetime. But the fact remains that in this particular story, Martha's burdensome sense of obligation and duty has cultural roots which Jesus doesn't confront on her behalf. Her anxiety doesn't come from nowhere; she lives inside a social and religious system that fully expects her to behave as she does, and the power of that system is formidable. In other words, Martha needs systemic change in order to live into the permission Jesus tries to offer her. She can't embrace such radical freedom by herself; she needs those in power to embrace it with her and for her.

So I wonder: What would it be like for us contemporary Christians to examine the systems and structures that still bind "Marthas" today? What would it cost us to dismantle those systems? What would it look like to create concrete opportunities for the overburdened in our midst to rest? To sit freely at Jesus's feet? To find support, community, and help as they struggle to become disciples? What would it look like to stand in solidarity with your nearest Martha as she unlearns a lifetime's worth of messaging about what makes her soul lovable, valuable, honorable, and holy?

The bottom line is, it's ridiculous to champion contemplation over action. The mystic over the activist. Worship over service. We need both. Our common life *requires* both. How would the church survive without people like Martha? The ones who bake the eucharistic bread, tend the flower beds, restock the votive candles, and sew the pageant costumes? After all, isn't it fascinating that Mary and Martha are sisters? Their differences can't erase the basic fact that they belong together. They *need* each other. They hold each other in balance. Right? Isn't this, finally, a story about balance?

I don't think it is. I don't think Jesus's ringing endorsement of Mary's "choosing the better part" will disappear so easily. Because the story is *not* about balance. The story is about choosing the one thing, the *best* thing—and forsaking everything else for its sake. The story is about single-mindedness. About a passionate and undistracted pursuit of a single treasure. Think of Jesus's most evocative parables; they all point in this same direction: the pearl of great price. The buried treasure in the field. The lost sheep. The lost coin. The lost son. Christianity is not about balance; it's about extravagance. It's not about being reasonable; it's about being wildly, madly, and deeply in love with Jesus.

As soon as Jesus enters Martha's house, he turns the place upside down. He messes with Martha's expectations, routines, and habits. He insists on costly change. Perhaps Martha's mistake is that she assumes she can invite

Jesus into her life—and then carry on with that life as usual, maintaining control, privileging her own priorities, and clinging to her long-cherished agendas and schedules. What is Jesus's response to that assumption? No. Absolutely not. That's not how discipleship works.

In contrast, Mary recognizes that Jesus's presence in her house requires a radical shift in her priorities, plans, and postures. A surrender. Every action, decision, and priority has to be filtered through this new love, this new devotion, this new passion. Jesus is no ordinary guest. He is the guest who will be Host. The Host who will provide the bread of life, the living water, and the wine that is his own blood to anyone who will sit at his feet and receive his hospitality.

It's easy for us to lose sight of Mary. In our work-frenzied, performance-driven lives, it's easy to believe that pondering, listening, waiting, and resting have no value. In our age of snark and cynicism, it's easy to roll our eyes at spiritual earnestness. In a world that is profoundly broken and unjust, it's easy to argue that we should leave contemplation to the monastics and throw all of our time and energy into social engagement. To be clear: we *are* called to work for justice. We are called to bring liberty to the oppressed and comfort to the afflicted. But every "work" we do must begin, Jesus insists, from "only one thing." It must begin with him. It must begin at his feet.

Jesus doesn't call Martha out for her hospitality. It is not her cooking, cleaning, or serving that bothers him. Notice the actual problem he names: "Martha, Martha, you are worried and distracted by many things."

The root meaning of the word "worry" is "strangle," or "seize by the throat" and "tear." The root meaning of the word "distraction" is a dragging apart of something that should be whole. These are violent words. Words that wound and fracture. States of mind that render us incoherent, divided, and un-whole.

Jesus finds Martha in just such a state of fragmentation, a condition in which she cannot enjoy his company, savor his presence, find inspiration in her work, receive anything he wishes to offer her, or show him genuine love. Instead, all she can do is *question* his love ("Lord, do you not care?"), fixate on herself ("My sister has left me to do all the work by myself"), and triangulate ("Tell her then to help me").

Does any of this sound familiar? Is your inner life so strangled, so incoherent, that you struggle to give and receive love? Are you quick to seethe in the places you call home? Has your busyness become an affront to the people you long to host and to love? Is your worry keeping you from being present, engaged, and alive? Have you lost the ability to attend? To linger? Are you using your packed schedule to avoid intimacy with God or with others?

My answer to many of these questions is yes. If yours is yes, too, then I wonder if we can hear Jesus's words to Martha, not as a criticism, but as an invitation. Not as a rebuke, but as a soothing balm. Jesus knows that we ache to be whole. He knows that we place brutal and devastating expectations on ourselves. He knows that our resentments, like Martha's, are often borne of envy.

Martha longs to sit where Mary sits. She longs to take delight in Jesus's words. She longs to surrender her heavy burden and allow Jesus to host her. Maybe we long for these good things, too. Here's the good news: there is need of only one thing. If we choose it, no one will have the power to take it away from us; this is the Host's promise. So choose it.

# The Widowed Prophet

## Mark 12:38–44

*A poor widow came and put in two small copper coins, which are worth a penny. Then he called his disciples and said to them, "Truly I tell you, this poor widow has put in more than all those who are contributing to the treasury. For all of them have contributed out of their abundance; but she out of her poverty has put in everything she had, all she had to live on." (Mark 12:42–44)*

"The Widow's Mite" is a classic Gospel story, a go-to narrative for church stewardship drives. Who hasn't heard the moving account of the widow who slips quietly into the temple, drops her meager offering into the treasury, and slips away? Who hasn't squirmed when a well-meaning pastor brings the story to its inevitable conclusion: "If a desperately poor widow can give *her* sacrificial bit, how much more should we—so comfortably wealthy by comparison—give out of our abundance?"

I'll admit it; I've squirmed. I've squirmed because this woman's brief appearance in Mark's Gospel haunts me; her story is sharp-edged and troubling. Something in me doesn't want her reduced to a moral or exploited for the sake of capital campaigns and annual budgets. Something in me feels indignant. I wish I knew her name. I wish we celebrated her fierceness, not just her generosity. I wish I could know for sure that she died in peace.

Died? Yes. She dies, probably mere days after she drops those two coins into the temple treasury. In case that's a surprise, consider again what Jesus says about her as she leaves the temple in Mark's narrative: "She out of her poverty has put in everything she had, all she had to live on." The Greek word behind "all she had to live on" is *bios* (from which we derive "biology.") It means "life." In other words, the widow sacrifices her whole life.

As far as I can tell from the Gospels, Jesus doesn't lie. If he says the woman gives everything she has, well, she gives everything she has. We know she's a widow in first-century Palestine, a woman living on the margins of her society. She has no safety net. No husband to advocate for her, no pension to draw from, no social status to hide behind. She is impoverished and vulnerable in every way that matters. Two pennies short of the end. If I'm getting the timing right, Jesus dies four days after the events in this story. I wonder if the widow does, too.

Here's why I'm troubled by her story: What does it mean to applaud a destitute woman who gives her last two cents to the temple before slipping away to starve? Is this really a story of selflessness? Or is it a cautionary tale about naivete? Should we cheer, weep, or complicate the story further?

Mark prefaces the widow's offering with an account of Jesus blasting the religious leaders of his day for their greed, pomposity, and crass exploitation of the poor. Beware of the scribes, Jesus tells his followers. They devour widows' houses and for the sake of appearance say long prayers. Their piety, in other words, is a sham, and the religious institution they govern is corrupt—not in any way reflective of a God who cares for orphans and widows.

Indeed, in the days leading up to the widow's last gift, Jesus offers one scathing critique after another of the economic and political exploitation he witnesses around him. He makes a mockery of Roman pomp and circumstance when he processes into Jerusalem on a donkey's back. He cleanses money-mongering with a whip. He refuses to answer the chief priests, scribes, and elders when they demand to know the source of his authority. He confounds religious leaders on taxes, indicts them with a scathing parable about a vineyard and a murdered son, defeats them on the question of resurrection, and bewilders them with riddles about his Davidic ancestry.

So why on earth would he turn around and praise a woman for endangering her already tenuous life to support an institution he considers corrupt?

The simple answer is, he doesn't. Read the story carefully; *he doesn't*. Centuries of stewardship sermons notwithstanding, Jesus *never* commends the widow, applauds her self-sacrifice, or invites us to follow in her footsteps. He simply notices her, and tells his disciples to notice her, too.

This is a moment in the story when I'd give anything to hear Jesus's tone of voice and to see the expression on his face. Is he heartbroken as he tells his disciples to peel their eyes away from the rich folks and glance in her direction instead? Is he outraged? Is he resigned? Does he tell one of his friends to run after the woman and offer her a bit of bread or a drink of water? What does it mean to Jesus, mere seconds after he has described the temple leaders as devourers of widows' houses, to witness just such a widow being devoured? And worse, participating in her own devouring?

Here's a telling postlude: immediately after the widow leaves the temple, Jesus leaves, too, and as he does, an awed disciple invites Jesus to admire the temple's mammoth stones and impressive buildings. Jesus's response is quick and cutting: "Not one of these stones will be left upon another; all will be thrown down" (Mark 13:2).

Ouch. I wonder if the widow is still on Jesus's mind as he predicts the destruction of the temple. He has just watched a trusting woman give her all to an indefensible institution, one that refuses to protect the poor. Is he saying that no edifice steeped in systemic injustice will stand?

Back to my earlier question: Should we cheer or weep in the face of this story? Or, here's a third alternative: Should we call out (as Jesus does) any form of religiosity that manipulates the vulnerable into self-harm and self-destruction? Any form of piety that privileges long-winded prayers over works of compassion and liberation? Any version of Christianity that valorizes suffering as redemptive? Any practice of faith that coddles us into apathy in the face of economic, racial, sexual, and political injustice?

Jesus *notices* the widow. He sees what everyone else is too busy, too grand, too spiritual, and too self-absorbed to see. For me, this is the only redemptive part of the story—that Jesus's eyes are ever on the small, the insignificant, the unloved, and the hidden.

What exactly does Jesus notice? I don't know for sure, but I'll hazard some guesses.

He notices the widow's courage. I imagine it takes quite a bit of courage for her to make her "insignificant" gift alongside the rich, with their fistfuls of coins. Even more to allow the last scraps of her security to fall out of her palms. And more *still* to swallow panic, desperation, and the entirely human desire to cling to life no matter what and face her end with hope.

Jesus notices her dignity. She has to steel herself when widowhood renders her culturally worthless—a person marked "expendable" even by the temple she loves. She has to trust that her tiny gift has value in God's eyes. In her astonishing generosity, Jesus recognizes a quiet power: those two coins are her gestures of defiance. They mark her subversive resistance to dehumanization.

And finally, Jesus notices her vocation. Whether she recognizes it or not, the widow's action in the temple that day is prophetic. She is a prophet in the sense that her costly offering amounts to a holy denunciation of injustice and corruption. Without saying a word, she speaks God's Word in the ancient tradition of Isaiah, Elijah, Jeremiah, and her other Hebrew ancestors.

But she is also prophetic in the messianic sense, because her self-sacrifice prefigures Jesus's. She, too, gives up her life in the face of an unjust system that exploits her. Perhaps what Jesus notices is kinship. Her story mirroring his. The widow gives everything she has to serve a world so broken, it kills her. Days later, Jesus gives everything *he* has to redeem, restore, and renew that same world.

# The Way of the Hen

## Luke 13:31–35

*"Jerusalem, Jerusalem, the city that kills the prophets and stones those who are sent to it! How often have I desired to gather your children together as a hen gathers her brood under her wings, and you were not willing!" (Luke 13:34)*

I f I asked you to draw a picture of Jesus, what would you draw? A blue-eyed shepherd holding a staff? A lion? A loaf of bread and a cup of wine? A door, a gate, a light, a bridegroom? What about a chicken? Would it occur to you to draw a chicken?

Growing up, I spent many summers visiting my grandparents in rural South India. Both of my grandmothers kept hens—whole flocks of the clucking, flapping creatures—and as a little girl raised in American suburbia, I found the birds hilarious. After all, they weren't the most elegant of creatures. They were squat and beady-eyed, nosy and boisterous. They couldn't fly to save their lives, and they made the funniest noises. Granted, they could be fierce when they wanted to be; I learned early on to keep my distance from their beaks. But there was something sad about their ferocity, too. Something defenseless. Something vulnerable.

To answer my own question: if I had to draw a picture of Jesus, no, I would definitely not draw a chicken. So I come to the story of Jesus grieving over Jerusalem and stumble at his self-description: "How often have I desired to gather your children together as a hen gathers her brood under her wings, but you were not willing."

Can you picture it? Jesus, the mother hen?

Here's the thing: if maternal power, acumen, or success are the characteristics Jesus wants to emphasize in his choice of metaphor, he has more impressive images to choose from in the Hebrew Bible. God as enraged she-bear (Hos 13:8). God as soaring mother eagle (Deut 32:11–12). God as laboring woman (Isa 42:14). God as mother of a healthy, happy toddler (Ps 131:2). God as skilled midwife (Ps 22:9–10).

But those are not the images he chooses. Instead, Luke invites us to contemplate Jesus as a mother hen whose chicks don't want her. Though she stands with her wings wide open, offering welcome and shelter, her children refuse to draw near. Her wings—her arms—are empty. This, in other words, is a mother bereft. A mother in mourning. A mother struggling with failure and futility.

In the verses that precede this heartbreaking description, a group of Pharisees warn Jesus to leave the area where he's teaching and healing, because Herod wants to kill him. Though Jesus knows full well that the tetrarch's displeasure is nothing to mess with (Herod is, after all, the villain who orders John the Baptist's arrest and beheading), he tells the Pharisees that he's not afraid of "that fox" (Luke 13:32). I have work left to do, he tells them, and I won't be deterred by the machinations of a bully.

At this point in the story, Jesus has set his course for Jerusalem, the city that rejects God's messengers and kills its prophets. Jesus knows exactly what fate awaits him there, but he won't change course. Not for Herod, not for anyone.

And yet, even as he stands up to a fox, Jesus is a mother keening in grief. What does this stunning image offer to us for our own faith journeys? Here are three things that strike me as I imagine a Mother Hen God:

First, we are called to embrace vulnerability. Yes, Jesus mocks Herod by calling him a fox. But he never suggests that the fox isn't dangerous. If a determined fox wants to kill a brood of downy chicks, he will find a way to do so. What Jesus the mother hen offers is not the absence of danger, but the fullness of his unguarded, open-hearted, wholly vulnerable self in the face of all that threatens and scares us. What he gives us is his own body, his own life. Wings spread open; heart exposed; shade, warmth, and shelter at the ready. What he promises, at great risk to himself, is the making of his very being into a place of refuge and return for his children. For *all* of his children. Even the ones who want to stone and kill him.

What would it take for us to embrace Jesus's vulnerability as our strength? To trade in our images of a conquering God for the mother hen of this Gospel passage? Maybe what we need most in this life is not a fox-like divinity who wields his power with sly intelligence and sharp teeth, but a mother hen who calls to us with longing and desperation, her wings held patiently and bravely open. A mother hen who plants herself in the center of her children's terror and offers refuge *there*, at ground zero, where the feathers fly and the blood is shed.

I've seen mother hens gather their chicks under their wings when a predator approaches. The way they swell with indignation, fear, and courage. The way they stand their ground. The way they prepare to die if they have to, their children tucked securely beneath their soft, vulnerable bodies. I can't imagine a more profound or radical picture of God. Can you?

Secondly, we are called to lamentation. You don't have to be a parent to mourn missed opportunities, broken promises, or crushed hopes. All of us, regardless of our circumstances, know what it's like to feel rejected. We know the pain of watching someone we care about slowly self-destruct before our eyes. We carry painful memories of unrequited love, unmet desire, unfulfilled dreams.

In this Gospel passage, Jesus grieves for his lost and wandering children. For the little ones who will not come home. For the city that will not welcome its savior. For the endangered multitudes who refuse to recognize the peril that awaits them. His is the lamentation of helpless yearning. "How often have I desired to gather you." It is a lamentation for all that could have been in this broken, resistant, clueless world. It is a lamentation for the real limits we live with as human beings. The lasting wounds. The lifelong losses. Sometimes, like Jesus the mother hen, we can't do what we most desire to do. We can't give what we deeply long to give. We can't save the loved ones we ache to save.

How might you be called to lamentation in the time and place you occupy? What do you yearn for that eludes you? What missed chances, failed efforts, or broken dreams tug at your heart and call you into mourning? How might we, the church, lament with Jesus over our homes, our cities, our countries, our planet? How might we stand with him in the Jerusalem of our lives and weep our sorrow into new hope?

Thirdly, we are called to return. "You were not willing," Jesus tells his wandering children. You would not come back. You would not relinquish your right to yourself, not even when your life depended on it. The image of chicks snuggling under a mother hen's wings is an image of gathering, of community, of intentional oneness. It requires a return. A surrender. A refusal to self-isolate.

In what ways are we unwilling to be gathered by God? Where and how have we chosen to go it alone, spurning divine love because we consider it too invasive? Too risky?

I won't lie; loving a vulnerable Mother Hen God is the riskiest thing some of us can imagine doing. We'd prefer the lion, perhaps. Or the infuriated bear. And yet, a yearning mother hen is the mother we belong to. She's the one weeping for us. She's the one calling us home. Her body and her heart are on the line, and yet her desire is fixed on us. She will not fold her wings and turn away. She will not leave us to die without sanctuary.

May the desire of Jesus become our desire, too. May the way of the mother hen—the way of vulnerability, sorrow, hope, and eternal welcome—guide us home.

# What Glory Looks Like

## Mark 10:35–45

*James and John, the sons of Zebedee, came forward to him and said to him, "Teacher, we want you to do for us whatever we ask of you." And he said to them, "What is it you want me to do for you?" And they said to him, "Grant us to sit, one at your right hand and one at your left, in your glory." (Mark 10:35–37)*

Y ou have to hand it to James and John for sheer nerve. In this Gospel story, Mark records what might be the boldest request recorded in the New Testament. The request is made by the guys Jesus calls, "Sons of Thunder," two brothers who leave their father's lucrative fishing business to become disciples. The nickname is an apt one for young men so hotheaded, they ask Jesus elsewhere in the Gospels to rain heavenly fire on a Samaritan village that refuses them hospitality (Luke 9:51–56).

As the story opens, Jesus is making his way to Jerusalem, all the while telling his disciples that torment and death await him there. Cue the Sons of Thunder: "Teacher, we want you to do for us whatever we ask of you." Astonishingly, Jesus responds to this presumption with patient curiosity: "What is it you want me to do?" "Grant us to sit," they respond without hesitation, "one at your right hand and one at your left, in your glory."

"Glory" isn't a word we use much nowadays. It's a churchy word we hear in sermons and hymns. But let's face it: we have our modern synonyms. Though our vocabulary differs, we recognize too well what James and John are asking for. Prestige, fame, praise, distinction, success, honor, renown. In short, the Sons of Thunder want to finish first, win big, and retire as privileged favorites with intimate access to Jesus's power and glory. In fact, they don't simply *want* these things; they're convinced that they *deserve* them.

It's easy to laugh, or to dismiss the two boys as fools. But Jesus takes the request seriously and engages in a conversation that is compassionate rather than condemning. Let's pause for a moment and consider what James and John get right in this story.

First, the two brothers place their full faith in the right person. Undaunted by Jesus's gloomy predictions of suffering, they cling to the belief that he will prevail in the end. Though they have no concrete idea what Jesus means by "resurrection," they trust him—his word, his power, his leadership, his mission. Given what they've seen, heard, and experienced, they can't conceive of a meaningful future apart from their teacher. Their personal hopes and dreams, imperfect though they might be, are rooted in Jesus.

Second, they are ambitious for the reign of God. They expect and want Jesus to be glorified; they expect and want the world's wrongs to be righted. They're not complacent about injustice, oppression, hatred, and violence; they actively long for Jesus to remake the world. Interestingly, Jesus does not criticize James and John for these ambitions. He doesn't say, "It's wrong of you to want greatness. It's sinful of you to strive."

Instead, he redirects their striving. He offers them a different definition of greatness. This suggests to me that God can and will work with our desires and ambitions. God *wants* us to want more, seek more, hope more, and need more. What's lethal to the spiritual life is apathy. Desires can be redirected. Ambitions can be purified. But an unwillingness to care? A numbness of soul? A refusal to hope because we fear disappointment? These are the dead ends. These are the roadblocks to grace and transformation.

Thirdly, James and John *ask*. They approach Jesus boldly and make their request with confidence. Is the request tacky? Yes. Is it borne of ignorance and immaturity? Yes. Are some of the motives behind the request selfish? Yes. And yet, *they ask.*

They engage in real relationship with Jesus and express an authentic desire to remain close to him. As I reflect on this, I am reminded of how often I don't ask, don't engage, and don't lean. How often I go through my days as if God doesn't exist, even as I profess to be God's child, God's follower, God's friend. Real relationships require honest engagement. They require love, affection, and an ongoing desire for intimacy. James and John exemplify all of these traits in their friendship with Jesus, and I would do well to follow in their footsteps. After all, the Sons of Thunder aren't just disciples; they're members of Jesus's beloved inner circle. Jesus allows them to witness many things the other disciples don't. There's something about their unguarded approach and demeanor that Jesus cherishes.

So, okay. The Sons of Thunder get some things right. But they also get a key thing wrong, and that's where the heart of this Gospel story lies. The easiest way to describe their error is to contrast the demand they make of Jesus with the question Jesus asks them in return. "Teacher," they say, "we want you to do for us whatever we ask of you." In other words: "We're entitled to something here, Lord. We're willing to wait patiently, but you'll need to give us our due in the end. After all, we've sacrificed a lot to be your disciples. What's in it for us?"

In return, Jesus asks the question he always asks: "What is it you want me to do for you?" Not, "Here's what I want," or, "Here's what I'm entitled to," but rather, "I am here to serve. How can I serve you?"

What James and John fail to understand is that service in the kingdom of God is not a second-class means to a first-class end. Service *is* the end. Service is abundance. Service is power. Service is glory. "Whoever wishes to be great among you must be your servant, and whoever wishes to be first must be slave of all" (Matt 20:26). By all means aspire to glory! But recognize that glory by Jesus's definition is not an accretion of privilege. It's not upward mobility. It's not permission to guard and hoard. Glory in God's kingdom is an exercise in subtraction. It's a movement downwards. It's the generous and perpetual expending of one's self in love.

I wonder if the fantasies of earth-shattering power and glory we impose on God are just that—our own fantasies. Maybe such a God is easier to deal with, more familiar, more palatable, more impressive. Why bother getting involved in the world's sorrows if God can wave a magic wand and fix everything while we wine and dine at some heavenly banquet? Why lean into our own creativity, why respond to our own deep longings for justice, why call each other out to engage in the slow, risky work of renewing creation, when "glory" means grabbing the fanciest seats in the throne room? Why contemplate a Jesus who glories in serving his guests—refilling their water glasses, warming up their leftovers, preparing their rooms, washing their feet—when we can worship Superman instead?

This story leaves us with two questions. Two options. James and John seek glory by privileging themselves: "Do *for us*. Grant *us*." Jesus epitomizes glory by privileging others: "What can *I* do *for you?*"

Dare we trade one question for the other? Dare we surrender privilege for glory? The invitation is to mature in a downward direction—to serve, serve, and serve some more. Can we find the courage to make Christ's trajectory our own?

# The Temple of His Body

## John 2:13–22

*The Passover of the Jews was near, and Jesus went up to Jerusalem. In the temple he found people selling cattle, sheep, and doves, and the money changers seated at their tables. Making a whip of cords, he drove all of them out of the temple, both the sheep and the cattle. He also poured out the coins of the money changers and overturned their tables. He told those who were selling the doves, "Take these things out of here! Stop making my Father's house a marketplace!" (John 2:13–16)*

A few years ago, I came across a hymn that stopped me in my tracks. Composed by Brian Wren, it's entitled "Good Is the Flesh." Here is just one of its many verses:

> Good is the flesh that the Word has become,
> good is the birthing, the milk in the breast,
> good is the feeding, caressing and rest,
> good is the body for knowing the world,
> Good is the flesh that the Word has become.[1]

"Good is the flesh" was not a phrase I grew up hearing in church. Though I learned early on that the Incarnation is central to Christian orthodoxy, I did not learn to link that doctrine to actual bodies, actual flesh. Much less did I learn to honor the sacred in skin, limbs, muscles, and hair—mine or anyone else's.

But that is precisely what Jesus does when he brandishes a whip, overturns the tables of the money changers, drives out the sheep and cattle, and dares his listeners to "destroy this temple" (John 2:19). They misunderstand, of course, and assume that Jesus is referring to the Herodian temple they're standing in. But no, John insists in this story. Jesus isn't referring to edifices

---

1. Wren, "*Good Is the Flesh*," 6.

63

built of stone or brick or wood. The home of the transcendent is not a court-yard, a parapet, or an altar. Rather, God resides in a different kind of temple altogether—the temple of Jesus's own body.

These days, I think a lot about what it means to honor human bodies as holy places. As homes for God. It's not an easy thing to do in a religious culture that too often views the body as shameful, irrelevant, or dangerous. But Jesus's encounter with the moneychangers in the temple suggests that there is a high cost involved in honoring human flesh as the home of the divine. What Jesus calls out when he "cleanses" the temple is not Judaism or its various forms of worship. It is a system of exploitation via exorbitant tithes and taxes that blocks access to the divine—that literally keeps the bodies of the poor outside the gates of the temple, forcing them into more and endless debt before they can approach and worship God.

In this story, Jesus interrupts worship for the sake of justice. He won't stand for the violation of sanctuary. He will not tolerate blocked access to God's house. He will not stomach any version of unfairness and cruelty to-wards the most vulnerable and beleaguered people in his society.

Jesus is a disrupter. A leveler. An up-ender. Zeal is what animates him. Fervor, not casualness. Depths, not surfaces. He is not impressed by "mar-ketplace" faith.

Where does this leave us? Perhaps we can begin by asking honest ques-tions about our reactions to the story itself. How do we feel about Jesus's posture, language, tone, and actions in the temple? Are we offended by his anger? His impatience? His violence? If yes, why? What cherished version of God, church, piety, or worship does Jesus threaten in this narrative?

And then: What are *we* passionate about when it comes to faith? What are we most inclined to defend or resist? What are we zealous for as mem-bers of the body of Christ? Is zeal even on our radars? Or have we settled for a way of being Christian that is more rote, safe, casual, and comfortable than it is disorienting, challenging, transformative, and missional?

We don't hear much about anger in mainline churches these days. We assume there's something unseemly about rage. Something unsophisticated, something crude. We don't consider it polite to get angry.

But Jesus—the temple of God—burns with zeal for his Father's house. He doesn't use love and forgiveness as palliatives; he allows a holy anger to move him to action on behalf of the helpless and the voiceless. In this story, there is nothing godly about responding to systemic evil with pas-sive acceptance or unexamined complicity. If human bodies are temples—holy places where heaven and earth meet—then it is incumbent upon us to protect these holy places from desecration. We need to stop believing that our highest calling is to niceness.

This cannot happen if we keep our faith lives tethered at the level of intellectual abstraction. If we live a Christianity of the mind without also living one of the flesh. After all, it is with our bodies that we experience pain, anger, terror, and joy. It's my chest that hurts when I mourn. It's my face that burns when I'm angry. It's my whole body that warms with pleasure when I'm happy.

As Christians who have inherited this story of Jesus enacting both anger and love, we need to ask ourselves where our commitment to embodied love has atrophied. Has our faith become so abstract that we no longer find it natural to rejoice with those who rejoice and mourn with those who mourn?

*Good is the flesh that the Word has become.* Do we believe this? Do we believe it enough to honor all bodies as temples of God? We dare not say a glib "yes," because Jesus's boldness in the temple hastens his death. If we follow the disrupter, if we upend the temple when it neglects to serve as the Father's house, if we burn with the passion that animates Christ's coin-scattering justice, our choices will cost us. At the same time, our churches will become houses of prayer and refuge, hope and transformation. Sanctuaries of welcome for all nations.

# But What Do *You* Think?

## Matt 16:13–23

> Now when Jesus came into the district of Caesarea Philippi, he
> asked his disciples, "Who do people say that the Son of Man is?"
> And they said, "Some say John the Baptist, but others Elijah, and
> still others Jeremiah or one of the prophets." He said to them, "But
> who do you say that I am?" (Matt 16:13–15)

In one of his famous "letters to a young poet," Rainer Maria Rilke encourages his protégé to sit with what he doesn't know. He writes:

> Be patient toward all that is unsolved in your heart. Try to love
> the questions themselves, like locked rooms and like books that
> are written in a very foreign tongue. Do not now seek the an-
> swers, which cannot be given you because you would not be able
> to live them. And the point is, to live everything. Live the ques-
> tions now. Perhaps you will then gradually, without noticing it,
> live along some distant day into the answer.[1]

In Matthew's Gospel, Jesus invites his disciples to live a question. "Who do
you say that I am?" he asks as they make their way through the villages of
Caesarea Phillipi. Who am I? Where do I stand in this life we're making
together? What do I mean to you?

Perhaps you're thinking, "Wait, that's not the kind of question Rilke is
talking about in his *Letters*. Jesus's question is not a question to *live* with; it's
a question to *answer*. It's a creed question. A doctrinal question. A question
requiring conviction and certainty. There's nothing 'unsolved' about Jesus, is
there? Isn't he the Way, the Truth, and the Life?"

Yes, he is. *And yet.* If his conversation with his disciples has anything
to say about it, we are *still* meant to live the question of who Jesus is. We're
not meant to "solve" God once and for all. We're not meant to land when it
comes to theology; we're meant to journey, wander, explore, and question.

1. Rilke, *Letters to a Young Poet*, 21.

As Matthew tells the story, Jesus prefaces his big question with an easier one: "Who do people say that I am?" What's the word on the street? What have you heard? What do the opinion polls suggest?

I don't know about you, but I can hear the schoolboy relief in the disciples' voices as they scramble to answer Jesus's question: "Oh, I know! People say you're John the Baptist! No, wait, they say you're Elijah! Actually, some folks think you're Jeremiah. Yeah, but others say you're one of the prophets!"

I'm guessing they go on for a while, each disciple trying to drown out the others with a more promising answer. Not coincidentally, the answers they come up with match the religious factions they're partial to. To put this in contemporary terms, imagine the disciples answering Jesus's question this way: "There's the Lutheran take on who you are. But here's the Calvinist one. Of course, the Anglicans say something else. No, wait, let's hear what the Evangelicals think. And the Catholics! Yeah, but what about the Pentecostals? Or the Orthodox? The agnostics and atheists have opinions, too."

Interestingly, Jesus neither affirms nor denies these answers. He simply listens, allowing his friends to offer up everything they think they know. As if to say: this is an okay place to begin. This is where all explorations of faith begin, in naming what we've heard, examining what we've inherited, and parroting back the certainties others have handed to us. These answers cost us little; they simply hearken back to tradition and offer us a foundation to build on. But we cannot stop there. At some point, the question of who Jesus is must become personal.

So Jesus presses on. "But who do *you* say that I am?" Looking at each disciple in turn, he awaits a more intimate answer, inviting them to set aside other people's theologies and articulate their own. It's as if Jesus asks them to consider carefully the life they've lived *with* him, in his company. The bread they've broken, the miles they've walked, the burdens they've carried, the laughter and the tears they've shared. "Who am I *to you?*" he wants to know. "How have *you* experienced me?"

Matthew doesn't offer much detail, but when I imagine what happens next, I see the disciples falling into an awkward silence. I imagine them avoiding eye contact with Jesus. Shuffling their feet. Casting anxious glances at each other. I imagine every one of them hoping that someone else will answer first.

Meanwhile, I imagine Jesus standing vulnerably in their midst through that long silence, waiting to hear what his closest friends will say. Do they know him? Have they learned to trust him? How much have they comprehended of his mission and vision, and how much are they willing to confess? Do they love him enough to speak a truth that might cost them?

Cue Peter. Bold, reckless, impetuous Peter. When the silence becomes unbearable, he throws himself forward and stakes his claim: "You are the Messiah, the Son of the Living God" (Matt 16:16).

A perfect, A-plus answer. The Truth with a capital "T." Right?

Well, sort of. Jesus commends and blesses Peter for the answer. He declares that he will build his church upon "the rock" of Peter's bold testimony. And he promises Peter "the keys of the kingdom of heaven" (vv. 18, 19). All of this is true and powerful and worth celebrating.

But it's not the end of the story. When Jesus goes on to describe the suffering and humiliation his messiahship must include, Peter backtracks, pulls Jesus aside, and tells him to shut up. Such morbid talk is not worthy of a real Messiah.

Peter's insistence that Jesus fit into his watered-down comprehension of divinity hits a nerve so raw, Jesus turns and rebukes him with words that shock us still, two-thousand years later: "Get behind me, Satan! For you are setting your mind not on divine things but on human things" (Mark 8:33).

As strange and stinging as this exchange is, I like what it teaches us about "living the questions" of faith. I like that Peter's confession— "You are the Messiah"—signals the *beginning* of his exploration of Jesus's identity, not its end. As soon as Peter thinks he has the answer to the question nailed down, Jesus shuts *him* up. Jesus challenges what he knows and nudges him back to the starting line: "Yes, I am the Messiah. But no, you have no idea what 'Messiah' means. In fact, you're not even *ready* to know what 'Messiah' means; you can barely tolerate my talking about it. There's so much more for you to learn, Peter. So many more answers for you to grow into. Be patient. Don't force the locked doors. Try to love what is unsolved. Keep living the question."

When I think about the whole of Peter's story—all the biographical details that we have the privilege to know and ponder—I'm stunned by the answers that Peter must have lived into as time went on. Answers he could not have articulated in the early years of discipleship.

"Who do you say that I am?" You are the one who found me in a fishing boat and gave me a new vocation. You're the one who healed my mother-in-law. You're the one who said, "Okay, walk on water." You're the one who caught me before I drowned. You're the one who glowed on a mountaintop while I babbled nonsense. You're the one who washed my feet while I tried to stop you. You're the one who told me—accurately—that I'd be a coward on the very night you needed me to be brave. You're the one I denied three times to save my skin. You're the one who looked into my eyes with pain and pity when the cock crowed. You're the one who fed me breakfast on a beach and spoke love into my humiliation. You're the one who gave me courage to preach to three-thousand people on Pentecost. You're the one who taught me that I must not call unclean what you have pronounced clean. You're the one who stayed by my side through insults, beatings, and imprisonments. You're the one I followed into martyrdom. You are the Messiah, the Son of the living God.

Who do *you* say that Jesus is? Who has he been to you in the past? Who is he now? Who do you hope he will be in the future? These are questions to ponder for a lifetime, questions that have so many others folded into them, we'll never exhaust the possibilities. What stories of Jesus have you inherited? What "truths" about him do you need to say goodbye to? What religious assumptions are you clinging to because they're familiar, safe, or easy? Why are you afraid at times to answer the question at all? Why does it fill you with shame? Is Jesus merely *the* Messiah? Or is he yours?

What Peter learns is that Jesus is just as powerfully present in the questions as he is in the answers. Maybe even more so. To love what is unsolved is to allow Jesus to enter more deeply into your heart than any impersonal claim about him will ever do. *Live the question.* That is Jesus's invitation, and he makes it over and over again to each one of us. An invitation of love.

# Wonders

"Earth is so thick with divine possibility that it is a wonder we can walk anywhere without cracking our shins on altars."

—Barbara Brown Taylor[1]

1. Taylor, *An Altar in the World*, 15.

# A Day in the Life

## Mark 1:29–39

*Now Simon's mother-in-law was in bed with a fever, and they told him about her at once. He came and took her by the hand and lifted her up. Then the fever left her, and she began to serve them. (Mark 1:30–31)*

In her 1989 book, *The Writing Life,* Annie Dillard offers us a disconcerting reminder: "How we spend our days is, of course, how we spend our lives. What we do with this hour, and that one, is what we are doing."[1]

I shouldn't be disturbed by this straightforward truth, but I am. Much of the time, I'm not impressed by how I spend my days, and I don't want them to "count" as my life. I tell myself that *this* day, or that shapeless string of days last week, or that dull six-month stretch two years ago, don't count. I erase them. What *will* count (I promise myself) are the days I *plan to live* in the future. Days filled with intention, purpose, and meaning. Days meticulously scheduled and faithfully executed. Days marked by attentiveness, order, devotion, and beauty. When I get around to living *those* days, I will sculpt my life.

It's a fantasy, of course, because Dillard is right. How we shape the quotidian is how we shape existence. Our mundane hours are not throwaways; they bear faithful, searing witness to what we care about. How we spend our days is how we spend our lives.

In the first chapter of his Gospel, Mark shows us a day in the life of Jesus. As the Messiah begins his public ministry, we follow him around for twenty-four hours, observing what he does, what he says, and what he prioritizes. In typical Markan fashion, this section of the Gospel races from one event to the next, favoring speed over depth. Still, if we look carefully, we can find moments to linger over and lessons to savor. The point isn't to compare our days to Christ's and despair at our inadequacy. The point is to

1. Dillard, *Three by Annie Dillard,* 568.

trust that we are saved not only by Jesus's death and resurrection, but also by his *life*. Reflecting on that life is nourishing and salvific; it moves us closer to Christlikeness and closer to the heart of God.

So. A day in the life. Here's how Jesus spends it:

*He makes home sacred:* Mark begins with Jesus leaving the synagogue after Sabbath worship, entering the home of Simon and Andrew and spending the rest of the day in that domestic space. This might sound like a trivial detail, but I like the fact that Jesus lingers at home, blessing a humdrum location with his presence and honoring it as a sacred site where the work of God goes forward.

We know from the rest of the Gospels that some of Jesus's most significant encounters happen in homes. He performs his first public miracle at a home in Cana. He raises Jairus's daughter in the synagogue leader's house. His friend, Mary, anoints him with oil at her home in Bethany. Salvation comes to Zacchaeus when the despised tax collector welcomes Jesus as a houseguest. The disciples on the Emmaus road recognize Jesus when he breaks bread at their dinner table.

Holy things happen in the places we call home. God's power and presence are not limited to official sacred spaces. Our living quarters are not second best when it comes to seeking and finding Jesus. If anything, Jesus delights in the domestic.

For me, this delight is a particular comfort during these days of CO-VID, when I am largely confined to my home. There have been so many days in the past year when I've felt restless, trapped, and in limbo, as if "real life" is suspended, and nothing spiritually significant will happen until the world's lockdowns and quarantines are over. I'm grateful to know that Jesus isn't put off by the mundane as I am; he does amazing work in spaces I consider dull and ordinary.

What would it be like for us to honor our homes as Jesus honors Simon's? To elevate our living spaces as sites for the sacred?

*He heals:* Jesus's first act in this chapter of Mark is to heal Simon's mother-in-law. Hearing that she's feverish and bedridden, he goes to her side, takes her by the hand, and lifts her up. Immediately, the fever leaves her body, and she is restored to health. Some hours later, the "whole city" gathers around Simon's door, likewise seeking healing from diseases and demons. Again, Jesus cares for them as a compassionate healer, curing many.

I'll be the first to admit that I don't always know what to do with Jesus's healing stories. Is it just me, or have things changed rather drastically since he walked the earth two-thousand years ago, ushering in God's kingdom with all manner of miraculous signs and wonders? Don't get me wrong—I love the healing stories in the Gospels. I love the power and compassion with which Jesus touches the sick and the suffering. But sometimes, I wish that Matthew, Mark, Luke, and John had included a few less dramatic stories in their books, too. Did Jesus ever, for example, visit a feverish woman, take her hand, and offer only the comfort of his presence, without curing her? Did he ever sit in the dark with a profoundly depressed man—just sit? Did he ever keep vigil at a deathbed and cry with the family as they said goodbye? No resurrection, just tears? Did he ever experience God's "no," or God's "wait," when he sought to heal someone?

Obviously, I don't know, but I hang onto these possibilities, because they describe the world I live in. What I *know* is that Jesus spent many hours of his life offering whatever compassion, healing, and liberation he could. In Mark's opening chapter, he heals "many," not all. He casts out "many demons," not all of them.

But somehow, the "not all" doesn't stymie him; he still touches everyone who reaches out for help, because touch in and of itself is an instrument of hope and healing. He doesn't assume that illness and demon possession are punishments from God. Instead, he loves without measure, because love cures many ills.

In short, he offers the sick and the broken his steady presence, his warm embrace, and the good news of a kingdom that is coming—a kingdom without sickness, without sorrow, without fear. And his offers are enough.

Maybe our task as healers isn't to perform magic. Maybe spending our days as Jesus spent his means living graciously and compassionately in this vast and often terrible in-between. To offer the comfort of our steady presence to those who suffer. To encourage those in pain to hang on, because the work of redemption is ongoing. To create and to restore community, family, and dignity to those who have to walk through this life sick, weak, and wounded— without cures. To make sure that no one who has to die—and that's all of us, in the end—dies abandoned and unloved, if we can help it.

*He liberates and commissions:* Mark's Gospel tells us that as soon as Jesus heals Simon's mother-in-law, she "begins to serve" (Mark 1:31). I'll be honest: my initial reaction to this detail was disappointment and frustration. *Of course,* I thought, the poor woman has to leap out of bed and serve the men in her house the second her fever leaves her. Of course no one allows her to rest and regain her strength for a few hours. Of course the men don't serve *her.* Isn't that so typical of this sexist world?

Maybe. Maybe what we're reading in this story is sexism, pure and simple. But I wonder. The verb Mark uses to describe his mother-in-law's service is the same verb the Gospels use to describe the angels who attend Jesus after his forty days in the wilderness. It is the same verb Jesus uses to describe himself when he washes his disciples' feet: "I am among you as one who serves" (Luke 22:27). It is the same verb the early church uses to commission deacons, the "servant" leaders of the church.

What if Simon's mother-in-law is not an undervalued woman in a patriarchal system, but the church's first deacon? The first person Jesus liberates and commissions into divine service?

If nothing else, it's interesting to note that this unnamed woman recognizes and pursues her calling *before* her son-in-law and his friends do. While Simon and his gang bumble around, getting in Jesus's way, this woman gets to work without hesitation or self-consciousness, engaging in grateful ministry alongside Jesus. In healing her, Jesus also liberates and commissions her.

Though we know little else about the woman's life, we can safely assume that her ministry is effective. In First Corinthians, we read that Simon Peter's wife accompanies him on his apostolic journeys after Jesus's resurrection and ascension. Clearly, Simon's mother-in-law has a long-term impact on the faith of her daughter and her extended family.

Insofar as we are invited to heal, we are also invited to free others for service. We're invited to pay attention, to notice, and to bless the gifts and abilities of those around us. We're meant to spend our days as liberators, commissioning the healed to become healers.

*He prays:* The next morning, Marks writes, while it's still dark, Jesus goes to a deserted place to spend time with God. This is not a one-off; we know from the other Gospels that prayer is one of Jesus's daily practices: "But Jesus often withdrew to lonely places and prayed" (Luke 5:16). "After he had sent the crowds away, he went up on the mountain by himself to pray; and when it was evening, he was there alone" (Matt 14:23).

In "minor" verses like these, we see glimpses of Jesus's deeply rooted spiritual life, the source of his strength and vision. We see his need to withdraw, his hunger for solitary prayer, his inclination to rest, recuperate, and reorient his heart. These glimpses take nothing away from Jesus's divinity; they enhance it, making it richer and more mysterious. They remind us that the Incarnation truly is Christianity's best gift to the world. The Christ—the Messiah of the whole universe—prays, rests, reflects, and meditates. He needs time alone. He needs time alone *with God*. He is just like us.

Jesus understands the ongoing and necessary tension between compassion and self-protection in a world bursting with need. Jesus lives with this tension every day, and he is unapologetic about his need for solitude. Even as the crowds throng, he feels no shame in retreating when he needs a break.

This is an apt lesson for those of us who live in cultures where tireless striving is a virtue, and the need for rest is considered a weakness. It's also a challenge to those of us who *think* about prayer a lot, without actually set-ting aside time to pray. When our hours and days are measured, how many of them will we have spent alone with God?

*He moves on:* The story ends with Jesus leaving Simon's house so that he can take the good news to other towns, other synagogues, other homes. He makes this decision despite the fact that his disciples interrupt his prayer time to tell him that "everyone" is still searching for him back at Simon's house. Clearly, there are compelling reasons for Jesus to stay where he is, but his response is to set a boundary. To say no. To move on in keeping with his own sense of mission and timing.

Given Jesus's compassionate heart, I can't imagine that he makes this decision lightly. I imagine it costs him something. But after a morning of prayer and reflection, he recognizes and trusts the voice that says, "It's time to go."

What can we learn from Jesus's choice? Can we learn that sowing a seed and walking away is sometimes appropriate? Can we set boundaries in the face of pressing need? Can we relinquish fame and power, and choose obscu-rity? Can we risk the new and unknown? Can we hold firm to our sense of vocation even when our loved ones don't agree with our choices?

As we sculpt the hours that make up the days that make up our lives, who or what directs our decisions? Are we, like Jesus, able to let go and move on?

How we spend our days is how we spend our lives. Let's spend ours well.

# Same Old, Same Old

## Luke 5:1–11

*When he had finished speaking, he said to Simon, "Put out into the deep water and let down your nets for a catch." Simon answered, "Master, we have worked all night long but have caught nothing. Yet if you say so, I will let down the nets." (Luke 5:4–5)*

I t is early morning, and Simon Peter is cleaning his fishing nets after a miserable night on the lake. He and his partners have worn themselves out, casting nets from dusk till dawn. When the sun rises, they have nothing to show for their efforts but sore muscles and weary hearts; their nets are empty.

Just then, Jesus shows up, steps into Simon's boat, and tells his would-be disciple to "put out into the deep water." That is, to do the *same old same old* one more time, with no guarantee of better results.

Understandably, Simon protests: "Master, we have worked all night long." But then he obeys: "Yet if you say so, I will." As soon as Simon's net hits the water, everything changes. His emptiness gives way to epiphany.

I love this story for many reasons. First, I love that it describes failure so honestly. I'm no fisherman, but I know what it's like to work hard at something that matters, and have nothing to show for my efforts when I'm done. We all do. We all know what it's like to pour ourselves into a job, a relationship, a ministry, a dream, only to come away exhausted, thwarted, irritated, and *done*.

But if Simon's experience is representative, Jesus has a penchant for showing up at precisely such moments of loss and defeat. For reasons we often don't understand until later, he asks us to return to old sore spots of failure, and our spiritual health depends on how we respond to his invitation. Notice that when he asks, he doesn't stand at the shore and send us off; he steps into the boat and ventures into the deep water with us. Is his timing maddening sometimes? Yes. But maybe his timing is also perfect. Maybe we're most open to revelation when we've exhausted our own resources, when we've got nothing to lose in saying yes to one more attempt, this time with Jesus at our side.

Second, I appreciate the way the story honors the "same old same olds" of our lives. Jesus's call to Simon is specific and particular, rooted in the language, culture, and vocation the fisherman knows best. Simon and his partners understand the nuances of Jesus's "fishing for people" metaphor in ways I never will. They know from years of experience what depths of patience, resilience, intuition, and artistry professional fishing require. Simon knows the tools of the trade, the limitations of his body, and the life-and-death importance of timing, humility, and discretion. Most of all, he knows the water. He knows how to respect it, how to listen to it, and how to bring forth its best. When Jesus shows up and commissions the seasoned fisherman, Simon understands the call not as a directive to leave his experience and intelligence behind, but to bring the best of his knowledge and expertise forward—to become even more fully and freely himself.

This suggests to me that we're not called to follow Jesus in the abstract. We don't become Christians "in general," as if faith involves nothing more than attending church or being a nice person. If we're going to follow Christ at all, we'll have to do it in the particulars of the lives, communities, cultures, families, and vocations we find ourselves in. We'll have to trust that God prizes our intellects, our backgrounds, our educations, and our skills, and that God will bless and multiply the daily stuff of our lives for God's purposes.

In other words, Jesus's invitation to venture into deep water is a promise to cultivate us, *not* to sever us from what we love. It's a promise rooted in gentleness and respect, not coercion. It's a promise that when we dare to "go deep," God will enliven our efforts in ways we can't imagine.

Third, I love the liberation and abundance at the heart of this story. At a time when the fishing industry in Palestine is fully under the control of the Roman Empire, when Caesar owns every body of water, and all fishing is state-regulated for the benefit of the urban elite, Jesus dares to challenge the system. He knows full well that fishermen can't obtain licenses to fish without joining a syndicate. He knows that most of what they catch is exported, leaving local communities impoverished and hungry. He knows that the Romans collect exorbitant taxes each time fish are sold, and that to catch even one fish outside of this exploitative system is illegal.

How amazing (given this historical context) is an image of boats so laden with fish that even a weathered fisherman like Simon Peter finds the catch overwhelming. This is extravagant generosity. Food for all, food security for all, justice for all, nurture for all. In this eucharistic image of plenitude, Jesus shows Simon what God's kingdom looks like. God's kingdom is not Caesar's. God's kingdom suffers no empty nets, no empty tables. God's kingdom is good news for all.

Lastly, I love this story because it tells the truth about my fraught journey with faith: "Master, we have worked all night long but have caught nothing. Yet if you say so, I will let down the nets." I'm suspended in the gap between those two searing sentences. Is it just me, or do we all live in the gap between weariness and hope, defeat and faith, resignation and obedience? Though we're often reluctant to admit it, for fear of sounding ungrateful or irreverent, life can be a grind. A same old same old of monotony and failure. Even the most earnest and hardworking among us can land up on shore some mornings with empty, stinking nets tangled in our fingers, wondering what is wrong with us.

The hardest thing to do at such moments is to make the leap of trust that Simon makes. *"Yet if you say so, I will."* Yet if you say so, I will try again. Yet if you say so, I will be faithful to my vocation. Yet if you say so, I will choose depth instead of shallowness. Yet if you say so, I will trust that your presence in the boat is more precious than any guarantee of success.

Yet if you say so, I will cast my empty net into the water, and look with hope for your kingdom to come.

# They Have No Wine

## John 2:1–11

*When the wine gave out, the mother of Jesus said to him, "They have no wine." And Jesus said to her, "Woman, what concern is that to you and to me? My hour has not yet come." His mother said to the servants, "Do whatever he tells you." (John 2:3–5)*

"They have no wine." I doubt it's the line I'm supposed to fixate on, but I can't help it. I wonder how Mary says it. Does she pull her distracted son away from his friends before she whispers it in his ear? Is there an edge to her voice? Is her tone urgent, echoing the growing panic of the servants? I imagine she takes Jesus into an inner room, fixes his attention with a stern stare, and braces herself for pushback. *They have no wine.*

The wedding in Cana story is not—finally—a story about scarcity. It's a story about plenitude. About God's extravagant and limitless generosity.

Needless to say, there is much theological richness to mine in the story. The eschatological significance of a wedding as the backdrop for Jesus (our bridegroom's) first miracle. The importance of celebration, pleasure, and hospitality that Jesus affirms in conjuring 150 gallons of first-rate wine, just to keep a party going. God's desire and capacity to transform the ordinary into the sacred, the weak into the strong, the incomplete into the whole. The foreshadowing of the communion table in the sharing of wine.

But what strikes me is the pivotal role Mary plays in the story. Her line, "They have no wine," is a line I can get behind, because it's more than a statement of fact. It's an articulation of need. Of desperation. Of hope. Essentially, it's a prayer of intercession for a world that is not okay.

"They have no money." "She has no health insurance." "He has no friends." "I have no strength." Mary's line is a line I repeat daily, in endless iterations, for myself and for others. It's the line I cling to when I feel helpless, when I have nothing concrete to offer, when God seems to be a million miles away. It's a line that insists on the mysterious power of telling God the truth.

Mary's role in Jesus's first miracle is an odd and provocative one, but I'm grateful for it, because it allows me a place in what otherwise feels like an inaccessible narrative. I have no idea how to turn gallons of water into gallons of wine. But I do know how to say what Jesus's mother says. Sometimes, it's the *only* thing I know how to say. "There is need here." "Everything is not okay." "We're in trouble." "They have no wine."

So what does Mary do that we might learn from? How does she participate in Jesus's miracle of abundance?

*Mary notices.* In first-century Palestine, wedding feasts lasted for days, and it was the host's responsibility to provide abundant food and drink for the duration of the festivities. To run out of wine is a dishonor and a disgrace—a breach of hospitality the guests will remember for years.

I can easily imagine how the servants at Cana go limp with fear when the wine disappears; this is the kind of miscalculation that might cost them their jobs. We have no idea what Mary's connection is to the bride and groom; all we know is that she is one wedding guest among many. But she is the one who notices need. She sees what's amiss. She perceives the high likelihood of scandal and humiliation brewing beneath a seemingly glossy surface. If John's account is trustworthy, Mary notices and registers concern before Jesus does.

*Mary tells the right person.* John's Gospel doesn't include Jesus's infancy narratives. No angelic annunciations, no babe in the manger, no prophetic words or portentous stars. But the Mary this Gospel describes still knows her son. She knows what he's capable of and she trusts that he alone can meet the need she perceives. I love the assurance with which she brings her distress to Jesus. Given her thirty-year history with him, given the relationship they've cultivated, she is as certain of his ability and generosity as she is of the need itself.

*Mary persists.* This, for me, is the oddest and yet most encouraging part of the story. I don't know what to make of Jesus's reluctance to help when Mary first approaches him. "What concern is that to you and me?" he asks dismissively when he hears about the dwindling wine supply. "My hour has not yet come." Of course, Jesus is no fool; he knows that his countdown to crucifixion will begin as soon as he makes his identity known. Maybe he's reluctant to start that ominous clock ticking. Maybe he thinks wine-making shouldn't be his first miracle. Maybe there's a mysterious timeline he wants to follow—a timeline known only to him and to God.

Whatever the case, Mary doesn't cave in the face of his reluctance; she continues to press the urgency of her need into Jesus's presence. As if to say, "I don't care about your timeline! There's a desperate problem, right here, right now. Change your plans. Hasten the hour. Help!"

*Mary instills trust and invites obedience.* "Do whatever he tells you," she advises the household servants. She doesn't wait to hear the specifics of Jesus's plan. She doesn't pretend to know the details. She doesn't invent a roadmap. She simply communicates her longstanding trust in Jesus and invites the servants to practice the minute-by-minute obedience that makes faith possible.

The servants' task isn't easy. There's no running water in the ancient world, and those stone jars are huge. How many trips to the well, how much arm strength, how deep a resolve would such a task require? I imagine it's Mary's faith that helps the servants persevere when they feel bewildered and ridiculous. She acts as a catalyst, turning potential into action. She lays the groundwork for Jesus's instructions: "Fill the jars." "Draw some out." "Take it to the chief steward." She fosters a faith-filled atmosphere that becomes contagious. Instilling wonder in those around her, she ushers in her son's miracle.

Maybe I'm drawn to Mary because it's a hard business, holding the promise of God's abundance up against the agony of this world's scarcity, pain, and need. I love the miracle itself and all that it signifies. But I'm more acquainted with water than I am with wine. Many of us are, if we're honest. It doesn't matter what the particulars look like—chronic illness, physical pain, financial trouble, systemic injustice. Regardless of how we rewrite Mary's line to match our circumstances, it rings true for all of us, in some guise or another. *They have no wine.*

So what do we do? How do we participate in miracles of plenty? Maybe we can be like Mary. Maybe we can notice, name, persist, and trust. No matter how profound the scarcity, no matter how impossible the situation, we can elbow our way in, pull Jesus aside, ask earnestly for help, and ready ourselves for action. We can tell God hard truths, even when we're supposed to be celebrating. We can keep human need squarely before our eyes, even and especially when denial, apathy, or distraction are easier options. We can invite others to obey the miraculous wine-maker we have come to know and trust.

"They have no wine." "Do whatever he tells you." We live in the tension between these two lines. Let's live there well, sure of the one whose help we seek and confident that our asking matters.

# The Exorcist in the Synagogue
## Mark 1:21–28

*Just then there was in their synagogue a man with an unclean spirit, and he cried out, "What have you to do with us, Jesus of Nazareth? Have you come to destroy us? I know who you are, the Holy One of God." But Jesus rebuked him, saying, "Be silent, and come out of him!" (Mark 1:23–15)*

When was the last time an uninvited stranger walked into your church and took over the pulpit? How many exorcisms have you witnessed in the last month? How often do you spend Sabbath afternoons debriefing miracles? In this story from the Gospel of Mark, Jesus enters a synagogue, teaches with authority, astounds his listeners, casts out an unclean spirit, and becomes famous throughout the land. Can you relate?

Let's face it: this story is a tough one. How might we imagine our way into it? Can we picture ourselves as members of the ancient audience which hears Jesus speak? Can we align ourselves with the man possessed by the unclean spirit? Can we experience the story through Jesus's eyes? Each of these role plays will pierce us in different ways, so let's imagine:

*The audience.* We don't know their names, ages, or backstories. All we know is that they show up in the synagogue on the Sabbath, listen to Jesus teach, and find themselves astounded and amazed. I had to read the story half a dozen times before I realized something: I can't relate to these people. I can't remember the last time I was "astounded" and "amazed" by Jesus. Can you?

According to Mark, the people who hear Jesus in the synagogue are amazed because he comes with "a new teaching" and teaches "as one having authority" (Mark 1:21–28). The implication, of course, is that Jesus's audience is receptive to newness. Open to wonder. Am I? Do I approach my spiritual life with curiosity or boredom? Do I sit in the pew on Sunday mornings wanting to contend with something new? Or do I expect to be coddled and commended?

These are especially hard questions to ask ourselves if we've been Christians for a long time. The new becomes old. The fresh becomes familiar. The heart hunkers down for an unvarying long haul, and we forget that Jesus comes to make all things new. The audience in Mark's Gospel is "amazed and astounded" by the work of God because they allow Jesus to be unfamiliar in their midst. This need not be the anomaly. It *shouldn't* be. Jesus is amazing when we allow him to be. Amazement is the birthright of God's children.

*The man with the unclean spirit.* I'll get the obvious out of the way and admit that I have no idea what the "spirit" is in this story. Some commentaries recast the demon as a mental illness or a medical condition like epilepsy. Others insist on it being an actual spirit, a malevolent being that ensnares human souls. Still others argue that spirits in the New Testament are metaphors for anything that might "possess" or "control" us—anger, fear, lust, greed, hatred, envy.

I don't know which one of these explanations is true, and I'm not sure it matters. When I try to imagine my way into the life of the man with the unclean spirit, what disturbs me is not "who" or "what" the spirit is, but how utterly it ravages the poor man whose body and mind it possesses. The man has no voice of his own; the spirit speaks for him. The man has no control over his body; the spirit convulses him. The man has no community; the spirit isolates him. The man has no dignity; the spirit dehumanizes him.

Granted, this picture of "possession" is extreme. But all of us suffer under the bondage of "spirits" that diminish us. All of us know what it's like to lose agency and dignity to forces too powerful for us to defeat on our own. All of us know what it's like to cede control to demons that makes our lives unmanageable. Whether we regard such forces as spiritual, psychological, biological, or cultural, this story tells us true things about how "unclean spirits" affect and manipulate our lives.

In Mark's story, the unclean spirit goes to the synagogue and listens to Jesus. It recognizes "the Holy One of God" before anyone else does. It calculates the stakes, realizes that Jesus's presence signals its doom, and puts up a vicious fight before it surrenders.

Does any of this sound familiar? Sometimes our "unclean spirits" take up residence in our holy places. We carry our destructive habits and tendencies right into our churches, our friendships, our families, and our workplaces. Sometimes our demons—our fears, addictions, sins, and compulsions—recognize Jesus first because they know that an encounter with the holy will change everything. They make us recoil as soon as Jesus shows up in the guise of a loving friend or a provocative sermon or a wise book or a pricked conscience. Sometimes our lives actually get *harder* when we move towards healing, because unclean spirits always fight hardest when their time is up.

What possesses us? What wreaks havoc in our hearts and minds? What distorts our humanity? These forces might not leave our lives without a fight, but the Jesus of Mark's Gospel will do battle for us if we'll let him. Will we?

*Jesus.* Mark never tells us what Jesus teaches his audience that day. All we know is that he enters the temple, speaks with an authority his listeners find astonishing, and underscores that authority with an exorcism. Is this a character we can even approach, much less emulate?

I think the story offers a couple of plausible takeaways. First, Jesus doesn't use his authority to self-aggrandize or to consolidate power. He uses it only to heal, free, serve, and empower those around him. Maybe this is precisely why his audience finds him so compelling; his is the authority of a servant king. He has no political power. No earthly throne or kingdom to speak of. But he has an integrity that is irresistible.

Second, Jesus steps directly into the pain, rage, ugliness, and horror at the heart of this story. He isn't squeamish and he doesn't flinch. His brand of holiness doesn't require him to keep his hands clean. He is *in* the fear, in the sickness, in the nightmare, ready to engage anything that diminishes the lives of those he loves.

Yes, he preaches with great effectiveness to the faithful, but he also speaks the unclean spirit's language, listens to its cries, and rebukes it for the sake of a broken man's health and sanity. Consider the question the spirit asks: "What have you to do with us, Jesus of Nazareth?" There's only one answer: "Everything. I have *everything* to do with you." Wherever pain is, darkness is, torment is, *God is.* God has everything to do with us, even and maybe especially when we're at our worst.

May we, like the audience in the synagogue, recover holy amazement. May we, like the man with the unclean spirit, fight our way towards freedom. And may we, like Jesus, speak words of love and healing into the world's pain.

# Out on the Water
## Matthew 14:22–33

*And early in the morning he came walking toward them on the sea. But when the disciples saw him walking on the sea, they were terrified, saying, "It is a ghost!" And they cried out in fear. (Matt 14:25–26)*

I grew up with a fearless version of Christianity. A Christianity of brave fronts and polished surfaces that forbade the open acknowledgement of fear and anxiety. If you're not familiar with this brand of religion, here are some of its key platitudes:

"Fear not" appears in the Bible more often than any other imperative. It's a *commandment*. To disobey it is to sin.

Perfect love casts out fear. If you're afraid, you're not rooted in God's love.

You can't be fearful and faithful at the same time. Fear is a sign of faithlessness.

I wish I were exaggerating, but I'm not; I grew up hearing these supposedly devout responses to fear all the time, and I tried for years to live into them. But instead of inspiring courage, they coated my ever-present anxieties in guilt, shame, and hopelessness.

In Matthew's story of the disciples' sea crossing, Jesus's friends contend with deep, atavistic fear. Fear of the unknown. Fear of suffering. Fear of death. Fear of oblivion. The setting is the Sea of Galilee, a body of water surrounded by hills and prone to sudden, violent windstorms. It's nighttime, and the disciples are crossing on their own, as per Jesus's instructions. As the night wears on, the wind and waves intensify, and the disciples, still far from land, struggle against the turbulent water. Meanwhile, Jesus, having spent the previous day teaching and feeding the multitudes, is up in the hills, seeking renewal in solitude.

Sometime before dawn, he descends from the hills and approaches the boat. When the disciples see him walking on the water towards them, they're terrified. "It's a ghost!" they cry.

"Immediately," Matthew's Gospel tells us, Jesus identifies himself in an effort to reassure his disciples: "Take courage! It is I. Don't be afraid" (Matt 14:27). As far as we know, eleven of the disciples, frozen in fear, say nothing. But Peter—impetuous, over-the-top Peter—proposes a bizarre test to prove the would-be ghost's identity: "Lord, if it's you, tell me to come to you on the water." Jesus says, "Come," and out of the boat Peter goes (vv. 28, 29).

For a few luminous seconds, Peter walks on the water towards Jesus. Then he realizes what he's doing. He notices the vicious wind, the rising waves, the dark water, and fear overwhelms him. Beginning to drown, he cries, "Lord, save me!" (v. 30). Immediately, Jesus catches Peter, and delivers him to safety.

"You of little faith," Jesus says to the breathless, sopping disciple, once danger is past. "Why did you doubt?" (v. 31). We never hear Peter's answer, if he manages to offer one. But as soon as he and Jesus climb into the boat, the wind dies down, the sea grows still and calm, and the disciples recognize Jesus for who and what he is. "Truly," they say in awe, "you are the Son of God" (v. 33).

On the face of it, this story might appear to reinforce a "Fear Not!" version of Christianity. I've certainly heard sermons that declare as much: "See? When Peter exercises bold faith, he does the impossible! But when he gives in to fear, he nearly drowns."

I don't agree with this reading. In fact, I think this reading is dangerous. Nowhere in the Gospels are we called to prove our faith, or test God's character, by taking pointless risks that threaten our lives. Nowhere in the Gospels does Jesus teach us that bad things happen to us because we're too cowardly to earn God's protection. Whether we're talking about respecting the power of the sea during a vicious storm or heeding expert medical advice during a global pandemic, the same caution applies: recklessness is not faith, stupidity is not courage.

But then, what is this story teaching us? Notice carefully the timeline of events as Matthew's Gospel relates them. When the disciples see Jesus walking on the water, they're terrified. They don't recognize him; they think they're seeing a ghost. Naturally, they cry out in fear. At that instant ("immediately"), Jesus offers comfort and reassurance. He tells them exactly who he is. "Take courage! It is I! Don't be afraid."

We don't know if the silent eleven take Jesus at his word. But we know for sure that Peter does not. He sets Jesus an identity test. *"Lord, if it's you . . ."*

Can you hear the echoes of another famous identity test in Peter's words? The identity test Jesus faces in the wilderness, forty days after his baptism? *"If you are the Son of God . . ."* These are the tempter's words. Words that wed Jesus's identity to spectacle, to drama, to "proof."

What's at play here is not the morality or immorality of human fear. What's at play is *how* we respond to God's presence when we're afraid. What do we say, think, feel, and do when the divine comes to us in guises we don't recognize?

The disciples are not wrong to be afraid. Of course they're afraid! They're afraid because they aren't keen on drowning. They're afraid because gigantic waves in the middle of the night are scary. They're afraid because they lack the tools with which to process what they're seeing; human beings don't have the ability to walk on water.

There are so many ways to "drown" in this turbulent world. To find ourselves in over our heads. Fear comes when we face lethal viruses and failing economies, social isolation and political brokenness. Fear comes when unhealthy marriages, sick children, unfriendly neighbors, grinding jobs, and financial uncertainty threaten our lives. Fear comes when our bodies betray us into anxiety, panic, and depression.

The issue is not fear; the issue is where fear leads. Notice the first place Peter's fear leads him. It leads him straight to suspicion and distrust. His fear leads him to test and question Jesus's identity. Instead of taking Jesus's self-disclosure at face value, he demands proof. *"If it's you, enable me to do the impossible. If it's you, make magic happen so that I will be dazzled out of all doubt. If it's you, reorder reality and prove to me that you're God."*

Peter's fear response cuts right through me; I recognize it so well. Like him, I fail to recognize Jesus when the going gets rough. When I face fearsome circumstances, my go-to position is not trust; it's suspicion. I forget that my relationship with God is multifaceted and I reduce it to something crassly transactional: "Prove yourself to me."

Interestingly, Peter's test fails. Despite his initial boldness, he is not able to prove who Jesus is by walking on water. Why? Because Jesus doesn't calm the sea for Peter's convenience. Even though Peter steps out of the boat, his circumstances remain wild, turbulent, and dangerous. If Peter thinks he can manipulate Jesus into making faith easy, he learns otherwise. *Fast.*

To truly trust Jesus is to hold two pictures of God's kingdom in productive tension. Yes, sometimes Jesus demonstrates his power in miraculous Technicolor. At other times, we need to trust that his quiet, abiding presence in our wild, untamed lives is sufficient for the circumstances we face. Sometimes, Jesus's power is paradoxical; it comes to us in what looks like vulnerability, like weakness, like strangeness. The wildness of the sea is no proof of God's absence.

Once Peter is safe in the boat, Jesus asks him the question he can't answer: "You of little faith, why did you doubt?" I wonder if Jesus asks this question *not* because Peter gives way to panic and nearly drowns, but because his doubt compels him to make a foolish request in the first place. I wonder if Jesus's question means something like this: "Peter, as soon as you saw me, I told you exactly who I was. You heard my voice. I spoke words of assurance and comfort to you. Why didn't you believe me?"

Maybe, when Jesus asks us why we doubt, what he's really asking is: Why do you doubt *me?* Why do you not trust that I'll be honest with you? Why do you doubt that I am with you, for you, in you, and around you? After all this time, why do you still feel a need to test me?

In my mind, the power of this story doesn't lie in Peter's faith, doubt, courage, or fear. Peter's trajectory—fascinating though it is—is not the point of the narrative. *Jesus's* trajectory is the point because, unlike Peter's, it never changes. It is constant, focused, and relentless.

From the very beginning of the story, Jesus *moves towards* his disciples. He moves towards them when they're struggling at sea. He moves towards them when they decide he's a menacing ghost. He moves towards them when they're terrified by his approach. He moves towards them when they're reckless enough to set him a dare. He moves towards them when they begin to drown. He moves towards them when they ask for help. He moves towards them when they're shivering and sorry for their foolishness. He moves towards them when they realize who he is and what he is. He moves towards them when they worship him.

In other words, Jesus never stops moving towards the ones he loves. He never stops crossing the dark water to come to where we are. Neither our fearfulness nor our faithlessness alters his steady approach, because we are the ones he's bound for. Ours is the boat he climbs into and our flailing bodies are the ones he pulls out of the water. It is for us that he calls out across the terrifying waves, again and again and again: "Take courage. It is I. Don't be afraid."

# The Question That Hurts

## John 5:1–9

*When Jesus saw him lying there and knew that he had been there a long time, he said to him, "Do you want to be made well?" (John 5:6)*

I f you've spent any time reading the Gospels, you know that Jesus asks blunt questions. "Do you love me?" (John 21:15); "Why are you so afraid?" (Mark 4:40); "Are you also going to leave?" (John 6:67); "How long shall I put up with you?" (Matt 17:17); "Do you still not understand?" (Mark 8:21).

But the question he asks a man at the pool by the Sheep's Gate might be the most jarring of all. He asks it in Jerusalem, near the five porticoes by the pool, where people with chronic illnesses and disabilities lie waiting. Rumor, legend, or tradition has it that an angel visits the pool at random times, stirring up the water and giving it healing properties. The first person to step into the pool after the angel disturbs it receives healing.

Jesus visits this outdoor nursing home one day, finds a man lying by the pool who has been sick for thirty-eight years, and approaches him with a question. No introductions. No small talk. No sermon. Just a question: "Do you want to be made well?"

Is it just me, or is this an uncomfortable-making question? How would you feel if you were sick for close to four decades, and a stranger came along one day and asked if you *really* wanted to get better? Implying that your ongoing sickness is at least partially your fault. Implying that you are benefiting, consciously or unconsciously, from remaining sick. Implying that you are somehow invested in your brokenness, that you have stakes in it, that your identity is so wrapped up in your infirmity, weakness, or defeat, you can't imagine your life without your illness.

How would you feel? How would you respond? Would you hear insult in the question? Or would you hear a faint echo of the truth? The kind of truth that hurts?

Let me be clear: I don't believe that Jesus is victim blaming in this story. All four Gospels attest to his compassion for those struggling with illness and disability. Not once does he respond to physical or psychological suffering with mockery or condescension. Not once does he tell a sick person that her illness is her own fault. In fact, he *corrects* that cultural misunderstanding at every opportunity.

All of that to say: I trust Jesus's heart and his motives enough to take his question at face value. When he looks at the man who has been languishing by the pool for thirty-eight years, he sees more than sickness. He sees defeat. He sees resignation. He sees stagnation. He sees a man whose hope has dwindled. A man whose imagination has atrophied. A man who can no longer articulate what he wants for his future.

How do I know this? Well, notice that the man doesn't answer Jesus's question. "Do you want to be made well?" Jesus asks, and the man doesn't say yes. Isn't that odd? After thirty-eight years of suffering, he doesn't say yes. Instead, he gets defensive.

He explains the mechanics of scarcity in his nursing home: "I have no one to put me into the pool." He makes a case for the cutthroat unfairness of the world: "While I am making my way, someone else steps down ahead of me" (John 5:7). He invites pity, he hems and haws, he dodges. In short, he avoids answering Jesus's question, which isn't a question about the man's circumstances, but a question about his heart, his identity, and his desires: "What do you *want?*"

Have you ever considered this question? Have you squirmed under it? What do you want? Do you want to be made well from all that stymies, hobbles, paralyzes, and diminishes you? Do you want to stand up? Do you want to walk? Do you want to move?

How have you answered these questions in the past? How would you answer them today? Do you know?

For me, the question stings because I know exactly what it's like to *say* I want out, to say I want freedom, to say I want healing—and not quite mean it. I know what it's like to cling to brokenness because it's familiar. I know what it's like to make victimhood my identity. I know what it's like to benefit from the very things that cause me harm. I know what it's like to sink into self-pity and assume that everyone else has access to a magic pill I'll never get my hands on. I know what it's like to decide that I'm doomed to sit at the very edge of healing for the rest of my life and never attain it.

For me, the question stings because the very idea that God cares about what I want, that God is curious about my desires, and wants me to recognize and articulate them, blows me away.

But if I'm willing to sit with the uncomfortable truths at the heart of this Gospel story, maybe I can come to know that Jesus's desires for me aren't murky and fickle like mine are. He wants me to be made well. *Period.* He wants me to walk again. To thrive again. To live again. He wants to deliver me from the paralysis of my past, my baggage, my fear, my laziness. He wants me to *want,* and to want fiercely. He wants me to say yes. Do you want to be made well? *Yes.*

If there's anything more remarkable in this story than Jesus's question, it's what happens after he asks it. "Stand up, take your mat and walk," Jesus tells the man. And the man does exactly that. "At once," John tells us, "the man was made well, and he took up his mat and began to walk" (vv. 8–9).

Notice that the man never asks for healing. There's no indication in the story that he knows who Jesus is. Notice that Jesus makes no reference to belief, as he often does when he performs a healing miracle. He doesn't tell the man, "Your faith has made you well," because that would be a lie. Notice that Jesus doesn't dwell on the man's past; he doesn't dredge up the loss and waste of the thirty-eight years the man can't get back. And notice that he doesn't heal the man on the man's terms, by helping him into the pool when the angel stirs the water. Jesus simply tells the man to get up and walk. And he does.

What I take away from this story is that Jesus is always and everywhere in the business of making new and making well. His desire to heal is intrinsic to his character; it doesn't depend on me. In other words, "Do you want to be made well?" is a question he will never stop asking, because his heart's desire is for my wholeness, my freedom, and my thriving, and he understands that there is painful, surgical power in the question itself. Confronting the question of what we want—what we *really* want—is how the work of healing begins.

# Be Opened

## Mark 7:24–37

*Now the woman was a Gentile, of Syrophoenician origin. She begged him to cast the demon out of her daughter. He said to her, "Let the children be fed first, for it is not fair to take the children's food and throw it to the dogs." (Mark 7:26–27)*

What does it mean to call Jesus "perfect"? Does perfect mean sinless? Flawless? Whole? Complete?

The Jesus I grew up with was perfect in the sense that he never messed up, never fell short, and never had to say he was sorry. To question anything he said or did was to cast aspersions on his deity. If he happened to speak harshly? If he behaved in ways that were ethnocentric? If he called a pleading woman a dog? Well, his reasons for doing so were perfect.

The problem with this version of a "perfect Jesus" is that he doesn't appear in the Gospels. The Jesus of the New Testament is not *half* incarnate; he is as fully human as he is fully God. Which is to say, he struggles, he snaps, he discovers, he grows, he falters, he learns, he fears, and he overcomes. He's real, and he's authentically one of us. The good news of Christianity is not that Jesus is "perfect." It is that Jesus shows us—in real time, in the flesh— what it means to experience and embody the perfect grace of God. Over his lifetime, Jesus grows into the fullness of God's love, justice, compassion, and mercy. He learns obedience. In his full humanity, Jesus shows us what a life infused with God's love and loveliness looks like.

Christianity puts a lot of emphasis on "opening." Opening our hearts to Jesus's presence and salvation. Opening our eyes and ears to the broken world God wants us to see. Opening our minds to receive the truth.

But in the story of Jesus and the Syrophoenician woman, it is Jesus himself who must experience an opening. He has to have *his* eyes opened and *his* ears unstopped. It's the Son of God who must face his own blind spots, his own rudeness, his own prejudice, and allow himself to be opened to the full, glorious, and uncomfortable implications of the Gospel.

As the story opens, Jesus is far from home in the region of Tyre and Sidon (that is, Gentile country), on vacation or sabbatical. As far as we know, his friends aren't with him, and as the text makes clear, he wants to be left alone. "He entered a house and did not want anyone to know he was there" (Mark 7:24) We don't know for sure why he's keeping to himself, but we can assume that some combination of physical, emotional, and spiritual exhaustion has led him to seek solitude. For days he has fed the multitudes, healed the sick, liberated the demon-possessed, and confronted the Pharisees—all while putting up with his perpetually clueless disciples. For any number of understandable reasons, Jesus needs a break.

But a break isn't what he gets. Instead, he gets a Syrophoenician woman. An inconvenient outsider who barges into the house where he's staying, kneels at his feet, and begs him to cast a demon out of her daughter.

Anyone needing to protect "perfect" Jesus has to perform some serious gymnastics to justify what happens next, because it's disturbing. Jesus looks down at the Gentile woman, ignores the content of her plea, and dismisses her with words that make me wince: "Let the children be fed first, for it is not fair to take the children's food and throw it to the dogs."

Are there ways around the awfulness of this moment? Maybe. Maybe Jesus is bone tired and wants, just for once, to take care of himself before taking care of someone else. Maybe he's fed up with people begging him for gifts and favors. Maybe he's telling the truth about his mission: the healing he offers is for the children of Israel first. Maybe his ethnic slur is a test, a deliberate provocation to prove the woman's devotion.

These are all possibilities, but I don't think they do justice to the power of this story. What makes sense to me is that the Jesus we encounter here is fully human, a product of his time and place, shaped as we all are by the conscious and unconscious biases, prejudices, and entitlements of his culture. Yes, he is God incarnate. But he is also a Son still working out the scope and meaning of the divine vocation his Father has given him. He knows he's meant to share the good news. But as a human being, even he needs to "be opened" to how radically good that good news is.

So the Syrophoenician woman schools him. Turning his slur right back at the man who insults her, she replies, "Sir, even the dogs under the table eat the children's crumbs" (Mark 7:28).

It's a brilliant response, not least because it cuts to the heart of Jesus's boundary-breaking, taboo-busting, division-destroying ministry of table fellowship. After all, he's the Messiah who eats with tax collectors. He's the rabbi who breaks bread with sinners. His disciples are the ones who earn the Pharisees' contempt for eating with unwashed hands. The table is where Jesus shows the world who God is.

And so the table is precisely where the outsider, the Gentile, the outcast, the "Other," calls him out. As if to say, "Lord, where's *my* good news? Where's my place at the table? When will your goodness be good enough for me and for my daughter? If you are who you say you are, how can you be content while *anyone* goes hungry in the vicinity of your table? Look harder. Push further. See better. Expand the circle. Dissolve the boundaries. Widen the table. Preach your good news *to me*."

Here's the best part of letting our perfect Jesus go and letting the Jesus of the Gospels win our hearts instead: the Jesus of the Gospels accepts the instruction of the woman who challenges him. He allows her—the ethnic, religious, and gendered Other—to school him in his own gospel. To deconstruct his bias and entitlement. To break the barrier of his prejudice. To teach him compassion. The Jesus who never loses a verbal contest with anyone else in Scripture sits back in amazement and concedes the argument to an audacious, female foreigner: "Because of your teaching [in the Greek, your *logos*] the demon has left your daughter" (v. 29).

Jesus changes. He allows a perspective foreign to his own to move him from an attitude of prejudice to an attitude of inclusion. He allows himself to be humbled, rearranged, and remade. The Syrophoenician woman's faithful appeal teaches him that God's purpose is bigger than he has imagined.

I can almost hear Jesus's rueful laughter when he goes immediately from this encounter to his healing of a deaf man in the region of the Decapolis. Placing his fingers in a Gentile man's ears, Jesus looks up to heaven, sighs, and says, "Be opened" (v. 34). He *sighs*. Is the sigh ironic? Is it Jesus sharing a joke with God? As in, "Okay, I get it. Be *opened*. I hear you."

What would it be like to follow in the footsteps of a Jesus who listens to the urgent challenge of the Other? Who humbles himself long enough to learn what only a vulnerable outsider can teach? What would it be like to insist on good news for people who don't look, speak, behave, or worship like we do?

Be opened. Be opened to the truth that God isn't done with you. Be opened to the destabilizing wisdom of strangers. Be opened to God speaking from places you consider unholy. Be opened to the widening of the table. Be opened.

# When Daughters Go in Peace
## Mark 5:21-43

*Then one of the leaders of the synagogue named Jairus came and, when he saw him, fell at his feet and begged him repeatedly, "My little daughter is at the point of death. Come and lay your hands on her, so that she may be made well, and live." So he went with him. And a large crowd followed him and pressed in on him. Now there was a woman who had been suffering from hemorrhages for twelve years. She had endured much under many physicians, and had spent all that she had; and she was no better, but rather grew worse. (Mark 5:22-26)*

There aren't many Scripture verses that bring tears to my eyes as quickly as this one from Mark's Gospel: "But the woman, knowing what had happened to her, came in fear and trembling, fell down before Jesus, and told him the whole truth" (Mark 5:33).

The woman has been bleeding for twelve years. Her condition is a shaming one; it renders her ritually unclean, which means she can't enter the Temple, the heart and soul of her religious community. She cannot touch or be touched by anyone without making them unclean, too. By the time she approaches Jesus, she has spent every penny she owns on healthcare—"enduring much" (v. 26) under several physicians, only to have her condition worsen. She is a woman whose life circumstances have diminished and thwarted her. Her very body—its femaleness, its porousness—has become a source of isolation and disgrace. She is an outcast, an embarrassment, a pariah. Lonely beyond description.

Until one day, she makes a decision. A desperate and stunning decision to practice civil disobedience. To defy the religious rules of her day, and pursue healing from Jesus. She knows she has no business polluting the crowds with her presence. She knows she's forbidden to touch the healer everyone is raving about. She knows that even her fingertips on his cloak will defile him. But she decides to touch him, anyway.

If the story ended there, with a stolen touch, a quiet healing, and an invisible but still potent transformation of this woman's life, I would consider it miracle enough. But no. Jesus invites more. He *insists* on more. He insists that the woman, terrified though she is, come forward and tell her story. Her "whole truth." This is the part of the story that brings me to tears.

Jesus knows that the woman has spent twelve long years having other people impose their narratives on her. *Their* interpretations, assumptions, and prejudices. She's been reduced to caricature and shamed into silence. Jesus knows that even if the woman trembles, stammers, and takes all day to tell her story, she needs someone to listen, to understand, and to validate her "whole truth" in the presence of the larger community. This is what Jesus does. He creates space for her story. He listens. He allows her to speak her whole, complicated, painful truth, and by doing so, he restores her to fellowship, dignity, and humanity. "Daughter," he says when she is finally finished, "Daughter, go in peace" (v. 34).

Part of the reason I find this story so compelling is because I know firsthand the trauma of silencing and the power of risky truth telling. When I was nineteen years old, I tried to tell my family a "whole truth" about my childhood—a dark, secret truth I had carried alone for ten years. I still remember how hard my hands shook and my heart pounded as I sat my family down around our kitchen table and whispered the ominous words no one likes to hear: "We need to talk."

The truth I needed to tell was that I'd been sexually molested as a child and young teen. During the years the abuse was happening, I had no language for it, no narrative I could fit the violations into. All I understood was that something terrible was happening, something I must have caused and therefore deserved. I didn't know to call the abuse criminal; I took every shred of blame into my own bones. By the time the abuse ended, I believed that my body was polluted. Ugly, promiscuous, and dishonorable.

My attempt to tell my family the truth came after my first year away at college, a year during which I finally faced the trauma of the molestation and began the process of healing. I practiced telling for weeks, mouthing the awful words into the bathroom mirror or writing them down to get the sentences just right. Then, one weekend while I was home, I sat my family down, took many deep breaths, and asked them to listen.

They couldn't. My "whole truth" was too taboo to fit into any narrative they could understand. Some things were sayable, and some were not, and while my religious and cultural community could tolerate small doses of truth, whole truths involving sex, gender, abuse, and the female body were too dangerous to name. Whole truths like mine belonged in the shadows, and I was told to keep them there.

I was lucky, though, in that I eventually found people who could bear my story. They listened as I stumbled over my words, and with their help, I pulled the ugly truth out into the light. Over many months and years, these good people walked alongside me, carrying my whole truth with grace and compassion. With each shaky retelling, the story lost more of its sting. In the patient, tender company of loving listeners, I healed.

> *But the woman, knowing what had happened to her, came in fear and trembling, fell down before him, and told him the whole truth.*

Something beautiful happens when we give each other permission to tell the truth. Something festers, withers, and dies when that essential permission is denied to us. For me, the experience of having my loved ones turn away from my story was a trauma nearly as damaging as the abuse itself. It unhoused and unhinged me. But the experience of having people listen with compassion and wholeheartedness? That experience saved my life.

There's an intimacy and tenderness to this Jesus story that I find so compelling, even though the story takes place in public, in a crowd, with people pressing in on all sides. Somehow, in the midst of the noise and the chaos, Jesus stops, notices, and listens. He creates space. He amplifies and blesses what has been diminished.

The story of the bleeding woman in Mark's Gospel sits right alongside the story of another thwarted daughter. A little girl has fallen ill and died, and when her father pleads for help, Jesus enters the man's house, demands that the grieving bystanders not pronounce death where he sees resurrection, and approaches the dead child's bedside. Within minutes, the girl is raised and returned to her overjoyed family.

In each of these stories, Jesus returns a lost child of God to community and intimacy. In each of these stories, Jesus grasps the impure and the taboo (the menstruating woman, the dead girl's corpse) so that mercy can overcome shame and sorrow. In each story, a previously hopeless daughter "goes in peace," because Jesus finds value where no one else will.

What does love look like in the Gospels? It looks like the teacher in a crowd who notices the trembling tug of shaking fingers on his cloak. It looks like a heart that melts at the cry of a desperate father. It looks like the healer who visits a sick child and takes her limp body into his arms. It looks like the man who risks defilement to touch the bloody and the broken. It looks like the God who insists on the whole truth, however falteringly told. It looks like the Christ who waits with tenderness as a voiceless woman finds her voice. It looks like Jesus, who renames the outcast "daughter" and bids her go in peace.

# Legion

## Luke 8:26–39

*Then they arrived at the country of the Gerasenes, which is oppo-site Galilee. As he stepped out on land, a man of the city who had demons met him. For a long time he had worn no clothes, and he did not live in a house but in the tombs. (Luke 8:26–27)*

He haunts the places of the dead. Every night, the townspeople hear him, shrieking among the tombs. When they're quick enough, they catch him, wrap his wrists and ankles in chains, and haul his naked body back to town. But there's no containing what torments him; he escapes each time. Trailing broken chains behind him, he wanders the wilds, tearing at his skin until it bleeds, trading one kind of pain for another. If he has a name, no one knows it. If he has a history, no one remembers it. If he has a soul worth sav-ing inside his living corpse, no one sees it, because no one looks.

Until Jesus does.

The story of the "Gerasene demoniac" is a tough one for us twenty-first-century Christians, because it's full of details we find bizarre. Chatty demons. Suicidal swine. Instantaneous healing. Isn't this the stuff of horror movies?

I know that much ink has been spilt trying to address what contem-porary Christians find anachronistic about Jesus's exorcism stories. Was the man among the tombs really possessed by demons or "just" mentally ill? Isn't it dangerous to conflate psychological suffering with evil? If the demons were real, why did Jesus negotiate with them? Why did he show them mercy? What about those poor pigs? Why did they have to die to secure the demo-niac's healing? Didn't Jesus care about them or about the economic welfare of the townspeople whose livelihood disappeared over a cliff?

These are important questions, but I worry that focusing on the strange parts of the story prevents us from seeing how it can be *our* story, a story for here and now. Here's why *I'm* haunted (in good and necessary ways) by the healing of the Gerasene demoniac. Here's why his experience of Jesus makes me linger and recoil, repent and return.

First, I think the story is ours because it begins where we should begin, and that is with a question. "What is your name?" (Mark 5:9), Jesus asks the possessed man who approaches him. Notice that the man approaches—*not* to ask for help, but to push Jesus away. Maybe to *scare* Jesus away. In all likelihood, his approach is violent and feral. But Jesus asks for a name anyway, and by doing so, he begins to recall the broken man to himself. To his humanity, to his beginnings, to his unique identity as a child beloved of God.

*What is your name?* Has there ever been a more searching question? What would happen if you allowed Jesus to ask it of you? What would happen if you asked it of others? Who are you? Who are you, *really?* Beneath the labels and the diagnoses, the pretense and the piety, the fear and the shame? Who are you when no one is looking? What name do you yearn to be called in the lonely stretches of the night? Who were you before you lost yourself? Before someone hurt you? Before you withdrew from the pain? Do you remember?

Jesus begins where we must begin. With an honest questioning and naming of ourselves. Can we allow him to search us so deeply?

Second, I believe the story is our story because it tells us the unflinching truth about our condition. "Legion," the man says in response to Jesus's question (v. 9). My name is Legion. A multitude. A vast host. An incalculable swarm. Why? Because (Luke's Gospel tells us) "many demons" torment him. In other words, the sources of his brokenness are myriad. The assault on his mind, soul, and body is multi-pronged; it comes from many sources braided together.

Perhaps it doesn't matter how we explain the "demons." Regardless of what language we use (biblical, theological, medical, sociological), what we know for sure is that the man's condition strips him of agency, sanity, dignity, and community. It keeps him in isolation. It renders him anonymous. It encourages him to mutilate his own body. It deadens his soul and divides his mind. In short, it deprives him of self-control and propels him towards self-destruction.

The truth is, what ails us as human beings *is* legion. The evil that haunts us has many faces, many names. We are all—every one of us—vulnerable to forces that seek to take us over, bind our mouths, take away our true names, and separate us from God and from each other.

Some of us suffer from depression or anxiety. Some of us are addicted to sex, alcohol, wealth, or thinness. Some of us experience the world at a deafening volume in colors too lurid for our sensitive eyes. Some of us are slaves to the internet or marred by bitterness or caught up in cycles of dishonesty. Some of us can't shake traumatic memories. Some of us were abused as children. Some of us struggle with jealousy. Some of us are imprisoned within systems of injustice that stretch back so many centuries, we can't imagine liberation. Some of us experience our skin colors, accents, genders, or sexualities as magnets for other people's hatred. Some of us suffer illnesses that crisscross the boundaries of medicine and culture, nature and nurture.

If we expand the definition of "possession" to include everything that conspires to keep us dead when God wants us alive, then the story of the Gerasene demoniac is not an ancient oddity at all. It is the air we breathe. The zeitgeist we inhabit. It is the pandemic of our time.

That's the bad news. But it's not where the story ends. The third reason I consider the story "our story" is because it tells us where salvation lies, and it does so without hesitation or apology. When the demoniac sees Jesus, he falls down before him. When the townspeople come running to see what's going on, they find the man "sitting at the feet of Jesus, clothed and in his right mind" (v. 15). Salvation, in other words, lies in surrendering to the one the demons flee.

But is this the story we offer to the "possessed" who walk through our doors each Sunday? Is it a story we even believe anymore? Or has the long haul of this thing we call Christianity, with its stretches of unanswered prayer, its unhealed diseases, its too-frequent grinds of grief, loss, doubt, and boredom, worn out our souls?

The problem is, we live in the uncomfortable tension between the already-and-the-not-yet. Yes, Jesus has defeated death. Yes, the demons fear his name. Yes, we are right to look to God for healing and liberation. But no, the battle isn't over. The abyss hasn't swallowed the demons whole. The freedom we seek is not yet within our grasp.

But that doesn't mean the story is false. It means we have more to look forward to. It means our hope is grounded in what Jesus has already done, in the power he has already demonstrated. It means we are heirs of good news already.

If only we could stop there. But Luke goes one step further in his account of the Gerasene demoniac, so we must, too. The fourth reason to embrace this story as our own is because it illustrates an unpleasant truth about human relationships. When the townspeople see that the demon-possessed man is healed, they don't rejoice. They express no relief, no gratitude, no hospitality, no awe. Instead, they recoil in fear and beg Jesus to go away.

What does this mean? Maybe it means that we humans prefer to stick with demons we know, rather than embrace freedoms we don't. Maybe it means we need some people to be "bad" so that we can be good. Maybe it means the shackles and chains that bind so many of God's children are the instruments of our own making, the weapons we wield to manage our own fears. Maybe it means the Gospel doesn't always bring peace—it also brings upheaval and offense. Maybe it means resurrection comes along and kicks our butts so hard we ask Jesus to leave us alone, because we'd so much rather stay dead.

The story ends with Jesus commissioning the healed man to stay where he is and serve as the first missionary to his townspeople—the same townspeople who fear, shun, trap, and shackle him for years. I have to admit, this detail makes me laugh. Isn't this just like Jesus? To choose the very people we consider the most unholy, the most unredeemable, the most repulsive and unworthy—and commission *them* to teach us the Gospel? That is God all over.

Here, then, is a story about our truest names. Here is a story about resistance and resurrection. A story about the Jesus who finds us naked among the tombs, scatters our demons, and clothes us with dignity for the healing of the world.

# Enough and More

## John 6:1–21

*Then Jesus took the loaves, and when he had given thanks, he distributed them to those who were seated; so also the fish, as much as they wanted. When they were satisfied, he told his disciples, "Gather up the fragments left over, so that nothing may be lost."*
*(John 6:11–12)*

I grew up with parents who were always feeding people. I can barely remember a weekend when we didn't have family members, parishioners, college students, or neighbors sitting around our dining table. My earliest memories involve warm, bustling kitchens; my mom garnishing fragrant pans of lamb biryani with cashews and raisins for a church potluck; my dad presiding over hamburgers, hot dogs, and tandoori chicken at our annual Sunday School barbecue. Waking up to the fragrance of onion-ginger-garlic (India's culinary trinity) frying on our stove was almost a daily occurrence.

As a child, I had no idea how much time, effort, and commitment went into my parents' lifestyle of hospitality. Nor did I know that my parents valued feeding people because they knew firsthand what it felt like to go hungry. Only as a young adult did I learn that each of them experienced lean times back in India, times when drought, recession, or failed crops rendered food scarce. My father, in particular, has vivid memories of going to bed hungry as a little boy. As I came to appreciate later, it was my parents' own, acute awareness of hunger—of what it feels like to need and not get—that motivated them to extend an open table to others.

The story of Jesus multiplying loaves and fishes to feed a multitude is the only story that appears six times across the four Gospels. Clearly, this event meant a lot to the early church. But what does it mean to us, here, now, in the twenty-first century?

In its original setting, I can easily imagine how Jesus's actions resonate with the crowds who flock around him. They are colonized peasants.

104

Overworked, underpaid, and malnourished. They know the agony of an empty table. The agony of watching their children cry for bread.

Me? Not so much. I've never been hungry like that. I've never had to wait more than a few hours for a meal. Where is the resonance—the challenge, the indictment, the *power*—of this miracle for me?

When I was little, my parents, brother, and I often spent our summers in the villages where my parents grew up. There, too, food was central. I remember how my grandmother chased down poultry, haggled with the fishmonger, sent a farm-hand up a tree to cut down coconuts, gathered peppers and green beans from her garden, and hand-ground spices on a slab of stone in the backyard to make the mouth-watering curries she took such pleasure in feeding us.

In that world, food was a gift. To prepare it with care was an act of generosity and deep love. To receive it with gratitude was a matter of honor and respect. As my mother constantly reminded me when we had to visit several relatives in one afternoon, and every one of them stuffed treats into my mouth: "Eat *something*. At least a bite. There's no worse insult than to refuse someone's food."

In contemporary Western culture, though, it's harder to honor food as a gift. We tend to treat it like dynamite. We carry our beautiful *hors d'oeuvres* to our church potlucks, circle the laden tables with fear in our eyes, nibble a little here and a little there—afraid of who might be watching—and carry our beautiful, barely touched dishes home again.

I'm not judging anyone; we come by the problem honestly. Jesus's feeding miracles are intended to speak abundance into a culture of scarcity. But we live in a culture of excess. Excess messaging, packaging, consuming, and dieting. We hardly know how to hear the word "abundance" in a positive light; we're too scared of its dangers to see its beauty. For some of us, food is an idol. For others, an enemy. For still others, an addiction coated in secrecy and self-loathing.

How would we respond if Jesus performed a loaves-and-fishes miracle for us now? Would we enjoy his generosity? Or would we flinch? The Gospels tell us that the crowd in Jesus's day "ate and were satisfied" (Mark 6:42; Luke 9:17; Matt 15:37). Would we be able to say that? Or would we say something more like:

"We ate, and looked around to see if we'd eaten more or less than the people sitting next to us."

"We ate, and immediately started calculating: Seven-hundred calories? Nine-hundred? How long on the treadmill to undo this damage?"

"We ate, but only the fish, not the bread. You know. *Carbs.*"

"We *didn't* eat. We gorged."

When Jesus feeds the multitudes, people sit down together, taking only what they need so that everyone receives enough. The point is not to scheme, compare, conserve, or quantify. The point is to enjoy a lavish gift in the company of others. Abundance doesn't have to lead to gluttony. Food doesn't have to lead to fear, isolation, and shame.

When Jesus feeds the multitudes, he also acknowledges what we so often try to forget: that we are physical beings with legitimate physical needs. We're not fleshless spirits; we have bodies, and those bodies themselves are gifts from God. Gifts worthy of honor and care.

In fact, I would argue that Jesus performs the feeding miracles precisely *because* he takes basic human need so seriously. When his disciples look at the crowds, they see only their own insufficiency. Their own scant resources. The impossibility of their situation.

But Jesus allows himself to see genuine need, and he allows that need to hit him squarely in the gut. In the face of the crowd's deep hunger, despair isn't an option; someone has to act.

Maybe it's only when we get in touch with our own deepest needs—for nourishment, for companionship, for help, for love—that we can extend a generous table to others. Maybe we need to be felled by our own hungers before we can turn abstract compassion into life-saving action.

The crowds eat and are satisfied. Is this because they eat in the presence of Jesus? What would that be like? To invite him to the table? To let him watch and partake as we eat? To welcome the Christ into the intimate realm of our bodily hungers? Where might such brave communion lead?

In the end, Jesus's feeding miracles are self-revelations. He gives bread because he *is* bread. He feeds hungry bodies because he, too, inhabits and honors a body. May we know him in the breaking of the bread.

# When Jesus Weeps

## John 11:1–44

*When Mary came where Jesus was and saw him, she knelt at his feet and said to him, "Lord, if you had been here, my brother would not have died." When Jesus saw her weeping, and the Jews who came with her also weeping, he was greatly disturbed in spirit and deeply moved. He said, "Where have you laid him?" They said to him, "Lord, come and see." Jesus began to weep. (John 11:32–35)*

The story of the raising of Lazarus is one of the most dramatic and difficult in Scripture, and I confess that I don't understand it. I don't understand why Jesus dawdles when he receives word of Lazarus's illness. I don't understand why he tells his disciples that Lazarus is "asleep" rather than dead (John 11:11). I don't understand why he chooses to bring Lazarus back: Does a man who's been dead for four days *want* to come back? And I definitely don't understand why Lazarus virtually disappears from the Gospel narrative once his grave clothes fall off. Why is he never heard from again?

In so many ways, the story is shrouded in mystery. But there are two words in the story I understand very well, and they are the words I cling to: "Jesus wept." For me, this is the heart of the story: grief takes hold of the Son of God and breaks him down. Jesus—the most accurate revelation of the divine we will ever have—stands at the grave of his friend and cries.

It has taken me a long time to appreciate Jesus's tears in this story. When I was a little girl, I didn't understand why Jesus cried when he knew that Lazarus was about to come back to life. Why mourn when joy is minutes away? As a young adult struggling with my faith, I didn't understand why Jesus cried after *intentionally* staying away from Bethany during Lazarus's illness. Like some of the onlookers in the story, I responded to Jesus's grief with contempt: "Could not he who opened the eyes of the blind have kept this man from dying?" (v. 37).

Over time, though, I've come to cherish Jesus's tears, maybe even more than I cherish the miracle that follows them. Here are some of the reasons why:

*When Jesus weeps, he legitimizes human grief.* His brokenness in the face of Mary's sorrow negates all forms of Christian triumphalism that look down on sorrow, despair, and lament. Yes, resurrection is around the corner, but in this story, the promise of joy doesn't negate the essential work of grief. When Jesus cries, he assures Mary not only that her beloved brother is worth crying for, but also that she is worth crying *with*. Through his tears, Jesus calls all of us into the holy vocation of empathy. We are not faithless when we grieve; we are as honest and faithful as Christ.

*When Jesus cries, he honors the complexity of our gains and losses, our sorrows and joys.* Raising Lazarus will not bring back the past. It will not cancel out the pain of his final illness, the memory of saying goodbye to a life he loves, or the gaping absence his sisters feel when he dies. Whatever joys await his family in the future will be layered joys. Joys shaped by the sorrows, fears, and losses they've just endured. In Lazarus's case, his future will be nothing like his past. Forever afterwards, he'll be known in his village as the One Who Returned. Perhaps that bizarre fact will make him a hero. But maybe it will render him a pariah. Whatever the case, Jesus's tears honor the reality of human change: he grieves because things will never be the same again.

*When Jesus cries, he honors the complexity of faith.* At no point does he expect piety to be disembodied or sanitized. He recognizes that all expressions of belief and trust come with emotional baggage. Martha expresses resentment and anger at Jesus's delay, and in the next breath voices her trust in his power. Mary blames Jesus for Lazarus's death, but she does so on her knees, in a posture of belief and submission. Likewise, Jesus's face is wet with tears when he prays to God and resurrects his friend. This is what real faith looks like; it embraces rather than vilifies the full spectrum of human thought, emotion, and sensory experience.

*When Jesus weeps, he acknowledges his own mortality.* In John's Gospel, the raising of Lazarus is the precipitating event that leads to Jesus's own arrest and crucifixion. When word spreads about the miracle in Bethany, the authorities decide that enough is enough; Jesus must be stopped. Essentially, Jesus trades his life for his friend's. Given this fact, I imagine that Jesus's tears are an expression of grief over his own pending death. He knows that his end is near. He knows that his time with his friends is almost over. He knows that it's nearly time to say goodbye to the lakes, skies, mountains, beaches, stars, and gardens he loves. In crying, he asserts powerfully that it is okay to yearn for life on earth. It's okay to feel a sense of wrongness and injustice in the face of all that death takes away. It's okay to mourn the loss of vitality, intimacy, longevity. It's okay to cling to the gift of life here and now.

*And finally, when Jesus weeps, he shows us that sorrow is a powerful catalyst for change.* In Lazarus's story, it is shared lament that leads to transformation. Jesus experiences the devastation of death so acutely, he recognizes the immediate need to restore life. His shattering leads to resurrection. Perhaps Jesus's tears can provoke us in similar ways. What breaks our hearts? What splits us open? What enrages us to the point of breakdown? Can we mobilize into those spaces? Can we work for transformation in our places of devastation? Can our sorrow lead us to justice?

Yes, we can and should celebrate Lazarus's story as a story of resurrection. But I hope we can make Jesus's tears our guide, too. I hope his honest expression of sorrow will give us the permission, company, and impetus we need not only to do the work of grief and healing, but to move with powerful compassion into a world that needs our empathy and our love. Yes, we are in death, but we serve a God who calls us to life. Our journey is not *to* the grave, but *through* it. The Lord who weeps is the Lord who resurrects. We mourn in hope.

# Is It Good for Us to Be Here?

## Matthew 17:1–8

*Six days later, Jesus took with him Peter and James and his brother John and led them up a high mountain, by themselves. And he was transfigured before them, and his face shone like the sun, and his clothes became dazzling white. (Matt 17:1–2)*

All three Synoptic Gospels tell the story of the Transfiguration, underscoring its importance to the early church. Over the centuries, the event has accumulated meanings, most of them abstractly theological. Growing up, I was taught that the Transfiguration is important because it reveals Jesus's divine nature, foreshadows his death, secures his place in the stream of Israel's salvific history, exalts him above the Law (Moses) and the Prophets (Elijah), and prefigures his Resurrection.

Weighty and important stuff. But here's my confession: I'm not sure I *like* the Transfiguration. I'm not sure it serves us well. Here's why:

For as long as I can remember, I've measured the depth and success of my faith by the number of mountaintop experiences I can truthfully claim. Do I "feel the Spirit" in Sunday worship? Has Jesus spoken to me in ways I can be sure of? Do I see visions? Speak in tongues? Encounter God's living presence in my dreams?

Most of the time, the answer is no. Which means I've spent most of my life feeling like a spiritual failure. More mature Christians, I've assumed, have frequent experiences akin to Peter's on the mountaintop. They see visions and dream dreams. They have conversations with a God who speaks to them in audible English. Jesus reveals himself to them in spectacular ways they can't describe or deny. They don't have to squint and strain to discern God's presence; God shows up in their living rooms and blows their minds.

It's not true, of course. This hierarchy of holiness. This way of measuring piety. And yet it lingers in me, this yearning for a particular kind of affective experience to come along on a regular basis and validate my faith. The truth is, I like, want, crave, and covet Christian mountaintops.

Stories like the Transfiguration don't help. If Peter can see Jesus in his full, unfiltered glory, why can't I?

One of the many problems with my "God on the mountaintop" version of Christianity is that it prompts me to carve up and compartmentalize my life. To separate sacred from secular. The mountain from the valley. The spectacular from the mundane. As if God is somehow more present in a rousing worship song, a stirring sermon, or a silent retreat, than God is when I'm doing the laundry or walking my dog. The work of discernment is harder and messier in everyday life, yes. But that doesn't mean it's impossible. The God of the whisper is still God.

In its worst iteration, mountaintop Christianity is addictive; it leads us to spend our days pursuing a "high" we conflate with spiritual success. When we don't experience a high, we feel empty, unloved, or bored. Meanwhile, we don't notice the ever-present God in whom we actually live and move and have our being. Desperate for the mountain, we miss the God of the valley, the conference room, the school yard, the grocery store, the street corner. Worshipping the extraordinary doesn't make for a healthy faith.

In the Transfiguration story, Peter responds to Jesus's dazzling appearance with a proposal: "Lord, it is good for us to be here. If you wish, I will make three dwellings" (Matt 17:4).

*It is good for us to be here.* Is it? Well, in some ways, yes. In some ways, Peter is absolutely right. It *is* good to set aside times and places for contemplation. It is good to gaze upon Jesus, whenever and however he reveals himself to us. It is good to move out of our comfort zones and confront the Otherness of the divine.

Until the Transfiguration happens, Peter and his fellow disciples experience Jesus as a teacher, a storyteller, a healer, and a traveling companion. His face, his manners, his voice, his mission—all are familiar to them. Familiar, endearing, and safe.

Then one day, high up on a mountain, the unimaginable happens. Before their very eyes, Jesus changes, becoming at once both fully himself and fully unrecognizable. The man they think they know is suddenly more, suddenly Other. And the path that lies ahead of him—a path that must end on another high place, a hill called Golgotha—upends everything the disciples think they understand about Jesus.

Whenever we think we have God figured out, it's good to be reminded that we're wrong. Whenever we try to stuff Jesus into a theological, cultural, or political box for our own convenience, it's good to have the box blown open. Whenever we grow complacent, it's good to be brought to our knees by a God whose thoughts are not our thoughts and whose ways are not our ways. These are good reasons to encounter Jesus on the mountaintop.

On the other hand, it's not good to fixate on the sublime so much that we desecrate the mundane. Most of life is unspectacular. By which I mean, most of life doesn't come with special effects. But all of life contains the sacred. The challenge is to cultivate the kind of sight that perceives God in places murkier and more obscure than a mountaintop.

As soon as Peter has an epiphany, he tries to hoard it. What I hear in his plan to "make dwellings" is an understandable but ultimately misguided attempt to contain, domesticate, protect, and possess the sublime. To harness the holy. To make the fleeting permanent. To keep Jesus shiny, beautiful, and safe up on a mountain. After all, everything is so good up there. So clear. So bright. So unmistakably spiritual. Why not stay forever?

Well, because God says no. Even before Peter is finished speaking, God covers him in a thick cloud, and tells him to listen to Jesus, not to his own misconceptions about the life of faith. It's Jesus's way, the way of the valley, the way of the cross, the way of humility, surrender, and sacrifice, that Peter must learn to follow.

In Matthew's version of the Transfiguration event, the disciples are overcome with fear when God speaks to them out of the cloud. They cower in silence and fall to the ground. But then comes the part of the story I like: "Jesus came and touched them, saying, 'Get up and do not be afraid.' And when they looked up, they saw no one except Jesus himself alone" (vv. 7–8).

Jesus comes and touches his friends, and in that simple, ordinary, human encounter of skin on skin, the disciples catch their breath, shed their fear, and return to themselves. Finally, they see the divine in a guise they can bear. As it turns out, Peter, for all his eagerness and bluster, isn't made for unending Transfigurations. He can't handle too much of the spectacular. All he can actually take of God's glory is a tender human hand on his shoulder and a reassuringly human voice in his ear.

I still yearn for mountaintop experiences, and that's okay. They'll come and go according to God's will and timing, not according to my micromanagement. In that sense, sublime spiritual experiences are easy; they require little from me. I can't control them. What's hard is consenting to follow Jesus back down the mountain. What's challenging is learning to cultivate awe and wonder in the face of the mundane. What's essential is finding Jesus in the rhythms and routines of the everyday. In the loving touch of a friend. In the human voices that say, "Don't be afraid." In the unspectacular business of discipleship, prayer, service, and solitude. In the unending challenge to love my neighbor as myself.

As we make our way in the life of faith, we can't predict how God will speak, or in what guise Jesus might appear. But we can trust in this: whether on the brightest mountain, or in the darkest valley, Jesus abides.

Even as he blazes with holy light, his hand remains warm and solid on our shoulders. Even when we're on our knees in the wilderness, he whispers, "Do not be afraid."

Listen to the ordinary. Keep listening to it. It is good for us to be here.

# Teachings

"Jesus came to show us how to be human much more than how to be spiritual, and the process still seems to be in its early stages."

—RICHARD ROHR[1]

1. Rohr, *The Universal Christ*, 23.

# Bear Witness

## Matthew 10:5–15

*As you go, proclaim the good news, "The kingdom of heaven has come near." Cure the sick, raise the dead, cleanse the lepers, cast out demons. You received without payment; give without payment. (Matt 10:7–8)*

In the first chapter of his book, *Tokens of Trust: An Introduction to Christian Belief,* Archbishop Rowan Williams describes a young Jewish woman named Etty Hillesum. Etty was in her twenties when the Germans occupied Holland. She wasn't a conventionally religious person, but between the years of 1941 and 1943, as she watched her world descend into a nightmare, she became aware of God's hand on her life. Imprisoned in the transit camp at Westerbork before being shipped to the gas chambers of Auschwitz, Etty wrote these words in her diary: "There must be someone to live through it all and bear witness to the fact that God lived, even in these times. And why should I not be that witness?"[1]

Williams goes on to describe Etty's commitment this way: she decided to occupy a certain place in the world, a place where others could somehow connect with God through her. She took responsibility for making God credible in the world. She took responsibility for God's believability.

*Making God credible in the world. Taking responsibility for God's believability.* How do you feel, contemplating those phrases? What reactions, if any, do they trigger? Alarm? Excitement? Surprise? Fear? I ask, because I don't tend to think of my faith life as having much to do with God's credibility. It doesn't occur to me that my Christianity might have such public implications.

But what if Etty Hillesum was on to something? What if we are called to make belief in the kingdom of God credible for the world we live in? Not just when belief is easy, but also and especially when belief feels impossible?

1. Williams, *Tokens of Trust,* 22.

In the tenth chapter of Matthew, Jesus commissions his twelve disciples to liberate the "harassed and helpless" in their surrounding communities. Seeing vast multitudes of "sheep without a shepherd" (Matt 9:36), Jesus is deeply moved, and he tells his disciples, "Go" (Mark 16:15). Go and proclaim the good news of the kingdom. Go and cure the sick, raise the dead, cleanse the lepers, and cast out demons. Go and touch. Go and heal. Go and resurrect. Go and make peace.

Go and render believable the compassion of God.

Needless to say, this commissioning is for us, as well. Which—let's be honest—sounds daunting and scary. Especially if we attend to what else Jesus says to his disciples. He doesn't just tell them what to do; he tells them *how* to do it, and some of his operating instructions are appalling:

> You received without payment; give without payment . . . Take no gold, or silver, or copper in your belts . . . Take no bag, or two tunics, or sandals, or a staff . . . I'm sending you out like sheep in the midst of wolves, so be as wise as serpents and as innocent as doves. You will be dragged before governors. You will be handed over to councils and flogged . . . You will be hated by all because of my name. (Matt 10:8–10, 16–17, 22)

Let's see if we have this straight. Indulge me for a minute while I paraphrase what Jesus is saying:

*Prioritize those who have nothing.* Go to the people who have no one to advocate for them, no one to hear them, no one to care for their needs. Go to the harassed, the mistreated, the oppressed, and the exhausted. Knock on their doors, listen to their stories, and place yourselves at their service. When they tell you they're not okay, believe them. When they tell you they're dying, believe them. When they tell you that demons are stalking their steps, *believe them.*

*Choose poverty, simplicity, and vulnerability.* Carry no weapons. Stockpile no resources. Have no back-up. Abandon your ego. Do not parade in like a savior, basking in pomp and circumstance. Lead instead with quietness, gentleness, curiosity, and humility. Humbly accept the hospitality of those you wish to help and learn the art of depending on the very people you think you can save. Make your home in troubled places and engage those places deeply. Insofar as it depends on you, keep, make, and share the peace. Remember that power has been given to you for one reason and one reason only: so that you can give it away.

*Don't be foolish. Be wise.* Be attentive. Listen. Educate yourself and learn the complexities of the world you live in. Understand what's happening beneath the surfaces of people's fears, sorrows, and furies. Be pure of heart, but don't revel in ignorance or mistake naïveté for faith.

*When you've done all of the above—in other words, when you get all of this just right—expect life to get grim.* Know that lots of folks will distrust you. Understand that many well-meaning people will yell and scream at you. Expect to get rejected, called out, wounded, and beaten. Don't be surprised when your life gets uncomfortable. Discomfort is what success looks like.

*Don't despair. You are not alone.* The Spirit of God is with you, and the Spirit will give you the words you need and the courage you lack for the work you're called to. Remember, the Spirit shows up when you step out. You don't have to be eloquent; you just have to be willing. Grace will abound when you move out of your safe spaces. So don't lose heart. Don't be scared. And don't give up. Those who endure to the end will be saved.

Make no mistake: this is a confrontational gospel. It's hard. It's demanding. It's offensive. In it, Jesus asks us to surrender everything for the sake of making God credible to a world that's convulsing in pain, and he does so without reservation or apology. His harsh-sounding instructions suggest that there will be times when our faith requires us to violate cultural norms, fight uphill battles, and speak dangerous truths to power.

If our overriding priority as Christians is to secure our own comfort, then we cannot follow Jesus. The discipleship Jesus describes will disorient and disrupt us. It will make us the neighborhood weirdos. It will shake things up in our families, our friendship circles, our churches, our communities. It will expose evils in the status quo we cling to. It will humble us to our knees.

Why does Jesus ask so much of us? Because he gave us so much. "You received without payment. Now give without payment."

Jesus calls us only to what we were created for. He knows the cure for our brokenness, our malaise, our boredom. He knows that when we go out into the world in his name, healing what is diseased, resurrecting what is dead, and casting out what is evil, we participate in the transformation of our own souls.

What we're hearing in these days is the very heart of God within us, deep calling to deep, the Spirit crying out on behalf of a world desperate for love. The only question that matters is this one: Will we listen?

*Someone* has to live through it all and bear witness to the fact that God lived, even in these times. Ask yourself: Why shouldn't that witness be me?

# The Blessing and the Bite
## Matthew 5:1–12

*When Jesus saw the crowds, he went up the mountain; and after he sat down, his disciples came to him. Then he began to speak, and taught them, saying: "Blessed are the poor in spirit, for theirs is the kingdom of heaven." (Matt 5:1–3)*

B lessed are you who are poor, hungry, sad, and expendable. Woe to you who are rich, full, happy, and popular. The Beatitudes in a nutshell. *Boom.*

People who know little else about Jesus know the Beatitudes. Some folks read them as lines of poetry. Some consider them a rule of life. Others find them naïve and impractical. Having grown up in the church, I'm familiar with the ways the Beatitudes are often misread and misused. I want to start there, by naming what they are *not:*

*The Beatitudes are not sentiments.* It's easy in our consumerist culture to allow a word like "blessing" to become greeting card fodder, bland and meaningless. ("I'm so #Blessed.") But the Beatitudes are not meant to settle and soothe us; they're meant to startle us awake. Yes, they are pastoral, and yes, they give us hope. But Christian hope is not a sedative. Christian hope gets us up and out the door.

*The Beatitudes are not to-do items.* They are not suggestions, instructions, commandments, or quid pro quos. There is nothing transactional about them, nothing that smacks of a "should," a "must," or an "ought." It is emphatically not the case that if I try very hard to be poorer, sadder, meeker, hungrier, thirstier, purer, more peaceable, and more persecuted than I am right now, God will like, love, reward, and appreciate me more than God already does.

*The Beatitudes are not shame tactics.* The point is not to read Jesus's litany of blessings for the poor and the disenfranchised and walk away feeling like an overprivileged wretch. The takeaway Jesus intends for his

THE BLESSING AND THE BITE

listeners is neither shame nor self-condemnation. The last thing Jesus's Beatitudes should do is defeat us.

*The Beatitudes are not permission slips for passivity.* To use Jesus's teachings about sorrow, meekness, poverty, and persecution to keep oppressed people oppressed is to distort his words and intentions. There is nothing in the Beatitudes that excuses injustice, nothing that relativizes abuse, nothing that frees us to tell suffering people that their suffering is God-ordained and redemptive.

*The Beatitudes are not pie-in-the-sky promises.* When Jesus offers his listeners the "kingdom of heaven," he is not asking them to grit their teeth and wait for death to alleviate whatever hell they're living in. He is not handing out the afterlife as an opiate, as if our lives here and now don't matter. To possess the kingdom, to experience comfort, to inherit the earth, to be filled, to receive mercy, to see God, to be called the children of God, and to receive a reward in heaven—these are not just about life after death. The Beatitudes describe a kingdom that is already-and-not-yet, the realm of God that is present and coming. The promise is not an either/or, it's a both/and. The kingdom is coming. The kingdom is now.

If the Beatitudes are not these things, then what are they?

*The Beatitudes are blessings.* The first words Jesus offers his commissioned disciples, the first words the Gospel of Matthew records from Jesus's inaugural sermon, are words of blessing. Are we listening? Blessing comes first. We *begin* with blessing. Blessing, not judgment. Blessing, not terms and conditions. Blessing, not penance. Blessing, not altar calls.

Jesus launches his ministry by telling the disciples who and what they already are: they are blessed. Blessed, fortunate, privileged, favored. Why? Because they are near and dear to God's heart. Whatever else Jesus's first followers go on to learn or accomplish is the outgrowth of their ground-of-being, their identity, their foundation. God gifts their identities to them, without condition or measure. They are freely blessed, and so they're free to bless others.

What does this mean? It means we're not God's nine-to-five employees, working for blessing as our compensation. We don't endeavor to do justice, love mercy, and walk humbly in order to earn God's blessings. We do justice, love mercy, and walk humbly because we are always and already blessed.

What would happen if we who profess faith in Jesus actually followed his example and made it our first priority to bless others as we have been blessed? To *lead* with blessing? What would happen to our hearts, to the church, to the world, if we offered blessings to our neighbors as generously as God offers blessings to us?

I'll be honest, I'm not good at accepting blessings from others, and I'm pretty clumsy about giving blessings away. On the accepting end, I tend to get cringy and anxious: If I accept this blessing, will God think I'm arrogant? Shouldn't my posture as a Christian be self-deprecating? What right do I have to bask in blessing?

On the giving end, my fears are similar: Who am I to offer anyone else a blessing? What do I have to offer, anyway?

Both sets of fears come from a refusal to accept the core identity God has given me. It's not a matter of our deserving; it's a matter of God's astonishing love and generosity. Ours is an identity of blessedness. Can we accept that?

*The Beatitudes are reversals.* In the Sermon on the Mount, Jesus describes a universe turned on its head. A world where the usual might-makes-right, survival-of-the-fittest hierarchies, rules, and priorities don't apply. In the kingdom Jesus describes, the poor are the wealthiest of all. The mourners are the ones who receive comfort. The starving sit at laden tables. Those who live meekly inherit everything. The peacemakers are God's children. And the victims of persecution win choice rewards.

Again, it's important not to read these stunning reversals through the scrim of shame. Shame won't get us anywhere. It's important instead to allow these reversals to provoke and instruct us, because they reveal essential truths about who God is.

What Jesus bears witness to in the Beatitudes is God's unwavering proximity to pain, suffering, sorrow, and loss. God is nearest to those who are lowly, oppressed, unwanted, and broken. God isn't obsessed with the shiny and the impressive; God is too busy sticking close to what's messy, chaotic, unruly, and unattractive.

This is important to remember, because the first thing I tend to ask when I'm hurting is, "Where is God? Why has God abandoned me?" The Beatitudes assure me that God doesn't exit my life when I find myself in low places. If anything, God is most present in the shadows. Most attentive in the fire. God is always close to the destitute, the anguished, the lost, and the confused. God accompanies those who go days, weeks, months, and years, hungry for a sign, a word, a crumb, a drop. Our hunger is not indicative of God's absence; our hunger is the sign we seek. The blessing we chase resides in the shadows.

The Beatitudes challenge me to examine my life, and to consider where and how my privilege keeps me from seeking God. When things are going spectacularly well, do I feel much urgency about ultimate things? Not really. I can go for days without talking to God. I can go for days without thinking about God. It's easy for all things deep and divine to become afterthoughts, because God isn't on my radar when I'm floating along on my own comforts.

This isn't because I'm callous. It's because I am already "full." I have easy access to laughter, so I don't wonder what lessons honest tears might yield. I am primed by my cozy life to live in the shallows, unaware of the treasures that lie waiting in the depths. Most of the time, it doesn't occur to me that I would be lost without the blessings that sustain me.

I think what Jesus is saying in the Beatitudes is that I have something to learn about discipleship that my privileged life circumstances will not teach me. Something to grasp about the beauty, glory, and freedom of the Christian life that I will never grasp until God becomes my all, my go-to, my starting and ending place. Something to recognize about the radical counter-intuitiveness of God's priorities and promises. Something to notice about the obfuscating power of plenty to blind me to my own emptiness. Something to gain from the humility that says, "The people I think I'm superior to have everything to teach me. Maybe it's time to pay attention."

If the Beatitudes have a "bite" to them, this is it. God is in the business of reversing just about everything the world values and worships. Things are about to change. Hierarchies are about to be toppled. Priorities are about to be reordered. Am I ready? Am I willing? Am I paying attention? Where am I located, vis-à-vis God's great reversal?

*The Beatitudes are a vocation.* We make a mistake if we separate Jesus's words from his actions. We diminish him if we try to interpret his teachings through any filter other than the filter of his own life and ministry. Yes, Jesus pronounces blessings on the meek, the hungry, the impoverished, and the oppressed. But what does he do before and after this pronouncement? He empowers the meek, he feeds the hungry, he cares for the poor, and he demands justice for the oppressed.

Jesus spends every waking moment alleviating suffering. He never valorizes misery for its own sake. He doesn't tell the hungry to tighten their belts. He doesn't ignore the cruelty of the religious elite and the politically powerful. He doesn't turn a blind eye to the incarcerated, the colonized, the ostracized, and the demonized. He doesn't leave the sick to die, he doesn't abandon the dead to their graves, and he never, ever tells anyone to just "grin and bear" their pain because heaven's reprieve will fix things by and by.

Which is to say, Jesus acts. He doesn't simply speak blessing; he lives it. Through his words, his hands, his feet, his life, he brings about the very blessings he promises. Insisting that pain in and of itself is neither holy nor redemptive in the Christian story, Jesus works to bring healing, abundance, liberation, and joy to everyone who crosses his path.

This is the vocation we are called to. The work of sharing the blessings we enjoy is not the work of a distant someday. It is the work we're called to now. The Beatitudes remind us that blessing and justice are inextricably linked. If it's blessing we want, then it's justice we must pursue.

Blessed are you. And you, and you, and you, and you. So go. Become what you are, give away what you seek, bless what God blesses, and turn the world on its head. Rejoice and be glad, for you are God's children. The kingdom of heaven is yours.

# Go and Do Likewise

## Luke 10:25–37

*Just then a lawyer stood up to test Jesus. "Teacher," he said, "what must I do to inherit eternal life?" (Luke 10:25)*

I n her book-length study of Jesus's parables, *Short Stories by Jesus*, Amy-Jill Levine suggests that religion is meant "to comfort the afflicted and to afflict the comfortable." She goes on to argue that we would do well to think of the parables of Jesus as doing this afflicting. "Therefore, if we hear a parable and think, 'I really like that' or, worse, fail to take any challenge, we are not listening well enough."[1]

The difficulty for me is that Jesus's parables are overly familiar, so much so that I don't experience them as afflictions. I know them well, and therein lies the danger: they no longer challenge me. I read, I nod, I walk away.

The parable of the Good Samaritan presents exactly this dilemma. A man gets beaten and robbed, a priest and a Levite pass him by, and a Samaritan stops and helps. The Samaritan, showing mercy, exemplifies neighborliness. I should go and do likewise.

Would Jesus's original audience agree with this reading? Would they feel afflicted by it? We *are* called to imitate Christ, aren't we? Doesn't the Good Samaritan story offer us a great example of compassion and neighborliness?

It does. But is "go and do likewise" the only lesson of this parable, or does Jesus have something more provocative in mind?

Perhaps it will help to place the story in a fuller cultural context. As Luke tells it, a lawyer approaches Jesus with a million-dollar question: "What must I do to inherit eternal life?" I know that scholars often give the lawyer a bad rap for testing Jesus, but I like the boldness of his question. He wants to live fully. He's not messing around in the shallows with his query; he's deep-sea diving. "Show me the good stuff, Jesus. Show me the path to eternal life."

---

1. Levine, *Short Stories by Jesus*, 3.

But Jesus is too savvy a teacher to answer the question directly, so he turns it back on his would-be student: "What is written in the Law? How do you read it?" The lawyer (no fool himself) gives Jesus a concise answer: "You shall love the Lord your God with all your heart, with all your soul, with all your strength, and with all your mind; and you shall love your neighbor as yourself" (vv. 26–27).

Jesus congratulates the lawyer on his doctrinal precision: "You have given the right answer," and encourages him to take the essential next step: "Do this, and you will live" (v. 28).

But the lawyer—miffed, perhaps, that Jesus wants more than textbook theology—asks for further clarification. "Who is my neighbor?" (v. 29). Or, to put it crassly: "Who is *not* my neighbor? How much love are we talking here, Jesus? Can you be specific? Where can I draw the line? Outside my front door? At the edges of my neighborhood? Along the cultural and racial boundaries I was raised with? I mean, there *are* lines. Aren't there?"

I'm sure the lawyer would have loved to spend hours discussing the fine points of responsible neighborliness. But Jesus doesn't take the bait; he tells a story, instead. A story whose main character we know so well, we've named hospitals, nursing homes, relief agencies, and philanthropic organizations after him. In the US, he even has a law coined in his honor: any modern-day "Good Samaritan" who stops to help a stranger enjoys legal protections for her trouble.

As Jesus tells it, a man is walking down the road from Jerusalem to Jericho when he's attacked. Bandits rob, beat, strip, and leave him for dead. Soon afterwards, a priest comes by. Seeing the wounded man, he passes by on the other side of the road. A short while later, a Levite does likewise. Then a Samaritan comes along. Seeing the stranded victim, he feels pity, and draws close. He bandages the man's wounds, anoints them with oil and wine, carries him to the nearest inn, pays the innkeeper for the victim's further care, and promises to return with more money as needed.

"Which of the three was a neighbor to the man who was robbed?" Jesus asks the lawyer at the conclusion of the story. "The one who showed him mercy," the lawyer replies. "Go and do likewise," Jesus says again. "Do this and you will live" (vv. 36–37).

*Do this.* Draw close. Show mercy. Extend kindness. Live out your theology in hands-on care for other people. Don't just think love. Do it.

Okay, makes sense. But I'm not afflicted yet, are you? What are we missing?

We're missing the fact that the story changes, depending on where we locate ourselves within it. If you're like me, you locate yourself in the priest or the Levite on bad days, and in the Good Samaritan on better ones.

Sometimes you see a need and pass it by because you're busy or preoccupied. But the Good Samaritan is still the ideal you hope to live up to. He is your example. Your goal.

Unless he's not. What if he's not? What if Jesus's parable is more than an example story? What if it's a *reversal* story? A story intended to upset our categories of good and bad, sacred and profane, benefactor and recipient? If we too easily and comfortably identify with the Good Samaritan, we miss the point. Maybe the point of the Samaritan is that he is *not* us.

Jesus tells this story at a time when the enmity between Jews and Samaritans runs very deep. The two groups disagree about everything. Though *we're* inclined to love the Good Samaritan, we need to remember that Jesus's decision to make him the hero of the story shocks his first listeners.

After all, the Samaritan is the Other. The enemy of the Jewish people. The object of their fear, their condescension, their disgust, and their judgment. He is the heretical outcast.

Is there anything we can do to recover the scandal at the heart of this parable? Think about it this way: Who is the last person on earth you'd ever want to deem the "good guy"? The last person you'd ask to save your life? Whom do you secretly hope to convert, fix, impress, control, or save—but never need?

The enmity between the Jews and the Samaritans in Jesus's day is not theoretical; it is embodied and real. The differences between them are not easily negotiated; each believes that the other is wrong about everything that matters. What Jesus does when he deems the Samaritan "good" is radical and risky. Essentially, he asks his listeners to consider the possibility that their fellow human beings are more than the sum of their political, racial, cultural, and economic identities. He calls them to put aside the history they know and the prejudices they nurse.

Perhaps what we need to do is locate ourselves—not in the priest, the Levite, or the Samaritan, but in the wounded man, dying on the road. Notice that he is the only character in the story not defined by profession, social class, or religious belief. He has no identity at all except naked need. Maybe we have to occupy *his* place in the story first. Maybe we have to become the broken one, grateful to anyone at all who will show us mercy, before we can feel the unbounded compassion of the Good Samaritan.

Why? Because tribalism falls away on the broken road. All divisions of "us" and "them" disappear of necessity. When you're lying bloody in a ditch, what matters is not whose help you'd prefer, whose way of practicing Christianity you like best, whose politics you agree with. What matters is whether or not anyone will stop to show you mercy before you die.

If it hasn't happened yet, your encounter on that treacherous road, it will. Somehow, someday, somewhere, it will. In a hospital room? At a graveside? After a marriage fails? When a cherished job goes bust? After the storm, the betrayal, the war, the injury, the shooting, the court case, the diagnosis? Somehow, someday, somewhere. For all of us. It will happen.

When it does, it won't be your theology that saves you. It won't be your cherished affiliations that matter. All that matters will be how quickly you swallow your pride and grab hold of that hand you hoped never to touch. How humbly you'll agree to receive help from the enemy you fear. How long you'll persist in the Lone Ranger fantasy we all cling to before you allow an unsavory Other to bless you.

"Who is my neighbor?" the lawyer asks. Your neighbor is the one who scandalizes you with compassion, Jesus answers. Your neighbor is the one who upends all of your entrenched categories and shocks you with a fresh face of God. Your neighbor is the one who mercifully steps over the ancient, bloodied line separating "us" from "them" and teaches you the real meaning of "Good."

What shall I do to inherit eternal life? Do *this*. Do this and you will live.

# On Lostness

## Luke 15:1–10

*Now all the tax collectors and sinners were coming near to listen
to him. And the Pharisees and the scribes were grumbling and
saying, "This fellow welcomes sinners and eats with them." So
he told them this parable: "Which one of you, having a hundred
sheep and losing one of them, does not leave the ninety-nine in
the wilderness and go after the one that is lost until he finds it?
When he has found it, he lays it on his shoulders and rejoices."*
*(Luke 15:1–5)*

"I once was lost but now am found. Was blind but now I see." I can't count
how many times I've sung these famous lines from John Newton's
"Amazing Grace." I learned the hymn when I was a little girl, and I still
find its assured language moving and beautiful. But here's the thing: I'm
not convinced anymore that I can fit my faith into its neat before-and-after
story. *I once was lost but now am found.* The truth is, my lostness is not over.
Lostness remains a central feature of my relationship with God, and if Luke's
Gospel has anything to say about it, this is exactly as it should be.

As the story begins, Jesus is in trouble once again for hanging out
with the wrong people. As "all the tax collectors and sinners" come near
to listen to him, the Pharisees and scribes begin to grumble: "This fellow
welcomes sinners and eats with them."

In response, Jesus tells the scandalized religious insiders two parables.
In the first, a shepherd leaves his flock of ninety-nine to look for a single
lamb that is lost. He searches until he finds it, and when he does, he carries
that one lamb home on his shoulders, invites his friends and neighbors
over, and throws a party to celebrate.

In the second, a woman loses one of her ten silver coins. Immediately,
she lights a lamp and sweeps her entire house, looking for the coin until she
finds it. Like the shepherd, she calls her friends and neighbors and asks them

to celebrate the recovery of the coin: "Rejoice with me, for I have found the coin that I had lost" (v. 9).

The first thing that strikes me about these parables is how many years I've spent misreading them. For a long time, I thought that the lost lamb and the lost coin represented sinners—people outside the home country I call Christianity. But no. The lost lamb in the parable belongs to the shepherd's flock—it is *his* lamb. Likewise, the coin belongs to the woman before she loses it; the coin is one of her very own. In other words, these parables are not about outsiders finding salvation and becoming Christians. These parables are about us, the insiders. The churchgoers, the bread-and-wine consumers, the Bible readers. These are parables about lostness on the inside.

What does this mean? It means that lostness isn't an experience exclusive to non-Christians. Lostness happens within the beloved community. It's not that we cross over once and for all from a sinful lostness to a righteous foundness. We get lost over and over again, and God finds us over and over again. Lostness is not an aberration; it's part and parcel of the life of faith.

But what does it mean to be lost? It means we lose our sense of belonging, our capacity to trust, our felt experience of God's presence, our will to persevere. Some of us get lost when illness descends on our lives and God's goodness starts to look not-so-good. Some of us get lost when death comes early for someone we love, and we experience a crisis of faith that leaves us reeling. Some of us get lost when our marriages fail. Some of us get lost when our children break our hearts. Some of us get lost in the throes of addiction or anxiety or unforgiveness or hatred.

Some of us get lost within the very walls of the church. We get lost when prayer turns to dust in our mouths. When the Scriptures we once loved lie dead on the page. When sitting in a pew on a Sunday morning makes our skin crawl. When even the most well-intentioned sermon sucks the oxygen out of our lungs. When the table of bread and wine that once nourished us now leaves us hungry, cranky, bewildered, or bored.

We get lost. We get so miserably lost that the shepherd has to wander through the craggy wilderness to find us. We get so wholly lost that the housewife has to light her lamp, pick up her broom, and sweep out every nook and cranny of her house to discover what's become of us.

For the record, these versions of lostness aren't trivial. Notice that the searching in these parables is not a show. The shepherd doesn't *pretend* to look for the lost sheep. The woman isn't putting on an act with her lamp and broom. What's lost is really, truly lost—even though the seeker is God.

Can we pause for a moment and take in how astonishing this is? God faces genuine stakes when it comes to our lostness. God experiences authentic, real-time loss. God searches, persists, lingers, and plods. God wanders over hills and valleys looking for lost lambs. God turns her house upside down looking for her lost coin. And when at last God finds what God is looking for, God cannot contain the joy that wells up inside. So God invites the whole neighborhood over, shares the happy news of recovery, and throws a party to end all parties.

I'll admit it—this is not how I picture God. I can't easily imagine God as a foolishly love-hungry shepherd, leaving the ninety-nine to crawl through bushes and clamber over ledges in search of the one. I can barely conceive of God as a housewife bent over her broom, poking into dusty, cobwebby corners, hoping to spot a silvery glimmer in the shadows. I struggle to conceive of God as one who seeks the small, the seemingly insignificant, the hard-to-find, the just plain difficult.

Maybe the most scandalous aspect of these lost-and-found parables is not that I still get lost. Maybe what's most scandalous is what they reveal about the nature of God. God the searcher, the seeker, the determined and dogged finder. If Jesus's parables are true, then God doesn't hang out where I assume he does.

If Jesus's parables are true, then God isn't in the fold with the ninety-nine insiders. God isn't curled up on her couch polishing the nine coins she's already sure of. God is where the lost things are. God is in the wilderness, God is in the remotest corners of the house, God is where the search is at its fiercest. If I want to find God, I have to seek the lost. I have to *get* lost. I have to leave the safety of the inside and venture out. I have to recognize my own lostness and consent to be found.

This isn't easy. Not by a long shot. For one thing, it's hard for me to believe that I'm worth looking for. That I'm loved and desired enough to warrant a diligent search. It's hard to trust that God won't give up on me. That God does God's best work when I'm lost and unable to find myself. That God feels such joy at my recovery that God tells the whole world the good news and throws us all a party.

But this is in fact the case. Jesus tells these parables to religious insiders who won't admit their own lostness. He shares these stories with folks who can't reconcile their brand of piety with Jesus's bewildering claim that lostness has its virtues. In her book, *An Altar in the World*, Barbara Brown Taylor makes a strong case for these virtues. She suggests that lostness makes us stronger and softer at the same time. Lostness teaches us about vulnerability. About empathy. About humility. Lostness shows us who we are, and who God is.[1]

God looks for us when our lostness is so convoluted and so profound, we can't even pretend to look for God. But even in such bleak and hopeless places, God finds us. This is amazing grace. And it is ours.

---

1. Taylor, *An Altar in the World*, 69–86.

# Letters to Prodigals

## Luke 15:11–32

*Then Jesus said, "There was a man who had two sons. The younger of them said to his father, 'Father, give me the share of the property that will belong to me.' So he divided his property between them."
(Luke 15:11–12)*

"There was a man who had two sons." So begins one of Jesus's best-known stories about love and lostness, "The Parable of the Prodigal Son." I was a little girl in Sunday School when I first learned about the boy who ran, the boy who stayed, and the dad who threw the big party. I fell in love with it immediately, especially the details about the pigs and the party. (*Charlotte's Web* was my favorite novel at the time, and what kid doesn't love a big celebration?)

But as the years went by, and I heard the parable over and over again, it began to lose its power. The younger son's selfish greed, the older son's fury, the patient father's extravagant love—the story's rich layers started to collapse in on each other.

As a remedy, I've tried to re-enter the story with my imagination and write letters to the two sons in the parable. If I could ask them anything, if I could have honest conversations with them, what would I say? Here's what I came up with:

## To the Boy Who Ran,

I begin with you, because you feel inaccessible. Thoughtless. Careless. Demanding. So selfish, you take my breath away. How shall I relate to you? I've never run away, or squandered an inheritance, or given myself over to "dissolute living."

Nor have I felt the ardent, tear-soaked embrace of a lovesick father welcoming me home. Maybe this is why I dislike you. Am I envious because

God is tender? Am I hurt because the father's love is a wild, unfettered thing, unpredictable and unfair? Yes, I am. *Yes. I am.*

Here's what I'd like to know: Was your penitence genuine? Did you mean the pious speech you composed in the pigsty, or were you just a clever talker, well-versed on your father's soft spots? Did you feel bad about your adventure, or just bad that it failed?

Here's the other thing I'd like to know: Did you really get your act together once the party was over and the fatted calf was eaten? Did you get up early the next morning and pull your weight in the fields? Did you apologize to your brother? Take care of your father? Make peace with the villagers you scandalized? Did you understand in your heart that, really, there's no such thing as going home? Did you get that everything—*everything*—would have to change?

Here's what I *really* need to know: What is this bitter root in me that needs to see your penitence? That wants to make sure you understand just how much fear, destruction, and sorrow you caused, before I let you off the hook? Why do I need to withhold the forgiveness that alone might restore you?

I know that this is a problem. My spite. My withholding. Everything in me accuses you of having no empathy—of not giving a damn about how you ripped your father's heart out of his chest—but the truth is, I'm struggling to empathize with you. So I'm digging down, trying extra hard to find the tender places beneath your brashness. Who are you beneath the labels? Beneath "prodigal," "selfish," and "sinner"?

"Dying of hunger" (v. 17). That's how your story describes your final days in that far-off country. When your adventure was over, when your funds ran dry, when your so-called friends abandoned you. There among the pigs, covered in filth, you finally realized who and what you were. "Dying of hunger." May I give you a new label? A new name I can relate to? Aren't you, at the core, the Hungry One?

It was hunger, wasn't it, that first lured you away from a good life and a good father? A gluttonous hunger, maybe, but hunger still. For freedom? Self-expression? Novelty? Something in you—something wild and insistent—needed feeding.

But here's the thing that knocks the breath out of me: your father, in his vast, unorthodox wisdom, understood. He didn't hold you back. He didn't decide what your journey should look like. He let you go.

What did he know that I refuse to know? That you couldn't return home without leaving first? That you couldn't taste resurrection without dying? That maybe lostness is part of the deal—the prelude to the most magnificent finding? Can it be that I, too, need to know such hunger?

Know it on the tongue, in the gut, like a fire in my bones, before I can savor a father's feast?

Your father understood. What a remarkable thing that is, his deep and patient comprehension of how life actually works. He respected the hunger that pulled you away. He knew that a wiser, sharper hunger would bring you home.

Was it admirable? What you did? I don't know. But there is this: even though it cost you, even though it wounded your family, you honored your hunger. I can't speak to the rightness or wrongness of your decision, but maybe there is something in it that I should attend to. I usually ignore my hunger. When I can't ignore it, I hide, minimize, and vilify it. Is there a chance my hunger wants to point me to God?

Your journey ends in a passionate embrace. Unrestrained welcome, overflowing joy. Were you grateful? Were you indebted? Did you try extra hard in later years to earn the feast your father lavished on you? Or did you simply rest in his prodigal love, knowing you didn't need to earn it? It seems your father didn't care; he just wanted to hold you close.

There's so little of your experience I can applaud. Despite my best attempts to reconcile my heart with yours, my envy remains. Your father ran to welcome you. He cared for nothing in this world so much as having you safe and snug in his arms. No matter what the preachers say, this is not everyone's visceral experience. To hear we are loved is one thing. To feel ourselves embraced is another. You are fortunate. Do you know that? Something jealous in me wants to make sure you know it.

But something broken in me wants to reach you, too. To build bridges between your life and mine. What do you know that I know, too? I know what it's like to hunger. To hunger for life, for depth, for passion, for joy. I know what it's like to imagine an exotic Elsewhere, a more perfect nourishment miles away from my father's all-too-familiar table. I know lostness—the lostness of being small, stupid, and sorry in a world too big to navigate. I know what it's like to "come to myself" (v. 17) in the broken, impoverished places I create in my own heart. And I know what it's like to feel shame—shame that I've disappointed everyone, shame that I'm damaged goods, shame that I'll never be enough to earn the love I crave.

I still don't like you. But maybe we're not so very different after all.


## To the Boy Who Stayed,

My sympathies lie with you. Your story haunts me. Your resentments mirror mine. When I think of you standing outside your father's house, your brother's easy laughter ringing in your ears, I ache. I imagine you sore and sweat-stained after a day in the fields, longing to go inside for a shower, a meal, a bed. Longing for so many legitimate things—only to be thwarted by a robe, a ring, and a fatted calf. Not intended for you.

Theologians tell me I'm supposed to look at you and see self-righteousness, arrogance, and unholy spite. But I don't; I look at you and see pain.

I'm an oldest kid, too. Cautious, diligent, responsible. I like order and I don't mind work. But I'm a stickler about fairness. I care about fairness a lot. And I'm also a seether. I don't confront; I seethe. Just like you.

Tell me. How long did the bitterness fester? How many weeks, months, or years did you suffer in silence, mistaking restraint for righteousness? Did your father shrink in your eyes as your anger grew? Did every word he spoke, every request he made, every sigh he sighed, grate on your nerves? Did you lie in bed at night and wish you'd had the audacity to leave, too?

Or maybe it was another kind of courage you lacked. The courage to cry? To plead? To confess a need so insatiable and so secret, it made you burn with shame?

What would have happened if you'd looked your father in the eye and said, "I know that all you have is mine. But it's not enough. I can't explain why, but your 'everything' is not enough for me. I can't find contentment. I can't make my way to love. Somehow, even in your very presence, I am lost."

These are terrifying things to admit to yourself, much less to say out loud. But what if you had said them? What if you had said, "Something in me is broken. Something in me can't enjoy what's mine. Something in me doesn't understand the joy that lives in giving myself away. Help me. Wrap me in your arms and hold me. I am full of hatred, for myself most of all. Teach me what you know. Teach me how to love."

The challenge of your story is that you have rightness on your side. You are right to call for justice. Right to ask why your brother's sins incur no consequences. Right to ask why your own loyalty seems to count for so little.

You are right to find your father's version of love a bit much, a bit scandalous, a bit risky. Because it is. You've understood the point of your own story better than anyone. Yes, your brother squandered his inheritance. Perhaps, by hoarding and withholding, you've also squandered yours. But the real prodigal in this story is your father, is he not? Over-the-top, undignified, and hair-raising in his love? You're right to be appalled.

I don't know why your father never gave you a young goat. Or threw you and your friends a spontaneous party. I wish with all my heart he had; it makes me angry that he didn't. Was he waiting for you to ask? Were you, in turn, waiting for him to initiate? I know that mingy, self-protective mindset so well: "If I have to ask for it, then it doesn't count."

Maybe it does. Maybe there is something essential to be learned in the asking.

"We have to celebrate and rejoice" (v. 32). This is your father's final word to you as you stand out in the cold, your arms crossed, your fists clenched, your heart bleeding. Did you know, dutiful firstborn? Did you know you *have* to celebrate? Did you know that joy is a *must* in your father's house? That partying is a duty?

How astonishing that you lived within arm's reach of your father all these years, and never glimpsed the merriment that is at his core. "*We have to celebrate and rejoice.*" He insists. But there you stand, lover of justice. One-hundred percent right—and one-hundred percent alone.

What will it take for you to lean into celebration? To try out mercy as a balm? Some lessons can only be learned as you laugh. Some hearts will only be healed at the feast, in the dance, at the party.

Here's your vindication, yours and mine: the power in this story is the older child's. It's yours. Your brother is inside; he's done breaking hearts, at least for the time being. Now your father stands in the doorway, waiting for you. Waiting for *you* to stop being lost. Waiting for you to come home. Waiting for you to take hold at last of the inheritance that has always been yours. Did you know that your choices are so powerful? You get to write this ending.

It's getting cold outside. The sun is setting, and the party beckons. What will you do, as the music grows sweeter? What will we choose, you and I?

# The Extravagant Sower

## Matthew 13:1–13

*And he told them many things in parables, saying: "Listen!*
*A sower went out to sow." (Matt 13:3)*

S itting in a boat one day, Jesus looks out at the crowd gathered on the beach and tells them a parable: A sower goes out to sow. As he sows, some seeds fall on the path, and the birds come and eat them up. Other seeds fall on rocky ground, where they spring up quickly, but wither when the sun burns their shallow roots. Other seeds fall among thorns and are choked. Still other seeds fall on good soil and bring forth abundant grain.

If your experience is anything like mine, you've read the "Parable of the Sower" many times and focused exclusively on the four types of terrain Jesus describes. Perhaps you've thought about the people you preach to week after week, and worried over who is hardened, rocky, thorny, or "good." You've agonized over how to cultivate more fertile soil in your church or community. You've analyzed and quantified, assessed and judged. You've evaluated ministry plans and strategies, pruned leadership commissions and committees. You've bought special pots, invested in high-end fertilizers and weed killers, and counted, sorted, and planted your seeds with exquisite care, placing each bit of God's good news in its optimal place to guarantee an impressive harvest.

Or else you've read this parable and walked away, feeling bad about your own faith life. Feeling judged, inadequate, and anxious. You've wondered how to make your spiritual soil less rocky. You've designed all sorts of self-improvement projects to get rid of the thorns. More prayer. Less Twitter. More Bible study. Less cynicism. More church. Less television. You've read the parable as an indictment of your relationship with a sower who just can't seem to find an appropriately hospitable environment in your messed up heart.

There's nothing wrong with planning and pruning. There's nothing wrong with honest and humble self-assessment. But I think we miss

137

something when we read the parable as a lesson about the "Four Terrains."
Because that is not what it is. It is the parable of the *sower*. It is a parable about
the nature and character of God. God's kingdom, God's provision, God's extravagant generosity when it comes to us, his creations.

Consider again the actions of the sower as Jesus describes them: the
sower goes out to sow, and as he sows, the seeds fall everywhere. *Everywhere.* Imagine it: a sower blissfully walking across the fields and mead-
ows, the back alleys and sidewalks, the playgrounds and parking lots of
this world, fistfuls of seed in his quick-to-open hands. There is no way to
contain that much seed. No way to sort or save it. Of course it will spill
over. Of course it will fall through his fingers and cover the ground, scattering in every direction. How can it not?

But here's the surprising part of the story: the sower doesn't mind.
He's not obsessed with where the seeds land; all he cares to do is keep sowing, flinging, and opening his hands. Why? Because there's enough seed
to go around. There's enough seed to accomplish the sower's purposes.
There's enough seed to "waste."

As I imagine this profligate sower walking in, around, and through
the varied terrains of our lives, I can't help but notice my own contrasting
stinginess. The truth is, I don't believe that there's enough Good News to go
around. I don't begin with the generous assumption that every kind of soil
can benefit from the seed. I don't have confidence that God's Word will go
out from God's mouth and accomplish what God wills for it, no matter where
it lands. I don't trust in God's endless ability to soften hard ground, clear
away rocks, and cut through the most stubborn of thorns to make way for a
harvest. I don't care about the birds as much as God does.

In short, I forget that all the terrain—*all the terrain*—is finally God's.
Under God's provision and sustained by God's love. Who am I to tell God,
the Creator of the earth and all that is in it, what "good soil" looks like?
Who am I to decide who is worthy and who is not? Who am I to hoard
what I have been so freely and lavishly given? Who am I to look at God's
generosity and call it waste?

If only our failures as the church were the opposite of what they've
been in relation to this parable. How I wish we were known for our absurd
generosity. How I wish we were famous for being like the Sower, going out
in joy, scattering seed before and behind us in the widest arcs our arms
can make. How I wish the world could laugh at our lavishness instead of
recoiling from our stinginess. How I wish the people in our lives could see a
quiet, gentle confidence in us when we tend to the hard, rocky, thorny places
in our communities, instead of finding us abrasive, judgmental, exacting,
and insular. How I wish seeds of love, mercy, justice, humility, honor, and

truthfulness would fall through our fingers in such appalling quantities that even the birds, the rocks, the thorns, and the shallow, sun-scorched corners of the world would burst into colorful, riotous life.

In a world overshadowed by sickness, scarcity, anxiety, suffering, and loss, what does the world need more than a sower who is lavish? A sower who errs on the side of wastefulness? A sower who'd rather lose a bunch of seeds to inhospitable terrain than withhold a single one?

The thing about this parable is that at some deep, intuitive level, we recognize its wisdom. Whether we want to admit it or not, we know that Jesus is telling us the truth. We understand that seeds are mysterious. We know that the most elegant and carefully cultivated gardens sometimes fail, while profusions of weedy, vibrant wildflowers push through cracks in sidewalks and brighten depressed neighborhoods. We've seen how new life can spring from the most shriveled places in our lives—places we've given up on, places we've assumed are hardened beyond hope. We've witnessed inhospitable environments being altered by love. We know that joy follows from selflessness and generosity, not from caution and miserliness.

In the end, the problem is not our ignorance in the face of this gospel; the problem is our unwillingness to follow in the footsteps of the extravagant sower. His carefree generosity worries us. His seeming wastefulness offends us. Why won't he discriminate? Why won't he wait and withhold? Why won't he privilege the terrain that's more deserving?

Because that's not the kind of sower he is. Look at him, tossing seeds to the wind with a delighted smile on his face, inviting us to release our own handfuls and revel in his joy. He's too busy laughing to count seeds. Are we?

# Let Them Grow Together

### Matthew 13:24–30

*He put before them another parable: "The kingdom of heaven may be compared to someone who sowed good seed in his field; but while everybody was asleep, an enemy came and sowed weeds among the wheat, and then went away." (Matt 13:24–25)*

One of the gifts of Christianity is that it's full of paradoxes. Every facet of the religion, from its theology, to its ethics, to its holy book, to its founder's own identity, invites us to occupy in-between places, places of hard but life-giving ambiguity. Yes, I know: paradox doesn't always *feel* life-giving. We like simple, black-and-white clarity in our lives, and we often try to pummel Christianity into giving it to us. But God won't be pummeled. Despite our preferences, God gifts us with rich and rigorous contradiction.

Don't believe me? Here are some of the paradoxes I'm thinking of: God is One and God is Three. Jesus is divine and Jesus is human. Creation is good and creation is broken. To give is to receive. To die is to live. To pardon is to be pardoned. To be weak is to be strong. To serve is to reign. We're saved by grace, and faith without works is dead. We are in the world, but we are not of the world. The kingdom of God is coming, and the kingdom of God is within us.

My list is far from exhaustive, but hopefully it demonstrates how central paradox is to Christianity. Paradox is woven right into its fabric. At every point, Christianity calls us to hold together truths that seem bizarre, nonsensical, counterintuitive, and irreconcilable. And yet these contradictions are what give the religion heft, credibility, and verisimilitude. If I live in a world that's full of contradiction, then I need a religion robust enough and complex enough to bear the weight of that messy world.

But this means we have to teach ourselves to love the both/and, the in-between, the mystery. This isn't easy, especially for those of us who grew up believing that Christianity is a monolith, or a sure-fire formula for prosperity, or a set of propositions requiring our intellectual assent. It's not a coincidence that heresies often emerge from an unwillingness to sit with paradox: Jesus *can't* be fully God and fully human—so he's not! God can't be immanent and transcendent at the same time, so let's amplify one attribute over the other. It can't be the case that blessing includes suffering, so let's preach prosperity theology.

It takes courage to say, "This is true—*and this is true also.* I don't know how, but God does, and God will show me beautiful things if I venture into the tension of this both/and, and wait for more light, more wisdom, more truth."

In the Gospel of Matthew, Jesus invites us to lean courageously into paradox. A householder plants seeds in his field. While everyone is asleep, an enemy sneaks onto the field, sows weeds among the wheat, and goes away. When the plants come up, the householder's servants are baffled. "Master, did you not sow good seed in your field?" they ask him. "Where did these weeds come from?" The householder doesn't spare them the truth: "An enemy has done this" (vv. 27–28).

But when the servants offer to tear up the weeds, the householder stops them. "No, for in gathering the weeds you would uproot the wheat along with them. Let them both grow together until the harvest. At harvest time, I'll instruct my reapers to collect, bundle, and burn the weeds, and then I'll gather the wheat into my barn" (vv. 29–30).

As I ponder this parable, I see Jesus asking his followers to hold seemingly contradictory truths in tension. One: evil is real, noxious, and among us. Two: our response to evil must include both acknowledgment and restraint.

*Evil is real, noxious, and among us.* For many progressive Christians, this is the harder of the two truths to swallow. After all, "evil" is such an old-fashioned, heavy-duty sort of word. It has an ugly history within the church, a history of exclusion and wounding. Isn't it time we dispensed of such draconian language in favor of something softer? Gentler? More enlightened? Do we really need to call anyone or anything evil?

For what it's worth, Jesus doesn't share our squeamishness. He states without flinching that evil is real and insidious. Evil in the parable of the wheat and the weeds is not a mistake, an accident, or a fluke. The weeds Jesus describes are intentionally sown by an enemy whose motivations are loveless and sinister. Moreover, the literal weeds (which many scholars believe is darnel—"false wheat," or *Lolium temulentum*) are not harmless; they're poisonous. They mimic the look and color of grain, but they're fake, and their seeds can cause illness and even death if consumed in large quantities.

In other words, there is nothing wise or enlightened about denying the reality of evil. We are, like the field in the parable, both mixed and messy. The world contains wheat and weed, good and evil, the fruitful and the poisonous. We are all sinners, and we are all saints. To confess this is not to be draconian or puritanical; it is to be discerning and wise. It is to live in reality.

But there is more to be gleaned about evil from this parable than the fact that it is real and harmful. Jesus also says without apology that evil is doomed: "At harvest time, I'll instruct my reapers to collect, bundle, and burn the weeds." And again: "At the end of the age, the Son of Man will send his angels, and they will collect out of his kingdom all causes of sin and all evildoers, and they will throw them into the furnace of fire, where there will be weeping and gnashing of teeth" (v. 41).

Again, this is not a truth that sits well with many of us in the twenty-first century. Perhaps we need to ask ourselves why. If this parable offers unequivocally good news for the world's downtrodden, disenfranchised, tormented, wounded, and oppressed, then why are we uncomfortable with its sweeping promise? What does our discomfort say about us? About our location, vis-a-vis injustice, oppression, cruelty, and suffering? What version of divine "love" are we preaching if it doesn't include a finale of justice for the world's most broken and desperate people? What *is* compassion, in the end, without justice? Without an embodied realization of the good, the whole, the restored, and the abundant? If the gospel will never redeem the most victimized among us, then why are we bothering with it? Why are we calling it good news?

In this eschatological parable, Jesus promises his listeners that justice is both necessary for an abundant harvest and certain because God wills it. Yes, the weeds may win out in this lifetime—Jesus doesn't deny the grim reality of life here and now. Evil may claim victory for many seasons, lifetimes, and generations. But the passionate, protective, and deeply righteous love of God will not suffer evil to rule the world forever. Oppression will end. Injustices will cease. The wheat will thrive and the weeds will not. "All causes of evil and all evildoers," Jesus says, will be exposed and disempowered (v. 41). *All causes of evil.* The causes we condemn in others, and the causes we complacently excuse in ourselves. The causes that are personal, and the causes that are systemic. The causes we know about, and the causes we don't. All causes of evil. No exceptions.

In short, all that chokes, starves, breaks, distorts, poisons, and harms God's beloved will burn away. Not because God hates the world. But because God loves it.

And yet (here's the paradox): *Our response to evil must include both acknowledgment and restraint.* I have to laugh at the earnestness of the householder's servants in Jesus's parable, because it mirrors my own. Like the servants, I tend to get worked up about weeds. Weeds in my own life, and weeds in other people's. I tend to get eager, preachy, and zealous for the purity of the field. Possessive about the integrity of the householder. Impatient for a quick, clean harvest.

Also, like the servants, I tend to lead with confidence rather than humility when it comes to moral gardening: "Jesus, trust me, I know how to separate the weeds from the wheat. Let me at it, please, and I'll have that field cleared for you in no time!"

But Jesus says no. "No" and "wait." Jesus insists on patience, humility, and restraint when it comes to patrolling the borders of the field. He asks us, even as we acknowledge the pernicious reality of evil, to accept his timing instead of ours when it comes to destroying it. Why? Because there is no way we can police the wheat field without damaging the wheat. There is no way we can rid ourselves of everything bad without distorting everything good. When we rush ahead of God and start yanking weeds left and right, we do harm to ourselves and to the field. Our sincerity devolves into arrogance. Our love devolves into judgment. Our holiness devolves into hypocrisy. The field suffers.

The fact is the seeds of God's life in us are still young and growing. Our roots are delicate and tender, and they need time. They need *lifetimes*. This is not to say we should ignore evil, but it is to say that we should move gently and with great care, recognizing that our task is to grow the good, not burn the bad. Our job is to bless the field, not curse it. Remember, the field is not ours, it is God's. Only God knows it intimately enough to tend it. Only God loves it enough to bring it safely to harvest.

So once again we are called by Jesus to a complicated in-between. A paradox. Evil is real, noxious, and among us, and our response to evil must include both acknowledgment and restraint.

If this ambiguity worries you, then remember that we are braced by a God who is too big for one-dimensional truths, and this is a *good* thing. It's not that we hold paradox; it's that paradox holds us. We are held in a deep place. An ample place. A generous place. Though *we* might fear paradox, God does not. We're safe, even in the contradictions. Weedy, perhaps, but safe.

# Abide

John 15:1–8

*Abide in me as I abide in you. Just as the branch cannot bear fruit by itself unless it abides in the vine, neither can you unless you abide in me. I am the vine, you are the branches. Those who abide in me and I in them bear much fruit, because apart from me you can do nothing. (John 15:4–5)*

One day, when my daughter was two years old, her grandfather took her out for ice cream. After parking his car and lifting my daughter out of her toddler seat, my dad offered her his thumb. "You have to hold it tight until we're inside the ice cream shop," he told her. "This is a busy street." My daughter took one look at his outstretched hand, wrapped her left fist around her own right thumb, and said "No, thank you. I can hold my own."

"No, thank you, I can hold my own," might be the perfect slogan for Western Christianity. We are products of a culture that celebrates the individual and distrusts the communal. We package the Christian life as a one-on-one transaction between a single believer and her God: "*I* accepted Jesus as *my* Savior." We put a lot of stock in our personal spiritual experiences: *my* prayer life, *my* worship, *my* epiphany.

If we do align ourselves with a larger Christian community, we often do so with a consumer mindset, trusting that we're free to join up and free to quit as we please. We are, in other words, Lone Rangers. We believe in pulling ourselves up by our own spiritual bootstraps and encouraging others to do the same. We struggle not to view dependence as weakness. We cherish our personal space and feel claustrophobic when people press too close. We believe, of course, in loving our neighbors, but we feel most comfortable loving them from a distance, or at least with one eye trained on the nearest exit.

Given this reality, I can't imagine a more counter-cultural and challenging vision of the Christian life than the one Jesus offers in this Gospel. "I am the vine, and you are the branches," he tells his disciples. "Those who abide in me and I in them bear much fruit, because apart from me, you can do nothing." If those words aren't blunt enough, he continues: "Whoever does not abide in me is thrown away like a branch and withers; such branches are gathered, thrown into the fire, and burned" (v. 6).

Burned? Gulp.

I'm not much of a gardener, but I have a potted jasmine vine growing on my patio. It is fragrant and beautiful, but it doesn't care one whit about personal space. It's a messy, curly, jumbly thing. It stretches, spreads, and invades. It grows in all kinds of tangled up directions, and its densely interwoven tendrils are just about indistinguishable from each other.

If this is Jesus's metaphor for the spiritual life, then we need to shed our Lone Ranger mentality fast. We are meant to be tangled up together. We are meant to live lives of profound interdependence, growing into, around, and out of each other. We cause pain and loss when we hold ourselves apart, because the fate of each individual branch affects the vine as a whole. In this metaphor, dependence is not a matter of personal morality or preference; it's a matter of life and death. Branches that refuse to cling to the vine die.

My problem, of course, is that I don't believe this. I don't *want* to believe it, because it's inconvenient. It implies that my life is not my own. That my choices affect people I don't even know. That I am bound to the community of God's people whether such boundedness suits my temperament or not. Worse, it requires me to hold two seemingly contradictory truths in tension. One: the point of my Christian life isn't me—my growth, my catharsis, my contributions, my achievements. I am inextricably connected to a larger whole, and apart from that whole, my spirituality, profound and precious though it might feel to me, is without value. Apart from the vine, I am not only barren; I am dead. In other words, I'm not the fruit in this metaphor. I'm not supposed to be the end product of my own spiritual life.

And two: I matter more than I can possibly imagine. Every branch matters more than I can possibly imagine, because the fruitfulness of God's vine is no trivial thing; it constitutes the life and nourishment of the world. The best grapes are produced closest to the central vine, where the nutrients are the most concentrated. To cut myself off from the vine, then, is to diminish my fruitfulness. It is to deny the world the fruit of Christ's saving, cleansing, healing love.

I titled this essay, "Abide," because it's the key word in Jesus's metaphor, appearing eight times in the Gospel passage. If God is the vine grower, Jesus is the vine, and we are the branches, what should we do? We have only one task: to abide. To tarry, to stay, to cling, to remain, to depend, to rely, to persevere, to commit. To hang in there for the long haul. To make ourselves at home.

But "abide" is a tricky word. Passive on the one hand, and active on the other. To abide is to stay rooted in place. But it is also to grow and change. It's a vulnerable-making verb: if we abide, we'll get pruned. It's a risky verb: if we abide, we'll bear fruit that others will see and taste. It's a humbling verb: if we abide, we'll have to accept nourishment that is not of our own making. It's a communal verb; if we abide, we will have to coexist with our fellow branches. We will have to live a life that is messy, crowded, tangled. A life that's deeply rooted and wildly fertile.

I can't imagine that there was ever a time when Jesus's followers found the metaphor of the vine easy to apply in daily life. But it's especially challenging to do so now. We live in bitterly divided times. We have good reasons to be cautious and self-protective, even within the church. It's hard in our self-promoting culture to confess that we are lost and lifeless on our own. That our glory lies in surrender, not self-sufficiency.

Equally hard is the spiritual and imaginative leap we must make in order to trust the metaphor at all. As in, really? Jesus isn't just a wise teacher? A good role model? A provocative historical figure? He's the very source and sustainer of my life?

My dad and I had a good laugh over my daughter's attempt at independence when he brought her home from their outing. Needless to say, he didn't allow his two-year-old granddaughter to hold her own hand while crossing the street. He told her she had to grasp his thumb, or else miss out on the ice cream. In typical toddler fashion, my daughter threw a tantrum, waited a few minutes to see if my dad would relent (he didn't), and finally grabbed hold of his hand.

If only we would surrender our ferocious independence with no more than a quick tantrum. If only we would consent to see reality as it truly is. "*I am* the vine," Jesus tells his disciples. "You *are* the branches." It's a done deal. Whether we like it or not, our lives are bound up in God's and in each other's. The only true life we will live in this world is the life we consent to live in relationship, messy and entangled though it might be. The only fruit worth sharing with the world is the fruit we'll produce together.

# The Bothersome Widow

## Luke 18:1–8

*He said, "In a certain city there was a judge who neither feared God nor had respect for people. In that city there was a widow who kept coming to him and saying, 'Grant me justice against my opponent.'" (Luke 18:2–3)*

In Luke's Gospel, Jesus tells a parable about a widow who seeks justice against an oppressor. Day after day, she appeals to a judge, "who neither fears God nor has respect for people." Day after day, the judge refuses to help. But she persists, tirelessly bothering the judge until he's sick of her very presence. "I will grant her justice," he says to himself, "so that she may not wear me out" (v. 5). (In the Greek, "so that she won't give me a black eye.")

At the outset, the Gospel writer tells us that Jesus's parable is about "the need to pray always and not lose heart" (v. 1). But this is troubling. Are we supposed to harass God until we wear him down? Is that what prayer is? Being a pest? When I receive an answer to prayer, is it only because God is sick to death of hearing my voice and wants me to shut up?

Thankfully, the Gospel writer anticipates these questions and wards them off. In case we're inclined to think of God as the unjust judge, Jesus explains that the parable works by way of contrast: *Unlike* the heartless judge in the story, God "will quickly grant justice" to those who ask (v. 7).

But this explanation raises its own troubling questions, because our lived experiences contradict it. Often, God *does* delay, and our most fervent prayers—prayers for healing, justice, protection, peace—go unanswered. Often, our struggles with prayer lead us to experience God very much as the judge, turned away from the urgency of our requests for reasons we can't fathom.

So, what are we to make of this parable? For starters, I wonder if the story is less about God and more about us. I wonder if it's about the state of our hearts and the motivations behind our prayers. Maybe what's at stake

147

is not who God is and how God operates in the world, but who *we* are, and why we need to be people of persistent prayer.

I want to consider this possibility from two angles. First, what can we learn if we put ourselves in the place of the widow? The parable begins with an exhortation not to lose heart. What does this mean? What does it look like to "lose heart" in our spiritual lives? The words that come to mind are weariness, resignation, numbness, and despair. When I lose heart, I lose my sense of focus and direction. I lose clarity, and begin to doubt God's intentions. I get irritable and cynical. My spiritual GPS goes haywire, and all roads lead nowhere.

In contrast, the widow in Jesus's parable is the very picture of purposefulness, precision, and clarity. She knows her need, she knows its urgency, and she knows exactly where to go and whom to ask in order to get her need met. If anything, the daily business of getting up, getting dressed, heading over to the judge's house or workplace, banging on his door, and talking his ear off fortifies her own sense of who she is and what she's about.

Like many of the storied widows in the Bible (the widow of Zarephath, who feeds the prophet Elijah; Anna, the prophetess who awaits the infant Messiah; the generous widow whose two mites Jesus commends), there is nothing vague or washed out about this bold, plucky woman who drives the apathetic judge nuts with her demands. She lives in Technicolor, here and now: "Give me justice! I will not shut up until you do."

What happens when we pray like the widow? What is prayer for? I can only speak from experience, but I know that when I persist in prayer, *really* persist, with a full heart, over a long period of time, something happens to me. My sense of who I am, to whom I belong, what really matters in this life, and why—these things mature and solidify. My heart grows stronger. It becomes less fragile and flighty. Once in a long while, it even soars. And sometimes—here's the biggest surprise—these good and substantive things happen even when I don't receive the answer I'm praying for.

I don't mean to suggest that unanswered prayer doesn't take a toll. It does. Sometimes it breaks my heart. But maybe that's the point of the parable, too: the work of prayer is hard. The widow's predicament is not straightforward; she has to make a costly choice every single day. Will I keep asking? Dare I risk humiliation one more time? Do I still believe that my request is worthy of articulation? Can I be patient? Am I still capable of trusting in the possibility of justice?

Prayer is, finally, a great mystery. We can't know—it's not given to us to know—why some prayers are answered quickly and many others are not. We can't understand why our earnest pleas for justice, healing, or peace hit the wall of God's silence and sometimes remain there for weeks, months, years, or lifetimes. And yet, from the heart of this bewildering mystery, Jesus asks, "Will I find faith on the earth?" (v. 8). Which is to say, will I find men and women like the bothersome widow? Will I find such ferocity? Such tenacity? Such fortitude?

The widow's only power in this story is the power of showing up. The power of presence and grit. But the story suggests that this power is not to be taken lightly. Which is to say, prayer is not to be taken lightly. We can't always know what gets shaken, transformed, upended, or vindicated simply because we show up again and again in prayer.

But there is a second way to read the parable, too. It might seem like a stretch, but I'm offering it anyway, because it speaks to where I often find myself in my relationship with God. What if I am not the widow in the parable? What if I am the judge, and God (the pleading, persistent one) is the widow? The widow knocking down my door in the hopes that I will soften my heart and attend to the pain, injustice, and sorrow wounding God's very being?

Jesus describes the judge as a man who neither fears God nor has respect for people. Can I honestly say that I never fit this description? Can I profess that I'm never indifferent, irritable, closed off, or unsympathetic? Is it really the case that my heart is always open to the pain and brokenness of others? Don't I self-protect? Don't I say, "It's not my problem. Someone else will take care of it"?

Scripture attests to the fact that God not only hears the cries of the helpless; God is *in* the cries of the helpless. God dwells with the unseen, unheard, unloved, and unwanted. God is the wronged widow crying for justice, pleading with me to listen, to care, and to keep my heart open on her behalf.

The truth is the judge lives in me, and if the parable of the widow has anything to offer, it is that prayer alone will wear down my inner judge. It is through persistent prayer that my heart will soften. It is through persistent prayer that every obstacle I place before God—my fear, my shame, my woundedness, my inattentiveness—will be dismantled. In this sense, prayer is the fist that breaks down the doors of my resistance. Prayer is what enables the light of God's compassion to illuminate the dim corners of human life with hope and compassion.

In the end, this parable is about persistence. God delights in those who persist, those who dare to strive with the divine. Wrestling, as it turns out, is not a bad thing, because it's the opposite of apathy, the opposite of resignation. It's even the opposite of loneliness. To fight with God—to show up day after day in prayer, to wrestle with our resistance in the darkest hours of the night—is to stay close, to keep our arms wrapped tight around the one who alone can bless us. Fighting means we haven't walked away. Fighting means we still have skin in the game.

When the Son of Man comes, Jesus asks at the end of the parable, will he find faith on the earth? Faith that persists, faith that contends, faith that wrestles? This is the question that matters. Will God find such faith in us?

# When You Pray

## Luke 11:1–13

*He said to them, "When you pray, say: Father, hallowed be your name. Your kingdom come. Give us each day our daily bread. And forgive us our sins, for we ourselves forgive everyone indebted to us. And do not bring us to the time of trial." (Luke 11:2–4)*

Let's start with the hard stuff and acknowledge that this Gospel teaching is full of landmines: "Ask, and it will be given you; search, and you will find; knock, and the door will be opened for you" (v. 9). "Everyone who asks receives, and everyone who searches finds, and for everyone who knocks, the door will be opened" (v. 10). "I tell you, even though [the friend whose door you bang on at midnight to ask for bread] will not get up and give you anything because you are his friend, at least because of your persistence, he will get up and give you whatever you need" (v. 8).

When I call these famous words "landmines," I'm not saying that Jesus's teaching puts us in danger. I'm saying that interpretation matters. Read the wrong way, Jesus's teaching on prayer renders prayer transactional, inviting us to believe that God is a cosmic gumball machine into which we insert prayers like so many shiny quarters.

Like some of you, I was raised to believe in a gumball God. For years, I believed that fervent, persistent prayer heals diseases, prevents car accidents, feeds hungry children, fends off nightmares, prevents premature death, saves broken relationships, and "stops the bad guys."

But then life rose up and kicked me in the butt. Diseases didn't get better, car accidents happened, I had nightmares, babies starved, young people died, relationships disintegrated, and the bad guys thrived. When I asked other Christians to explain these discrepancies, I received two answers: (1) You need to pray harder, longer, and with more faith, or (2) God *did* answer your prayers; God said no.

Both of those answers broke my heart. No, worse than that: the answers *hardened* my heart. Over time, prayer, which used to be easy, became excruciatingly hard. These days when I sit down to pray, I often do battle with a persistent question: "Why bother?"

All of that to say: I come to Jesus's teaching with caution, afraid of doing harm, afraid of reopening old wounds. To ask what role prayer plays in the face of ongoing tragedy, injustice, and oppression in our world is to raise the hardest questions I can think of about God—questions I don't know how to answer. Does God intervene directly in human affairs? Can prayer "change" God? Do our prayers have tangible effects on other people, even when those people have no idea that we're praying for them?

To be fair, I know plenty of people for whom these questions are irrelevant and even heretical. I have friends and family members who pray with full confidence for everything from parking spots and lost house keys to cancer remission and Ivy League acceptances for their children. They pray expecting answers, and they apparently receive them. Or so I am told, and who am I to question them? All I can say is that my experiences with prayer have never been so seamless.

If your prayer life is equally fraught, then what can we honestly make of Jesus's teaching in this Gospel passage? What can we carry away with integrity? Here are a few possibilities:

"Lord, teach us." The reading begins with a disciple approaching Jesus and asking for instruction. "Lord, teach us to pray." It's a simple, straightforward request, but here's what surprises me: I've never made it. Have you? Have you ever asked Jesus to *teach* you to pray? Has it ever occurred to you that such a thing is askable? Or that your asking might give God joy?

Remember, the disciples are not ignorant or inexperienced when it comes to prayer; they're devout Jews who have most likely grown up attending Sabbath services, lifting their hands in worship, or lying prone on the ground to make their confessions. They know how to pray. What they seek is not better technique.

So, what is it? What do they observe in Jesus when he prays? We can't know for sure, but I'll hazard some guesses: Intimacy. Belonging. Trust. Peace. A closeness to God that is transformative and nourishing. Fresh vision, renewed perspective, greater strength, and deeper empathy. "Lord, teach us to pray."

In other words, teach us to attain what you have attained. Teach us to be with God as you are with God. To commune as you commune. To communicate as you communicate. Teach us to unlearn those false beliefs and false promises that keep us from praying as you do. We confess that we are impatient and self-absorbed creatures, greedy for quick answers and even quicker gains. Unmake all of that. Help us to start afresh. Teach us to pray.

*When you pray.* "When you pray," Jesus says to his disciples in response to their request—and already I'm in trouble. *When* I pray? Shoot.
How about, "*If* I pray?" Because really, when do I pray? When it's January
1st, and I've made yet another New Year's resolution to have a "daily quiet
time" with God? When I've read my millionth book on the theology, history, psychology, or neurology of prayer, and I decide to give the practice
another shot? When I promise to "keep you in my thoughts and prayers,"
because your situation scares or saddens or paralyzes me so badly that I
can't think of anything else to say? When I'm in full panic mode, and the
only options available are prayer or collapse?

"When you pray," Jesus says casually, as if prayer is a given. A matter
of course. A practice so natural and so intrinsic, he might as well say, "when
you breathe," or, "when you blink," or, "when your heart beats." Prayer is not
a special activity reserved for special times, places, or people. Prayer is not
the private property of a pious few; prayer is ordinary. Prayer is what we're
wired for. Prayer is what God's children *do*.

If we can pause and think about it for a minute, this is a reason to
both relax and rejoice. What Jesus offers is an invitation to enter into
prayer gently, with quiet confidence. To trust it as we trust oxygen, food,
or water. To lean into it as we lean into the strength of our own bones,
tendons, and muscles. Prayer will hold us because it is *for* us. We know
and are known in prayer.

*Ask, seek, knock.* Yes, back to the landmines. But what if we begin
with a possible synonym for Jesus's famous ask-seek-knock trifecta? What
about "yearn"? Or "hunger"? Or "want"? What if Jesus's lesson here is a
lesson of permission? Permission to name our longings? To acknowledge
the desires which drive and haunt us? To state without reservation or embarrassment that all is not okay, that we are not yet full, that even though
it's midnight and we know our door-pounding is mightily inconvenient to
the surrounding universe, we don't care and we're going to keep pounding
because we still need bread *right now?*

Ask. Seek. Knock. Keep knocking. Go to your friend's house and
wake him up. Don't let him go back to sleep until he hauls himself out
of bed. When you pray, say, "Your kingdom come." When you pray, say,
"Give us each day our daily bread." When you pray, say, "Forgive us our
sins." When you pray, say, "Do not bring us to the time of trial." Ask. Seek.
Knock. Keep knocking.

Notice that there is nothing dainty or delicate about this teaching from
Jesus. His invitation is muscular, assertive, aerobic, and pushy. It is longing
named, named, and named again. It is a holy yearning insisting on itself to a
God who can more than handle our ferocity. It is *imperative.* I wonder how

my prayer life would change if I accepted Jesus's call to prayer as a call to contend with God. Apparently, this God is not invested in my politeness.

*How much more.* Read the lesson carefully, and you'll find another surprise. There is only one promise in it. Only one, and it is not the one I was raised to desire or expect. Jesus concludes his teaching on prayer with a striking sentence: "If you then, who are evil, know how to give good gifts to your children, *how much more* will the heavenly Father give the Holy Spirit to those who ask him!" (v. 13). What Jesus promises us in answer to our prayers is the Holy Spirit. That's it. That's all. There is no other promise or guarantee.

How the church devolved from this to prosperity theology is beyond me, but here we are, here's the actual promise: when we pray, when we persist in prayer, when we name our longings in prayer without fear or compromise, God will never fail to give us God's own, abundant, indwelling and overflowing self as the answer we actually need. When we contend in prayer, God will not withhold God's loving, consoling, healing, transforming, and empowering Spirit from us. When it comes to no-holds-barred, absolutely self-giving generosity, God's answer to all of our prayers will always be yes.

Maybe this yes is what the disciples sense in Jesus when they watch him pray. Maybe the presence of the Spirit radiating through Jesus is what compels them to go deeper in their own prayer lives. Whatever the yes is, it suffuses Jesus's whole being. However the Spirit manifests herself in Jesus's life, she is so beautiful and so compelling, the disciples want to experience her, too.

Here's the question for us: Do we consider the yes of God's Spirit a sufficient response to our prayers? If God's guaranteed answer to our petitions is God's own self, can we live with that?

Sometimes I can, and sometimes I can't. It's not easy to let go of my transactional, gumball God—idol though that God is. It's hard to persist in prayer and not receive the answers I'm hoping for. It's hard to accept the Holy Spirit as God's perfect gift when I'd rather receive physical healing, or an end to the toxicity that governs American politics, or lasting freedom from anxiety, or commonsense gun control, or realistic hope in the face of climate change. My love for God is thinner than I thought it was; often I want *stuff from God* much more than I want God. I want God to sweep in and fix everything much more than I want God's Spirit to fill and accompany me so that I can do my part to heal the world. Resting in God's yes requires vulnerability, patience, courage, discipline, and trust—traits I can only cultivate in prayer.

So, we pray. We pray because Jesus wants us to. We pray because it is what God's children do. We pray because we yearn and our yearning is precious to God. With words, without words, through laughter, through tears, in hope, and in despair, our prayers usher in God's Spirit and remind us that we are not alone in this broken, aching world. God's Spirit is our yes. God's Spirit is our guarantee.

# On Fairness

## Matthew 20:1–16

*"Am I not allowed to do what I choose with what belongs to me?
Or are you envious because I am generous?' So the last will be
first, and the first will be last." (Matt 20:15–16)*

A few years ago, Sarah Brosnan and Frans de Waal, two zoologists at
Emory University, decided to study the evolution of fairness. They
wanted to explore where our distaste for unfairness comes from. Do we
learn it, or is it hardwired?

To study this question, Brosnan and de Waal designed an experiment
using capuchin monkeys. Pairs of monkeys were placed in adjacent cages
where they could see each other, and trained to take turns giving small
granite rocks to their human handler. Each time a monkey relinquished a
rock, she would receive a piece of cucumber as a reward.

Capuchins love cucumbers, so both monkeys found this arrangement
satisfactory, and handed over their rocks with enthusiasm. Then the handler
changed things up. After a few fair and even exchanges, the handler rewarded
the first monkey with a chunk of cucumber as usual, but gave the second
monkey a grape—the equivalent of fine wine or caviar in the monkey world.

Seeing that the game had changed for the better, the first monkey
perked up, and very eagerly handed over another rock, expecting, of
course, to receive a grape, too. But no, the handler gave her another piece
of cucumber. To make things worse, the handler then gave the second
monkey another grape for free!

The results, which you can see on YouTube, were striking.[1] The first
monkey just about lost her mind. Not only did she refuse to eat the cucumber; she hurled it at the handler's face. She then proceeded to bang against
the bars of the cage, throw her remaining rocks in every direction, and make
furious gestures at her grape-eating companion.

1. Brosnan, in TED Blog Video, "Two Monkeys Were Paid Unequally."

The experiment has since been repeated using other primates, and the results have been similar. Scientists have also studied the development of fairness in human babies, and found that infants as young as nine months old will react strongly and negatively to perceived unfairness. Clearly, as Brosnan and de Waal concluded after their experiment, fairness is a concept that is deeply rooted in the human psyche.

Which brings us to Jesus's "Parable of the Generous Landowner," and the thorny question about fairness that lies at its heart: Am I not allowed to do what I choose with what belongs to me? Or are you envious because I am generous?

The parable begins with a landowner going out several times in the course of a day to hire laborers for his vineyard. When the workday is over, the landowner pays every worker the exact same wage, regardless of how many hours they worked. The laborers who put in a full day complain that this is unfair. In response, the landowner deflects their accusations and asks them if they are envious because he is generous.

Writer Mary Gordon, in her book *Reading Jesus,* answers the landowner's question with painful honesty. *Yes,* she says. "I am envious because you are generous. I am envious because my work has not been rewarded. I am envious because someone has gotten away with something. Envy has eaten out my heart."[2]

I appreciate Gordon's candor, because this parable is offensive. We know what fairness is, and we know how it's supposed to play out. Equal pay for equal work is fair. Equal pay for unequal work is *not* fair. Having our sincere efforts noticed and praised is fair. Having them ignored is *not* fair. Rewarding hard work and ambition is fair. Rewarding sloth and sloppiness is *not* fair.

I live in high-strung Silicon Valley, where children learn early that the only place in the world worth standing is at the front of whatever line they happen to be in. Academic, musical, athletic, pre-professional. Why be second when you can be first? Why be mediocre when genius pays so handsomely? Why bother with your neighbor's needs when resources are scarce and time is flying? Work hard. Work harder. Happiness comes to those who slog the longest to achieve the highest success. Because that is how the world works. That is *fair.*

But God—if the landowner in Jesus's parable represents God—is not fair. At least, not according to our inherited beliefs. God, it turns out, does *not* believe that the best place to be is at the front of the line. God isn't interested, as we so often are, in showing favor to the best, the biggest, and the

2. Gordon, *Reading Jesus,* 14.

brightest—the workers with the most elite educations, astonishing professional achievements, and fanciest zip codes.

In fact, the landowner in Jesus's story doesn't judge his workers by their
hours. He doesn't obsess over why some workers are able to start at dawn
and others are not. Perhaps the late starters aren't as literate, educated, or
skilled as their competitors. Perhaps they have learning challenges, or a tough
home life, or children to care for at home. Perhaps they're refugees, or don't
own cars, or don't speak the language, or can't get green cards. Perhaps they
struggle with chronic depression or anxiety. Perhaps they've hit a glass ceiling
after years of effort, and they're stuck. Perhaps employers refuse to hire them
because they're gay or trans or disabled or black or female.

Whatever the case may be, the landowner doesn't ask them to defend
themselves. All he cares about is that every last person in the marketplace
finds a spot in his vineyard—the early bird and the latecomer, the able-
bodied and the infirm, the young and the old, the popular and the forgotten.
When the workday is over, what concerns the landowner is not who de-
serves what. He simply wants every worker to end the day with the dignity
and security of a living wage. The capacity to go home and feed a family.
Sufficient security and peace of mind to sleep well. A solid grasp on hope. A
reliable sense of accomplishment, belonging, and dignity.

"Are you envious because I am generous?" asks God. Or literally, in the
Greek: "Is your eye evil because I am good?"

It embarrasses me to admit this, but ever since I was a little girl, I
have assumed that if I lived in Jesus's time, I would be one of the early
birds in the landowner's vineyard. I'd be first in line and ready to go before
the sun comes up. I'd work the hardest and the longest. Of course I would!
I'm Type A! I'm a morning person! I'm a "J" on the Myers-Briggs and a six
on the Enneagram!

But consider this: the parable reads very differently if we situate ourselves at the *end* of the line. The workers who get more than they expect
to—the ones who receive twelve times the pay they know they deserve—are
ecstatic at the end of their workday. Ecstatic, stunned, thrilled, and grateful.
Their experience is one of utter blessing, and I'll bet that what goes on at
their end of the line is one big raucous party.

The other stuff? The envy? The bitterness? The grumbling? The dis-
satisfaction? All of that murky stuff belongs to the "deserving" folks at
the front of the line. They can't party; they're too busy feeling miffed and
offended. They can't take satisfaction in their hours of good work. They
can't delight in the fruit of the vineyard. They can't relax into their time off
and enjoy the gifts of leisure. Though the landowner honors his agreement
with them, though they receive their daily bread and lack no good thing,

they waste their off-hours in resentment and anger. Like the monkey in Brosnan and de Waal's experiment, they take a perfectly good reward and hurl it into the empty air, fists raised.

Maybe, if God's generosity offends us, it's because we don't have eyes to see where we actually stand in the line of God's grace and kindness. Where would we rather stand? At the front of the line, where bitterness and judgment poison the air? Or at the back, where joy has won the day?

I don't think it's a coincidence that the landowner insists on paying his workers in reverse order, thereby making sure that the first workers see what the last receive. He wants them to experience what radical generosity looks like. He wants them to relinquish their anger and join the party. He wants them to use their plenty to build longer tables, not higher walls.

Needless to say, this is a story for our times. As I sit here writing this essay, the air outside my door is so polluted from California's ongoing wildfires, it's unsafe to leave my house. Human-caused climate change has done this. Meanwhile, COVID-19 is casting shadows of death, fear, hunger, unemployment, and misery all around the world, and many of our collective responses to the pandemic are intensifying the losses. People of color in the US and around the world are starving for equality and justice, and some of us are still refusing to honor and address their pain.

Could it be any more obvious that we are wholly dependent on each other for our survival and well-being? That the future of creation itself depends on human beings recognizing our fundamental interconnectedness, and acting in concert for the good of all? That what's "fair" for me isn't good enough if it leaves you in the wilderness to die? That my sense of "justice" is not just if it mocks the tender heart of God? That the vineyards of this world thrive only when everyone has a place of dignity and purpose within them? That the time for all selfish and stingy notions of fairness is over?

Are we willing to see this yet? Are we willing to live it?

Two-thousand years after Jesus first asked, the question remains: Are you envious because God is generous? Live into the discomfort of the asking. So much depends on our answer.

# The Story of the Bridesmaids
## Matthew 25:1–13

*Then the kingdom of heaven will be like this. Ten bridesmaids took their lamps and went to meet the bridegroom. Five of them were foolish, and five were wise. (Matt 25:1–2)*

T he parable of the ten bridesmaids has never been one of my favorites. When I first heard it as a child, I annoyed my Sunday School teacher by asking all the "wrong" questions: Why do the bridesmaids have to bring their own light to a wedding reception? Why are the "wise" bridesmaids so stingy? Why doesn't the groom show up for his own wedding until midnight? Why does the bride—whom we never even get to meet—put up with such a ridiculous delay? Why, after keeping his poor bridesmaids waiting for hours, does the groom blame *them* for lateness and shut his door in their faces?

These questions still bother me, so much so that I can't tie the pieces of this particular parable into a colorful interpretative bow. All I can do is keep the pieces scattered and examine them by turns. Or (to switch metaphors), to turn the parable around and around in my fingers as if it's a diamond, and see what it reveals from each angle, in each facet. I won't pretend that my various discoveries cohere. But maybe this is what we're supposed to do with Jesus's parables. Maybe we're supposed to let their meanings open out, wider and wider and wider. Maybe the truths the parables reveal are various and infinite, impossible to lock down.

In any case, here we go. Here are some interpretative possibilities for the story of the bridesmaids:

*There is going to be a wedding someday. No, really, there is.* Here's a potentially uncomfortable question: When is the last time you heard (or preached) a sermon about the second coming of Jesus? Do you remember? When is the last time you thought to yourself, "What if it's today?! What if *today* is the day when God's kingdom comes in all of its fullness, and our broken earth is restored and made whole?"

The truth is, many of us have grown accustomed to the bridegroom's absence. Accustomed and indifferent. His absence and delay are our norms, so much so that deep in our hearts, we no longer believe he's going to return. We no longer believe there's going to be a wedding. After all, isn't that sci-fi, children's story, parting-of-the-clouds stuff embarrassing? Won't people think we're delusional if we take it seriously?

Maybe. But the problem with letting go of the eschaton is twofold. One, we have to make Jesus a liar in order to do it. Jesus *said* that he will return, just as surely as he said he would be crucified, buried, and resurrected on the third day. On what grounds shall we choose to disbelieve a stated promise of the risen Christ?

Second, the coming of God's kingdom in all of its healing, justice-making fullness is the yardstick against which we must measure all of our own healing, justice-making work. The wedding feast is our ideal, our goal, our destination. Without it, we have no standard. No accountability. Nothing to lean into, nothing to work towards, nothing to anticipate as we labor in God's name.

The parable of the bridesmaids ends with a wedding. It ends in celebration and joy. We dare not abandon this glorious ending because we've grown tired of waiting.

*It's not going to go the way you think it's going to go.* In the parable, the bridesmaids have to wait so long for the groom's arrival, they fall asleep. Obviously, they don't *want* the party to begin at midnight. It's not their choice or desire to wait. But the five bridesmaids who carry extra oil in their flasks prepare themselves for the long haul, just in case. They consider and take seriously the possibility of surprise, of delay, of hardship, of unpredictability. They don't allow their preconceived ideas about the groom or the party to distract them from what's actually in front of them. They remain open and adaptable to the circumstances they find themselves in.

Do we? Are we ready for the long haul? Do we have the flexibility to handle the unexpected, or are we clinging to rigid, narrow notions of what God's presence looks like, such that we miss God when God actually shows up? Can we bear an unpredictable bridegroom? A bridegroom who surprises us? If Jesus's notion of time, faithfulness, fulfillment, and celebration look different from ours, will we still follow him into the wedding hall—or will we bail?

*Sometimes, doors close. Do what is needful now.* I don't like the fact that the five "foolish" bridesmaids in the parable arrive too late to gain entrance to the wedding. I don't like the fact that the groom closes his doors. I don't like the fact that the story leaves five women out in the cold.

But whether I like these things or not, they happen. Windows close. Chances fade. Time runs out. We know this; we experience it regularly. The opportunity to mend the friendship, forgive the debt, break the habit, write the check, heal the wound, confront the injustice, embrace the church, relinquish the bitterness, closes down. Opportunities end.

We hate this, of course, so we tell ourselves it isn't true. We tell ourselves that there's always tomorrow. That we'll get to it—whatever "it" is—eventually. Because there will always be more time.

What if there isn't? What if this parable is telling us to be alert now, awake now, active now? What if it's inviting us to live as if each day—singular and fleeting—is all we have? Tomorrow, if it comes, will be its own gift, its own miracle, its own challenge. Don't presume that it belongs to you. Do what is needful now.

*You're more valuable than your oil supply, so stick around.* As far as I can tell, the fatal mistake the five "foolish" bridesmaids make is that they leave. They assume that their oil supply is more important to the groom than their presence at his party. So, they ditch the scene at its most crucial moment and go shopping, depriving themselves of a wonderful celebration and depriving the bridegroom of their companionship, support, and love on his special day.

This is a point I want to press into, because I understand the foolish bridesmaids' rationale in this narrative moment. I get how hard it is to stick around when my "light" is fading and my reserves are low. I get what it's like to scramble for perfection, to insist on having my ducks in a row before I show up in front of God or the church or the world. After all, it's scary and vulnerable-making to linger in the dark when my pitiful little lamp is flickering, my once-robust faith is evaporating, and my measly, leaky flask is filled with nothing but doubt, pain, grief, and weariness. Only a bridesmaid who trusts in the groom's unconditional compassion, only a bridesmaid who knows that the groom has light and oil to spare, only a bridesmaid who understands that her presence is of intrinsic value to the groom, will find the honesty and courage to stay.

The bridesmaids in the parable lack this courage. They scatter, and I believe the wedding procession suffers as a result. Five fewer lights brighten the groom's path. Five fewer voices cry out with joy at his arrival. Five fewer friends dance and sing the night away in honor of the groom and his bride. The loss is communal, extensive, and real. This is not a situation to celebrate or endorse; it's a situation to grieve.

Perhaps the lesson of this parable is: don't allow your fear or your sense of inadequacy to keep you away from the party. Be willing to show up as you are, complicated, disheveled, half-lit, and half-baked. The groom delights in *you,* not in your lamp. Your light doesn't have to dazzle. Remember, God created light. God *is* light. And Jesus is the light of the world. Your half-empty flask of oil isn't the point. You are. So stay.

*Scarcity isn't a thing in God's kingdom. Quit hoarding.* Ironically enough, the "wise" bridesmaids in Jesus's parable distrust the sufficiency, generosity, and love of the bridegroom as much as the "foolish" bridesmaids do. Operating on the basis of scarcity and fear, they refuse to share their oil. Smug in their own preparedness and "wisdom," they forget all about mercy, empathy, kinship, and hospitality. They forget that the point of a wedding celebration is *celebration.* Gathering. Communing. Joining. Sharing. It doesn't occur to them that their stinginess has consequences. That it sends their five companions stumbling into the midnight darkness. That it diminishes the wedding, depriving the bridal couple and their remaining guests of five lively, caring companions.

I'm not sure what it will take for us Christians to live fully into the abundance of God. But it's clear that our assumptions about scarcity are killing us. We're so afraid of emptiness, we idolize excess. We're so worried about opening our doors too wide, we shut them tight. We're so obsessed with our own rightness before God, we forget that "rightness" divorced from love is always wrong. We live in dread that there won't be enough to spare. Enough grace. Enough freedom. Enough forgiveness. Enough mercy. Somehow, we would rather shove people into the night than give up the illusion of our own brightness.

What would it be like to stop? What would it be like to care more about the emptiness in our neighbor's flask than the brimming fullness of our own?

*What if Jesus isn't the door slammer?* It is possible, given the context in which Matthew's Gospel was written, that Jesus isn't the bridegroom in this parable. We know that the Matthean "Jesus movement" of the first century was in conflict with local religious leaders who considered their Christian peers heretical and deviant. It is likely that there was much discussion around who belonged and who didn't, who was "in" with God and who wasn't.

Sound familiar? One of the great tragedies of the Christian story across history is that we are better known for policing our borders than welcoming our neighbors. We are quick to say, "I don't know you," to those who believe or practice differently than we do. We feel safer and more pious behind closed doors than we do with open arms. Maybe this parable is showing us the ugliness of the closed door.

As I wrote at the start, these are interpretative *possibilities* for Jesus's parable of the bridesmaids. Surely there are other angles. Other facets. Which ones speak to you? Where do you see yourself in the story, and where do you see Jesus, looking at you? Locate yourself and locate him. Start talking. The doors are open and the wedding hall is full of holy light.

# Salty

## Matthew 5:13–20

*You are the salt of the earth; but if salt has lost its taste, how can its saltiness be restored? It is no longer good for anything, but is thrown out and trampled under foot. (Matt 5:13)*

When I was seven years old, my mother decided that I was old enough to start helping her in the kitchen. My first tasks as her assistant included grating coconuts, chopping onions, and peeling what felt like an infinite number of garlic cloves. But there was one culinary lesson Mom stressed over all others. Before she'd let me preside over an actual pot of curry, I had to learn—or, rather, my mouth had to learn—how to check for salt.

Under Mom's tutelage, I learned that it is possible to get every ingredient in a recipe just right—to combine perfect amounts of cumin, turmeric, paprika, ginger, garam masala, and cayenne—and still ruin the dish with salt. Too little salt, and the curry remains bland and lifeless, all of its zest and kick subdued. Too much salt, and the curry loses its complexity to an unbearable bitterness.

In this Gospel reading from Matthew, Jesus says, "You are the salt of the earth; but if the salt has lost its taste, how can its saltiness be restored? It is no longer good for anything, but is thrown out and trampled underfoot."

Living as most of us do in cultures of plenty, we take household goods like salt for granted. But until fairly recently in human history, salt was one of the most sought after commodities. The ancients believed that salt would ward off evil spirits. Religious covenants were often sealed with salt. Salt was used for medicinal purposes, to disinfect wounds, check bleeding, stimulate thirst, and treat skin diseases. Roman soldiers were sometimes paid in salt—hence our English word, "salary." Brides and grooms rubbed salt on their bodies to enhance fertility. The Romans salted their vegetables, as we do salads. Around ten-thousand years ago, dogs were first domesticated using salt; people would leave salt outside their homes to entice the animals. And of course, in all the centuries before refrigeration, salt was essential for food preservation.

We still use salt for all sorts of purposes. Salt accentuates flavors, melts ice, softens water, and hastens a boil. It soothes sore throats, rinses sinuses, eases swelling, and cleanses wounds. In some contexts, salt has more than a flavor; it has an edge. It stings, burns, abrades, and irritates. If we don't have enough salt in our bodies, we die. But if we have too much? We die.

I know that it's possible to take a metaphor too far. No single descriptor in the Bible—salt, light, bride, clay, sheep, branch, dove, soil—captures or contains the entirety of what it means to live as followers of Christ. But when Jesus calls his listeners "the salt of the earth," he is saying something profound, something easy to miss in our twenty-first century context.

First of all, he is telling us who we are. We *are* salt. We are not "supposed to be" salt, or "encouraged to become" salt, or promised that "*if* we become" salt, God will love us more. The language Jesus uses is 100 percent descriptive; it's a statement of our identity. We are the salt of the earth. We are that which enhances or embitters, soothes or irritates, melts or stings, preserves or ruins. For better or for worse, we are the salt of the earth, and what we do with our saltiness matters. It matters a lot. Whether we want to or not, whether we notice or not, whether we're intentional about it or not, we impact the world we live in.

Second, we are precious. Again, it's easy to miss the import of this in our modern world where salt is cheap and plentiful, but imagine what Jesus's first followers hear when he calls them salt. Remember who they are. The poor, the mournful, the meek, the persecuted. The hungry, the sick, the crippled, the frightened. The outcast, the misfit, the disreputable, the demon-possessed. "You," he tells them all. "You are the salt of the earth. You who are not shiny and well-fed and fashionable, you who've been rejected, wounded, unloved, and forgotten—you are essential. You are worthwhile. You are treasured. And I am commissioning *you*."

For all of us who've spent months or years trying to earn divine favor, believing that our piety alone makes us precious in God's eyes, I hope this metaphor stops us in our tracks. Jesus knowingly names a commodity that is priceless in his time and place. He confers great value on those who do not consider themselves valuable. In fact, he does this, still. Now.

Third, salt does its best work when it's poured out. When it's scattered. When it dissolves into what is around it. I would have done my mother's curry recipes no favors if I'd kept our salt shaker locked in a kitchen cabinet. Salt is meant to give of itself. It's meant to share its unique flavor in order to bring out the best in all that surrounds it. Which means that if we want to enliven, enhance, deepen, and preserve the world we live in, we must not hide within the walls of our churches. We must not cluster and congregate for our own comfort. We must not retreat into our theological bubbles.

Salt doesn't exist to preserve itself; it exists to preserve what is not itself. Another metaphor for this? A metaphor Jesus used all the time? Dying. Jesus calls us to die to self. To die in order to live. Remember—we *are* salt. It's not a question of striving to become what we are not. It's a question of living into the fullness of what we are.

Lastly, salt is meant to enhance, not dominate. Christian saltiness heals; it doesn't wound. It purifies; it doesn't desiccate. It softens; it doesn't destroy. Even when Christian saltiness has an edge—even when, for example, it incites thirst—it only draws the thirsty towards the living water of God. It doesn't leave the already thirsty parched, dehydrated, and embittered.

One of the great tragedies of historic Christianity has been its failure to understand this distinction. Salt *fails* when it dominates. Instead of eliciting goodness, it destroys the rich potential all around it. Salt poured out without discretion leaves a burnt, bitter sensation in its wake. It ruins what it tries to enhance. It repels.

This, unfortunately, is the reputation Christianity has these days. We are known as the salt that exacerbates wounds, irritates souls, and ruins goodness. We are considered arrogant, domineering, obnoxious, and uninterested in enhancing anything but ourselves. We are known for hoarding our power, not for giving it away. We are known for shaming, not blessing. We are known for using our words to burn, not heal.

This is not what Jesus intends when he calls us the salt of the earth. Our preciousness is not meant to make us proud; it's meant to humble and awe us.

Our vocation in these times and places is not to lose our saltiness. That's the temptation—to retreat. To choose blandness over boldness and keep our love for Jesus an embarrassed secret.

But that kind of salt, Jesus tells his listeners, is useless. It is untrue to its essence. We are called to live wisely, creatively, and in balance. To learn, as my mother put it when I was a little girl, how to check for salt. Salt at its best sustains and enriches life. It pours itself out with discretion so that God's kingdom might be known on the earth—a kingdom of spice and zest, a kingdom of health and wholeness, a kingdom of varied depth, flavor, and complexity.

In his Sermon on the Mount, Jesus makes concrete the work of love, compassion, healing, and justice. It's not enough to believe. It's not enough to bask in our blessedness while creation burns. To be blessed, to be salt, to be followers of Jesus, is to take seriously what our identity signifies.

We are the salt of the earth. That is what we are, for better or for worse. May it be for better. May your pouring out—and mine—be for the life of the world.

# Mysteries

"I mean, let's face it, 'nothing' is God's favorite material to work with."

—NADIA BOLZ-WEBER[1]

---

1. Bolz-Weber, *Pastrix,* 106.

# My Broken Hosanna

### John 12:12–19

*The next day the great crowd that had come to the festival heard that Jesus was coming to Jerusalem. So they took branches of palm trees and went out to meet him, shouting, "Hosanna! Blessed is the one who comes in the name of the Lord—the King of Israel!"* *(John 12:12–13)*

Like most cradle Christians, I've celebrated Palm Sunday every year since I was a little kid, so I know the drill. I know how to make crosses out of palm branches. I know how to shout "Hosanna!" at the top of my lungs as Jesus makes his triumphant entry into Jerusalem.

But what I didn't know until recently is what the word "hosanna" actually means. All these years, I thought it meant some churchy version of "We adore you!" or, "You rock!" or, "Go, king!" It doesn't. In Hebrew, it means something less adulatory and more desperate. Less generous and more demanding. It means, "Save now!"

Confession: this year, I come to Holy Week tired, scared, and hungry. Tired of God's hiddenness and tired of my own unsteady heart. Scared of all the stones sealing all the graves I don't believe a miracle will roll away. Hungry for a would-be gardener God to find me at the tomb and call my name. Hungry for a million small, large, ordinary, and extraordinary resurrections.

This is me, cloak and palm branches at the ready, waiting with a mile-long list of expectations for a mighty king to come down the mountain and rock my world. This is the meaning of my hosanna. Save now. Not, "I love you." Not, "Your will be done." Not, "I will praise you as you are." *Save now.*

If the Palm Sunday story is about anything, it's about disappointed expectations. A story of what happens when the God we want and think we know doesn't show up, and another God—a less efficient, less aggressive, far less muscular God—shows up instead. When that happens, when our cries of "save us now" are met with heartbreaking silence, our hosannas go dark and our palm branches wither. We walk away, we close our hearts, and we betray the image of God in ourselves and in each other. If push comes to shove, our hosannas give way to hatred, and we strike to kill.

Historians tell us that Jesus knows exactly what he's doing when he asks his disciples to secure a donkey for his journey down the mountain into the holy city. In their compelling book, *The Last Week: What the Gospels Really Teach About Jesus' Last Days in Jerusalem*, Marcus Borg and John Dominic Crossan argue that *two* processions enter Jerusalem on that first Palm Sunday.[1] Jesus's is not the only Triumphal Entry.

Here's the backstory: every year during Passover—the Jewish festival that swells Jerusalem's population from its usual 50,000 to at least 200,000—the Roman governor of Judea rides up to Jerusalem from his coastal residence in the west. He comes in all of his imperial majesty to remind the Jewish pilgrims that Rome demands their loyalty, obedience, and submission. The Jewish people can commemorate their ancient victory against Egypt if they want to. But if they try any real time resistance, they will be obliterated.

Now picture the scene. As Pilate clangs and crashes his imperial way into Jerusalem from the west, Jesus approaches from the east, looking (by contrast) ragtag and absurd. Unlike the Roman emperor and his legions, who rule by force, coercion, and terror, Jesus comes defenseless and weaponless into his kingship. Riding on a donkey, he declares without words that his rule will have nothing to recommend it but love, humility, long-suffering, and sacrifice.

So often, I think I know exactly what kind of savior I need. The savior of the swift repair, the majestic intervention, the tangible presence, the butter soft landing. But that savior is not Jesus.

If there's a single day on the liturgical calendar that illustrates the dissonance at the heart of our faith, it's Palm Sunday. More than any other, this festive, ominous, and complicated day of palm fronds and hosanna banners warns us that paradoxes we might not like or want are woven right into the fabric of Christianity. God on a donkey. Dying to live. A suffering king. *Good* Friday.

These paradoxes are what give Jesus's story its shape, weight, and texture, calling us at every moment to embrace truths that seem counterintuitive. But the question remains: Will I choose the humble and the real, or will I insist on the delusions of empire? Will I accompany Jesus on his ridiculous donkey, honoring the precarious path he has chosen? Or will my impatience undermine my journey?

In reference to Palm Sunday, Frederick Buechner writes this: "Despair and hope. They travel the road to Jerusalem together, as together they travel every road we take—despair at what in our madness we are bringing down

---

1. Borg and Crossan, *The Last Week*, 1–30.

on our own heads and hope in him who travels the road with us and for us and who is the only one of us all who is not mad."[2]

Buechner is right: we are mad with despair and hope, both, so much so that we don't know what to do with the story of a God who comes to die so that we can live. For those of us who struggle to reconcile the role of God's will in the death of Jesus, Palm Sunday offers us a beautiful, terrible clue: it was the will of God that Jesus declare the coming of God's kingdom. A kingdom of peace; a kingdom of slow, self-emptying love; a kingdom of radical embrace, radical patience, and radical risk that demands from us a degree of trust, vulnerability, and courage that empire can't even imagine.

Jesus dies, not because a furious Father in heaven needs to kill his precious son in order to love us, but because Jesus unflinchingly fulfills the will of God. He dies because he exposes the ungracious sham at the heart of all human kingdoms, holding up a mirror that shocks us at the deepest levels of our imaginations. Even when he knows that his vocation will cost him his life, he sets his face like flint towards Jerusalem. Even when he knows who'll get the last laugh at Calvary, he mounts a donkey and takes Rome for a ride.

I don't mean for a minute to write glibly, as if the Jesus to whom I daily cry, "Save now!" doesn't break my heart. He does. Every time I pray my yearning hosanna and Jesus doesn't give me what I long for, my heart breaks again. The truth is, I want and I want and I want, so much more than I praise and I praise and I praise. I know that I'm supposed to love the God-on-a-colt who overturns all my expectations of what divinity should look like and act like. In theory, I *do* love him. But in practice, I daily pass God over, train my eyes on the horizon, and hold out hope for the emperor.

In the end, my solace is this: I am held by a God who sticks with me even when I won't stick with God. A God who accepts my worship even when it is mingy, half-baked, and selfish. A God who knows all the reasons my heart cries, "Save now!" and carries those broken, strangled cries to the cross.

Who knows how many deaths lie waiting around the corner? How many sorrows, disappointments, farewells, and jagged endings I or you must face before resurrection comes? I can't imagine, but Jesus can. If anything in the Christian story is true, then this must be true as well: Jesus will not leave us alone. There is no death we will die, small or big, literal or figurative, that Jesus will not hold in his crucified arms.

Here we are, and here is our God. Here are our hosannas, broken and unbroken, hopeful and hungry. Blessed is the One who comes to die so that we will live.

2. Buechner, *A Room Called Remember*, 78.

# Do You Know?

## John 13:3–15

*Then he poured water into a basin and began to wash the disciples'*
*feet and to wipe them with a towel that was tied around him.*
*(John 13:5)*

"Do you know what I have done to you?" (v. 12).
Jesus asks his disciples this question right after he washes their feet, just a few hours before his arrest. I think we can safely answer the question of their behalf: no. They have no idea what he has done to them. No idea that he has marked them for a new and radical kind of ministry. No comprehension that he has upended forever the relationship between power and humility, sovereignty and service. No idea that the God of heaven and earth has knelt before each one of them, showing them the way of love with his own hands. No. They do not know what Jesus has done.

Do we? When we gather on Maundy Thursday to mark the "night on which Jesus was betrayed," do we understand what's transpiring?

First, in sharing a quiet evening with his disciples over a loaf of bread, a jug of wine, a basin of water, and a damp towel, Jesus takes the things we write off as routine and commonplace, and makes them shimmer with God's presence. After Maundy Thursday, there is no such thing as "ordinary" anymore; Jesus makes it impossible for us to compartmentalize sacred from secular. Ours is a God of tepid water, dusty toes, cracked heels, and un-pedicured feet. A God of basins and towels; a God of small, upper rooms; a God of the single candle burning on a cluttered kitchen counter that maybe no one else will see but you. Ours is the God who comes into our smallness, our messiness, our not-nearly-good-enough-ness, and transforms it all with grace.

When I worry that my life is too mundane to be of significance to God, it helps me to remember what Jesus does on the night when he is betrayed. He lifts up the commonplace. He infuses the ordinary with God's presence. He shows us the sacredness of our everyday lives.

Second, Jesus teaches us to lean into what we can't change. The Gospel writer tells us that "Jesus knew that his hour had come to depart from this world" (v. 1). He knows that even though he wants the cup of suffering to pass from him, it will not. Friday will dawn, bringing with it the cross, the whips, the thorns, the pain. So he leans in. He surrenders. He allows himself to be humbled, stripped down, reduced, and laid bare.

For many of us right now, this lesson might feel particularly relevant. We, too, are being reduced. Stripped down to our essentials. Laid bare in our fears and vulnerabilities. Even though we don't want to, we're having to sit day after day with local and global circumstances we can't control. We're facing death and illness, depression and anxiety, economic reversals and professional upsets. We're having to face what we're really made of, what we honestly become when so many of the trappings of our lives—mobility, social connection, favorite forms of entertainment, and ready access to material comforts—are taken away.

What does Jesus do to us in such moments? He instills a discipline of acceptance. Of trust and long-suffering. Beyond that, he promises sustenance in times of fear. Yes, Good Friday must come. Yes, we will face loss, pain, and even death. But on a night like this, Jesus invites his friends to gather at the table. Come, he says. Take and eat. Be washed and refreshed. We will endure together.

John's Gospel tells that Jesus is able to lean into a time of suffering because he believes that he comes from God and will return to God. He knows that nothing—not even death—can separate him from the Father who loves him. This is no less true for us. Sometimes, accepting what we haven't chosen is sacred work.

Third, Jesus demonstrates what power looks like, and what it's for. In Jesus's day, the work of foot-washing belongs to the lowliest of slaves. What Jesus does in washing his disciples' feet is beyond radical; it's scandalous. Maybe it's even horrifying to his disciples, who fully expect Jesus to behave like a king. This is why Peter refuses at first: he doesn't know what to make of a Jesus who behaves more like a servant than a sovereign. Worse, when we remember that Jesus washes *Judas's* feet as well—the feet of a man who threatens his life—*we* might consider Jesus's act offensive. It turns our well-worn hierarchies upside down.

Lastly, Jesus commands us to love, not by our own definitions of love, but by his. On this night, even as the atmosphere darkens, even as death draws near, even as Jesus foresees his own agony, he spends time caring for the most basic needs of his friends. The need for food and drink. The need for refreshment and rest. The need for touch and intimacy.

When Jesus washes feet, he shows us that love doesn't have to look glamorous to be revolutionary. In fact, it's often the humblest acts of love which speak the loudest. A phone call to a person you don't usually think to call. A check-in over Zoom or email. A meal left at a door. An encouraging smile to the stranger standing near you in Costco's endless queue.

Jesus's last acts before his death remind us that when we fill hungry stomachs, quench parched throats, clean dirty feet, and ease people's fears, God's presence overflows and fills the spaces between us. When we move out into the world, compelled by Jesus's example to make sure that no one within our reach is hungry; no one is denied access to basic shelter, cleanliness, and health; no one is denied the nourishing gifts of bread, wine, water, soap, a towel, or a loving hand on an exhausted body; then, the world sees God.

On his knees, looking up as our dusty feet rest in his soon-to-be-pierced hands, Jesus says, "Love one another like this. Hands-on and no-holds-barred. Love until you surprise people. Love until the powerful of this world feel the threat of your love. Love until the broken of the world are healed, and the starving of the world are fed. Love until love becomes your signature, your trademark, your calling card, your identity. Love until you understand what I have done to you. Love until the world understands who I am. Remember me, and remember this: I have made you for love. Do you know what I have done to you? What I have done *for* you? What I long to do *with and through you?*"

As we ponder the self-giving of Jesus, may these questions burn within us. May we find our way to brave and honest answers. May we kneel before each other and learn the mystery of love.

# A Crucified God

## Matthew 27

*Then the soldiers of the governor took Jesus into the governor's headquarters, and they gathered the whole cohort around him. They stripped him and put a scarlet robe on him, and after twisting some thorns into a crown, they put it on his head. They put a reed in his right hand and knelt before him and mocked him, saying, "Hail, King of the Jews!" They spat on him, and took the reed and struck him on the head. After mocking him, they stripped him of the robe and put his own clothes on him. Then they led him away to crucify him. (Matt 27:27–31)*

Jesus was and is many things: teacher, healer, companion, Lord. It is essential that we experience him in all of these ways; each way complements and complicates the others. But the heart of who he is, is revealed at the cross.

We twenty-first century Christians are not scandalized by crosses. We worship in front of them on Sunday mornings. Some of us cross ourselves with our hands when we pray, or display decorative crosses in our homes, or wear tiny golden crosses around our necks.

There's nothing wrong with this, but we would do well to remember that reverence is *not* what Jesus's first disciples felt when they encountered his cross two-thousand years ago. For them, the cross held no religious meaning whatsoever. No veneer of holiness, no hint of redemption, no connection to God. For them, the cross was an instrument of the state. An instrument of torture, humiliation, and death. Imagine for a minute if the central symbol of our faith was an electric chair, or a lethal injection chamber, or a lynching tree.

Historians tell us that it was not uncommon for the road to Jerusalem to be lined with crosses in Jesus's day, each of them bearing a body. Anyone who traveled from their home to the market, or from the market to the temple, or from the temple to a friend's house, would have no choice but to encounter these grim instruments of capital punishment on a regular basis.

Imagine what life was like for the people who lived in the shadow of those crosses. Imagine how their hopes shriveled under the constant threat and terror. Because of course, that was the point. The crosses were *meant* to intimidate. The crosses were the Roman Empire's illustrated sermons, and the message of those sermons was clear: "You can have your religion. You can worship what you want. But don't forget, even for a minute, who *really* holds sway over your life. Go to temple if it suits you, call on your God if it makes you feel good, but don't even think about resisting the power structures that actually control your world. If you do, we'll hang you up, too."

We know that the disciples' great hope was that Jesus would lead them in a military revolution and overthrow their Roman oppressors. Jesus was the one who was supposed to pull down the crosses, not die on one of them.

I know that there's so much to be asked, pondered, and debated about the theological meanings of the cross. What happened when Jesus died? What did his crucifixion accomplish? What can we know for sure about sin, sacrifice, death, atonement, and eternity in light of Christ's death?

For me, the way to approach these questions is to stay as close to the story as possible. The story of betrayal, denial, and abandonment. The story of unjust trials, false accusations, and Jesus's mysterious silence. The story of floggings. The story of thorns. The story of bloodied wounds and oxygen-deprived lungs.

For those of us who've grown up in the church, it might very well be the case that the horror of Jesus's death has faded into over-familiarity. We've seen so many icons of Christ crucified that we barely notice them. But what would happen if we shook ourselves out of this familiarity for a few minutes and saw the story with fresh eyes? What if we could look at the cross and see what Jesus's first followers saw? Scandal? Wretchedness? Godlessness? Shame?

The Jesus we find in Matthew's Gospel is not a man who presides over his final chapter. He is a man who suffers in ways language can't describe. When he prays in Gethsemane, he "throws himself on the ground," and pleads for his life (Matt 26:39). His flogging at the hands of Pilate's soldiers weakens him so much, he can't bear the weight of his own cross. His last word is hardly a "word" at all; it's a howl. A wrenching cry of defeat and abandonment: "My God, my God, why have you forsaken me?" (Matt 27:46).

Embracing this forsaken God, much less following him, is the work of lifetimes. It's not a one-time decision we make during an altar call. It's not a single promise we make when we're baptized or confirmed. It's a slow journey on a steep and winding path, a journey of infinite wanderings, infinite returns.

Consider, after all, what Jesus bears on the cross and invites us to bear, as well. He bears the violence, contempt, and hatred of the world. He declares solidarity for all time with the abandoned, colonized, oppressed, accused, imprisoned, beaten, mocked, and murdered. He bursts open like a seed so that new life can grow and replenish the earth.

In other words, he unveils the poison. *Our* poison. He reveals what our human kingdoms always become unless God in God's mercy delivers us. In the cross, we are forced to see what our refusal to love, our indifference to suffering, our craving for violence, our resistance to change, our hatred of difference, our addiction to judgment, and our fear of the Other must wreak. When the Son of Humanity is lifted up, we see with chilling clarity our need for a God who will take our most horrific instruments of death, and transform them, at great cost, for the purposes of resurrection.

Think once again about those crosses that lined the road to Jerusalem in the first century. Think about the fundamental passivity those crosses were meant to instill in the people who gazed at them. And then think about Jesus willingly taking up one of those crosses and saying, "*I will not stop for you. I* will not choose safety at the expense of injustice and evil. I will not save my own skin while you keep killing the people I love."

In contrast, I live in such crippling fear of suffering and death that I use up a huge amount of my mental, spiritual, and physical energy trying to stave off both. To be fair, contemporary Western culture encourages me to do this. What would Jesus say to the multi-million-dollar industries that invite me to deny my mortality through cosmetics, fashion, leisure, sex, entertainment, real estate, sports cars, and weight loss? What would he say to a culture that glorifies violence but cheapens death? What would he say to a global economy that rapes and pillages the planet, instead of stewarding it with tenderness and wisdom? What would he say to a notion of personal liberty that encourages me to insist on my "rights," while ignoring my civic and communal responsibilities on this profoundly interconnected planet?

What would he say to my frightened heart that so often prioritizes self-protection over everything else that matters?

The cross is a lifelong challenge precisely because it is *not* about remaining passive. The cross is not about admitting defeat. The cross is not about opting out. The cross is about shaking things up. About rattling the system to its core. About confronting sin with the power of grace, love, and surrender.

Here and now, the cross is about saying: "It's not enough that my children are safe and sheltered if yours are not. It's not enough that I have clean air to breathe when my neighbors two towns over do not. It's not enough that I'll have dinner to eat tonight if you will not. It's not enough that my raced and gendered body feels safe on the streets when yours does not. It's not enough that my zip code grants me privileges while yours does not. It's not enough that I feel welcomed and nourished by the church if you do not."

To take up a cross as Jesus did is to stand, always, in the center of the world's pain. Taking up the cross means recognizing Christ crucified in every suffering soul and body we encounter, and pouring our energies into alleviating that pain, no matter what it costs us. It means accepting—against all the lies of our culture—that we *will* die, and following that courageous acceptance with the most important question any of us can ask: How shall I spend this one, brief, singular, God-breathed life? Shall I hoard it in fear, or give it away in hope? Shall I push suffering aside at all cost, and in doing so, push Jesus aside, too? Or shall I accompany the one I call "Savior" on the only road that leads to resurrection?

To be clear, there *are* versions of Christianity out there that deny the centrality of the cross to the life of faith. Versions that say: "You don't *have* to do the hard thing. You don't have to take this faith business so seriously. You don't have to engage deeply or take any real risks. You don't have to die."

It's true. We don't. But let's not pretend that spectator Christianity is what Jesus calls us to. Let's not fool ourselves that standing on the sidelines will grant us immunity, safety, meaning, or joy. To believe in the saving power of the cross involves far more than intellectual assent. Yes, we believe and we rejoice in the mystery of the salvation Jesus secured for us through his death. But the cross is not a historical artifact. The cross is a way forward. It is our *only* way forward.

As Christians, we love because the cross draws us towards love. Its power is as compelling as it is mysterious. The cross pulls us towards God and towards each other, a vast and complicated gathering place. Whether or not we want to see Jesus shamed and wounded, here he is, drawing us closer and closer to the holy darkness where divine light dwells. This is the solid ground we stand on. This is the path we are invited to walk. Stark, holy, brutal, beautiful.

# Father, Forgive Them

## Luke 23:32-37

*When they came to the place that is called The Skull, they crucified Jesus there with the criminals, one on his right and one on his left. Then Jesus said, "Father, forgive them; for they do not know what they are doing." (Luke 23:33-24)*

I n Luke's account of the crucifixion, Jesus's first words from the cross are words of forgiveness. Why is that? Why is forgiveness the first word?

Jesus has just endured a night of abuse. Accused, abandoned, mocked, and misunderstood, he has been separated from his companions, robbed of his dignity, and beaten to near-death. Now he hangs on a cross, surrounded by people who hate him, and the first word he utters is a word of forgiveness.

I'm tempted to dodge the question with theology. As in: *of course* Jesus's first word is forgiveness. Isn't forgiveness what he's all about? Isn't his job as our high priest to do exactly this—to stand in the gap and make intercession for us? What else *would* the Son of God do, but use his final moments to practice what he preaches?

The theology isn't wrong, but the danger is that we'll use it to spare ourselves. To withdraw into the cocoon of our own fallibility and say, "Sure, forgiveness is nice, but the Jesus of the Gospels is divine. He has a mission to fulfill, and an atonement to work out, so naturally, he remains true to his calling even when he's dying. We're impressed. But we're not God."

If you google the word "forgiveness," you'll get several million hits. Obviously, it's a word we can't say enough about. Much of what's online focuses on what forgiveness is *not*. Forgiveness is not denial. It's not pretending that an offense doesn't matter or that a wound doesn't hurt. Forgiveness isn't forgetting, or acting as if things don't have to change, or allowing ourselves to be victimized over and over again. Forgiveness isn't the same as healing or reconciliation. Healing has its own timetable, and sometimes reconciliation isn't possible. Sometimes our lives depend on us severing ties with our offenders, even after we've forgiven them.

So what does Jesus mean when he forgives his tormentors? What is he doing when he utters this first of his seven last words from the cross? I don't know for sure, but here's a possibility that gives me hope: maybe he's asking for help, and the help he needs is for himself.

According to Luke's account, Jesus doesn't *declare* forgiveness. He doesn't announce to the crowd that their sins are absolved, or that his suffering isn't a big deal, or that he feels affectionate towards the soldiers gambling at his feet. In fact, he doesn't address the crowd at all; his first word is addressed to God. In the form of a request. A plea. "Father, forgive them. They don't know what they're doing."

Some Greek scholars have argued that Jesus makes this prayer several times as he awaits death. Over and over again, like a mantra. "Father, forgive them. Father, forgive them. Father, forgive them." I like this possibility, because it suggests that forgiveness is not an event but an orientation, a posture we can't maintain on our own strength. Perhaps Jesus is saying, "Father, I'm finding forgiveness difficult. It slips away from me, and I can't hang onto it without you. I need your help now. And now. And *now.*"

Here's why I struggle with Jesus's first word. It's not that I dislike forgiveness. It's that I want to make forgiveness the eighth word, or the twelfth, or the three-hundred-and-twenty-seventh. As in, "Hang on a second. I need to sit you down first. I need you to understand how badly you've hurt me, because unless you comprehend that, you won't feel appropriately sorry, and I won't feel appropriately vindicated. As soon as I know for sure that you're remorseful, I'll forgive you."

Maybe Jesus's first word is forgiveness because it's the word that makes all the other words possible. Words like grace, tenderness, freedom, and joy. If I'm consumed with my own pain, if I've made injury my identity, if I center my rights and my anger in every interaction I have with people who hurt me, then I'm destroying myself.

To pray Jesus's prayer is to say, "I choose to uncross my arms and unclench my fists. I choose to release myself from the tyranny of bitterness. I choose to give up my frenzied longing to be understood. I choose to cast my hunger for justice deep into God's heart, because justice belongs to God, and God is the only one trustworthy enough to secure it."

Jesus bases his prayer of forgiveness on the ignorance of his attackers. "Forgive them, for they do not know what they are doing." What does it mean to forgive people, *not* because they've comprehended their guilt, but because they're clueless? Isn't that a moral cop-out? Doesn't it let sinners off the hook too easily?

Maybe. But here's another option: maybe it's just the plain truth about who we are and how we function. Maybe I *don't* know what I'm doing.

Maybe, even when I think I'm at my most enlightened, my most discerning, my most self-aware, maybe even then, I can barely wrap my head around the ways in which I harm myself, or you, or my spouse, or my children, or my neighborhood, or my church, or this planet. Maybe my vision is far more limited than I realize. Maybe at some level you and I can only be sacred mysteries to each other. If that's the case, maybe our best bet is to love each other poorly and forgive each other repeatedly.

Christianity teaches me that God's forgiveness is a given. It's the foundation for all of God's dealings with us. This is why, I think, forgiveness has to be the first word. It comes *first*. Before we know, understand, or repent, Jesus's prayer assures us that forgiveness *is*. Yes, it's hard, and yes, it's costly, and yes, we'll mess it up. But we can ask for it, nevertheless. Over and over again. Father, forgive them.

# Today with Me

## Luke 23:39–43

*Then he said, "Jesus, remember me when you come into your kingdom." He replied, "Truly I tell you, today you will be with me in Paradise." (Luke 23:42–43)*

What happens when a dream dies? When something you've longed for fails to materialize? A meaningful career, a fulfilling marriage, a healthy body? What happens when you're forced to let these go?

The story of the two thieves who die alongside Jesus is a story of two crushed dreams. Two men, guilty of the same crime, condemned by the same empire, and facing the same death. Two thieves looking at Jesus through the filter of the same crushed hope, but seeing very different things.

According to tradition, the thief who hangs to the right of Jesus—the one who defends him—is named Dismas. The thief to the left—the one who insults Jesus—is named Gestas. We don't know specific details about their crimes, but the fact that they die by crucifixion in first-century Jerusalem tells us enough.

The Romans reserved crucifixion for the most extreme political crimes. Jesus is crucified because he calls out the injustice of the Roman Empire and proclaims God's counter-kingdom of love. If Dismas and Gestas are condemned to the same type of death, it's because they are revolutionaries. Freedom fighters. Traitors. Like the thorn-crowned man dying between them, they dare to dream of a better world.

Though we don't know the specifics, we do know that their particular dream, whatever it entails and whatever crimes it leads them to commit, don't survive the Roman crosses of Good Friday. Whatever change they long for with all their hearts fails to come.

The first voice in the story is the voice of Gestas, the thief on the left. "Aren't you the Christ?" he mocks Jesus in a voice calculated to humiliate. "Save yourself and us!" (v. 39).

It isn't hard to distance myself from this voice. Indeed, Christian tradition makes it too easy: we call Gestas the "bad" or the "unrepentant" thief. But if I'm honest, I have to confess that I know Gestas's voice rather well. I know what it's like to mock what I don't understand. I know what it's like to mask my pain and vulnerability with contempt.

Gestas's voice is the voice of bitterness. Gnarled and desiccated, it's the voice that speaks when hope dies and hearts harden. We've been there, most of us. We've looked to our Messiah to behave in ways we recognize, only to have him appall us with his strangeness. We've asked him to enact particular kinds of salvation on our behalf and received silence in return. Like Gestas, we've faced disillusionment, and turned on Jesus: "You're not the God I thought you were. You must be no God at all."

The second voice in the story belongs to Dismas, the thief on the right. He, too, struggles with disillusionment. His dream, too, has been nailed to a cross. But unlike Gestas, who refuses to surrender his dream, Dismas allows his dream to die. He admits that the kingdom he's striving for is an illusion, so he turns to Jesus and asks the only thing left to ask: "Remember me when you come into *your* kingdom" (v. 42).

*Remember me.* Not, "Get me down from this cross." Not, "Fix my life." Not, "Vindicate me before this crowd." Remember me. Hold my story in your heart, lest it be lost. Allow me to live on in you. Consider that I also dreamed of a kingdom; I just didn't know until this moment that the aching heart of my dream was you.

One reason I cherish this story is because it's big enough for both voices. Both Gestas and Dismas get their say, and Jesus, who hangs between them, hears them both. He tolerates the terrible tension between despair and hope, absorbing both into his heart.

The other reason I love this story is because its third voice—the voice of Jesus—offers a hope so paradoxical, it transforms our suffering and changes our lives: "Today," Jesus says to Dismas, "You will be with me in Paradise" (v. 43).

In the Bible, paradise is depicted as a garden, a place of ancient wisdom and ceaseless beginnings. A place where seeds fall to the earth and die only to live again, a thousand times over. A place of sweet communion with God.

What does it mean to enter paradise while hanging on a cross? In his book, *Tattoos on the Heart,* Jesuit priest Gregory Boyle notes that ancient monastics, when faced with hopelessness and despair, would recite Jesus's promise as a mantra: "Today, with me, Paradise."[1] As if to say, God's

---

1. Boyle, *Tattoos on the Heart,* 159.

kingdom is far more than a promise for the distant future. It's also here, now, within and among us.

He's not the God we thought he was. But he's a God who remembers us. A God whose kingdom is a fragrant, life-giving garden. Can we entrust ourselves to the God who hangs in the gap between our hope and despair? The God who carries our dreams to the grave and beyond?

Today. With Me. Paradise.

# It Happens in the Dark

## John 20:1–18

*Early on the first day of the week, while it was still dark, Mary Magdalene came to the tomb and saw that the stone had been removed from the tomb. (John 20:1)*

Over the past few years, I've lost two close friends to sudden cardiac death. Both of them were active and healthy, with children ranging in age from ten to sixteen. Both deaths came with no warning, no symptoms, no time to say goodbye. One minute, they were alive and thriving in the world, and the next, they were gone.

In the days, weeks, and months that followed each death, I flailed. I grieved for the husband and children each friend left behind. I experienced panic attacks. I slept poorly. Most of all, I raged at the randomness of the deaths, the futility and unfairness of a world in which stories—beautiful, rich, layered life stories—get cut off mid-sentence, without sense or explanation. These friends of mine were hopeful, vivacious women. They wanted to see their children graduate from high school and college. They looked forward to planning their daughters' weddings and welcoming grandchildren into their arms. They wanted to celebrate silver and golden anniversaries with their spouses. They wanted to write, teach, worship, celebrate, love, laugh, dance, serve, travel, explore, *live.* They wanted to live.

I know that I write these words from a position of privilege; I made it through four decades of my life before death hit close to home. I'm well aware that there are babies whose mothers exit this world just as they enter it. Parents who lose their toddlers to cancer or their school-aged kids to gun violence. Men, women, and children around the world who regularly confront death from starvation, terrorism, war, disease, poverty, abuse, neglect, crime, or natural disaster. My experience of loss is neither unique nor dramatic; it is the human condition. Even in the midst of life, we are in death.

What does it mean to reflect on Easter when we are "in death"? Easter, the highpoint of our liturgical year. The season of trumpets and lilies, packed pews and "Alleluia" banners. It's a season of proclamation. The dawning of a new day, filled with new hope. "He is risen! He is risen, indeed!"

I believe in the joy of resurrection with all of my heart, but as I continue to grieve the deaths of my friends, I am drawn to other aspects of the Easter narrative. I am drawn to what Frederick Buechner calls "the darkness of the resurrection itself, that morning when it was hard to be sure what you were seeing."[1]

The Gospel of John describes the disciples stumbling in the half-light on that third day after Jesus's crucifixion, running here and there in their confusion. Is it an angel, sitting in that unlit tomb? Are those shadows grave clothes? The stranger lingering outside—is he the gardener? *"Early in the morning, while it was still dark . . . "* (Mark 1:34). That's where Easter begins. It begins in the dark.

When I was growing up, the key fact to proclaim was that Jesus rose—physically, bodily, literally—from the dead. As long as I believed that, I was on solid ground. If I could speculate on the *how* of the bodily resurrection, "proving" its plausibility with a good scientific theory or two, I could really congratulate myself.

The fact is the resurrection happens in total darkness. Sometime in the predawn hours of a Sunday morning, a great mystery transpires in secret. No sunlight illuminates the event. No human being witnesses it. Even now, two-thousand years later, no human narrative can contain it. It exceeds all of our attempts to pin it down, because it's a mystery known only to God. Whatever the resurrection was and is, its fullness lies in holy darkness, shielded from our eyes. All we can know is that somehow, in an ancient tomb on a starry night, God worked in secret to bring life out of death. Somehow, in the utter darkness, God saved the world.

Earlier in my life, this ambiguity would have frustrated me. Now it doesn't; it seems exactly right. Why? Because what I have learned in the process of grieving my friends' deaths is that no story my fragile mind can contain would be big enough to redeem such catastrophic loss. Death is *such* an abyss, such a horror, such a violation, that nothing I can understand or explain will make it okay. Only a mystery as huge as the resurrection will suffice. Having seen death up close, I cannot rest in certainty any longer; certainty isn't enough. I can only rest in mystery. My grief can only bear fruit in the dark.

In John's resurrection story, Mary Magdalene sees Jesus first because she chooses to remain in the darkness. Peter and John leave when they

---

1. Buechner, in Lawton, "Frederick Buechner Extended Interview," para. 12.

see the empty tomb, but Mary stays, bewildered and bereft. She stays even when staying feels unbearable.

In my own life, clarity, hope, and healing come when I am willing to linger in hard and barren places, places where the usual platitudes fall flat, and easy answers prove inadequate. Jesus comes in the darkness, and sometimes it takes a long time to recognize him. He doesn't look the way I expect him to look. He doesn't let me cling to my old ideas of him. He disappears again just as I grab hold of him. But he comes and calls my name, and in that instant, I recognize both myself and him.

As I continue to struggle with the loss of my friends, what matters isn't the theology or the science of resurrection. What matters is encounter. What matters is encountering the risen Jesus and finding in the mystery of his rising the hope I need for my own. Often, it's only in retrospect, only as I look back at the "gravesides" of my life, that I find the beginnings of new life.

Come Easter, may the Christ who rose in the darkness lead us into new life, light, and hope. May we know him in the half-lit places, the shadowy places, the hard places. May we dare to linger at the graveside until he calls our names. Christ is risen. He is risen, indeed.

# Embodied

## Luke 24:36b–48

*While they were talking about this, Jesus himself stood among them and said to them, "Peace be with you." They were startled and terrified, and thought that they were seeing a ghost. (Luke 24:36–37)*

In a much beloved poem, rabbi and liturgist Chaim Stern writes, "'Tis a fearful thing to love what death has touched."[1] What a fitting line to describe the dilemma Jesus's disciples face when he shows up in their midst, fresh from the horrors of crucifixion, and invites them to journey back from fear to love.

"Peace be with you," Jesus says in Luke's Gospel, no doubt with an affectionate, amused smile on his face. I'm guessing the disciples mutter, "Not so fast, buddy. You were dead. As in, *dead*. You're going to have to give us a minute."

I think Jesus will have to give all of us a minute. Or several. Aren't we, just like the disciples, afraid to touch, to trust, to love, and to hope in this world that's staggering under the weight of so much death? Don't we also tremble before the empty tomb, hesitating, wondering, disbelieving? Don't we tell ourselves to be cautious and careful, modest and moderate, keeping our joys and enthusiasms in check—because, *come on*. How can news this good be true? How audacious would we have to be to lean into it. Or—God forbid!—proclaim it? How shall we, here, now, in the company of the broken and the bleeding, embrace resurrection?

I cherish the Gospel stories we read in this season of Easter, because they show us a way forward. They show us how to do this hard and holy thing: to love and not despair, trust and not retreat. Even in the face of destruction and death.

---

1. Stern, "'Tis a Fearful Thing," 330.

Imagine for a moment what you'd do if you found yourself facing Jesus's bizarre, post-Easter predicament. Imagine showing up in a room where your friends have gathered to grieve the loss of *you* and having to convince them that you're alive. Imagine their terrified faces as you say the appalling thing over and over again: "I'm not a ghost! Honest! It's really me!"

How would you make your case? What would you do to calm their fears?

Jesus presents his scars. He offers his friends his vulnerability—his broken body enlivened and transformed by the high cost of love. He offers them—not a scientific treatise on resurrection, not a dazzling display of pyrotechnics, not an eloquent sermon—but his body. The *narrative* of his body. Its scars, its trials, its losses, its defeats. "I have history, just as you do," he shows his loved ones in the evidence of his hands and feet. "I am alive not just to triumph and victory, but also to pain and sorrow. I don't float somewhere above you, a safe, sanitized distance from where you dwell; I am here *with you* in the searing heart of things where the grace of God makes its home. Touch me. Touch me and see."

When Jesus's hands and feet aren't quite enough to convince his friends, he offers up his tongue, teeth, esophagus, stomach, and intestines, too: "Do you have anything to eat around here?" he asks.

The disciples hand him a piece of fish and watch in puzzled, joyful fascination as he chews and swallows it. As the moments pass, and the fish disappears, the dissociated disciples return to their bodies, their senses, their memories of shared appetites and shared meals. They lose enough of their fear to hear what Jesus is saying to them, and in that open-hearted hearing, they change. By the end of the encounter, the disciples are no longer frightened spectators; they are "witnesses." Witnesses with skin in the game, witnesses confident of their testimony, witnesses bursting with a story of resurrection so powerful, they cannot keep their mouths shut.

By sharing his scars, expressing his hunger, and accepting their hospitality, Jesus turns his disciples' trauma into communion.

I love this story for the way it grounds divine revelation in the concrete and the ordinary. It is in the presence of skin and bones, taste buds and nerve endings, that the disciples find a way to begin again. Which is why, perhaps, all of Jesus's post-resurrection appearances in the Gospels center on bodies. He receives the tearful embrace of Mary Magdalene, who clings to him as tightly as she can. He makes footprints on the Emmaus road with two of his bewildered friends. He tears into hunks of bread at their dinner table until at last they recognize who he is. He chews on broiled tilapia. He makes a campfire on the beach and cooks breakfast for his friends.

I know that we usually talk about Incarnation during Advent—not Easter—but for me, the Jesus of Easter *is* the Jesus of the Incarnation. The Jesus who develops in a womb, slides through a birth canal, sleeps in a feeding trough, and nurses at a peasant woman's breast. The Jesus who soaks in the waters of baptism, hungers for bread in the Judean wilderness, weeps at Lazarus's grave, basks in scented oils on his feet and head, sweats blood in the garden of Gethsemane, and asphyxiates on a Roman cross. This is the same Jesus—human, embodied, and incarnate—who shows up in Luke's Gospel and says, "Touch me and see" (Luke 24:39).

If even at the height of resurrection victory, Jesus's witness is a witness of visible scars and named hungers, then maybe we should pay attention. Maybe when the world looks at us to see if *our* faith is authentic and trustworthy, it needs to see our scars and hungers, too. Our vulnerability, not our immunity. Our honesty, not our pretenses to perfection. What would it look like for us to offer our stories of scars and graces, hungers and feasts, in testimony to this world? How might our embodied lives become a way of love? Naming our hungers, widening our tables, sharing our scars and our feasts—what if *this* is practicing resurrection? Maybe more is at stake in a piece of fish, or a glass of water, or a loaf of bread, than we have yet imagined.

When the disciples feed Jesus, he feeds them in return. In the encounter of skin to skin, their eyes are opened, death flees, and the resurrected Jesus comes alive in them. Belief doesn't come first. Scars come first. Food comes first. Bodies come first.

It is painful to write about bodies at a time when so many are suffering around us. How shall we speak of empty tombs when precious, singular, God-breathed bodies are dying because the powers-that-be around us and within us insist that they don't matter? I imagine you are like me; you wake up these days afraid to look at your newsfeeds, because what the headlines tell us about the expendability of bodies—black bodies, Asian bodies, trans bodies, immigrant bodies, indigenous bodies, unhoused bodies, women's bodies—is soul-crushing.

We are a resurrection people, but we're also a people in pain. If we begin to count all the ways in which the story of the crucifixion—a story of state-sanctioned violence, mass apathy, loveless legalism, clerical corruption, and collective spiritual anemia—reverberates right now across our global landscapes, we might collectively fall to our knees. Jesus and his scars are everywhere.

I recognize that in some circles, it's unfashionable to "need" the empty tomb and the risen Christ. I know that the resurrection is sometimes dismissed as a crutch, an opiate, a naive refusal to dwell in the here and now. But here's the thing: we don't cling to the resurrection in order to escape the here and now. We cling to the resurrection to embody new life *in* the here and now. We rest in the resurrection so that we can pour out our lives for the vulnerable, the threatened, the hopeless, the lost, and the dying.

It's so much easier to ideate. To abstract. To wax eloquent on the poetic beauty of resurrection as metaphor. All of that has its place. But here is Jesus, holding out to us his hands and his feet, his scars and his hungers, and saying, "Be my *body*."

Be my body in the shadow of the lynching trees. Be my body in the institutions of power and influence you inhabit. Be my body in all the locations where hatred, white supremacy, violence, and trauma rule the day. Be my body in all times and places where death mocks and diminishes my children, and with the power of the resurrection within you and around you, stand firm and say, *enough.*

Enough.

The resurrection is not a platitude or a line in a creed. The resurrection is fire in our bones, steel in our blood, impetus for our feet, a song of lamentation, protest, and ferocious hope for our souls. The resurrection is God's clarion call to the church. God's insistence that we speak, stand, and work for life in a world desperate for fewer crosses, fewer graves, fewer landscapes littered with the desolate and the dead.

In the resurrection, as God declares that death will not have the last word, we stand at the empty tomb and declare with God that all must be enlivened, vindicated, healed, and raised by the death-defying love and wholly restorative justice of a God who formed us from dust and called that dust good.

"You are witnesses of these things," Jesus says at the end of this Gospel story (v. 48). You are witnesses to an ancient and ever-living story of embodiment, a story of hands and feet, scars and hungers, skin and bone, death and new life. Witnesses bear a responsibility. Witnesses must *speak.*

It is a fearful thing to love what death has touched. But we can do it. We *must* do it. We must do it because the love of God that conquered a grave two-thousand years ago conquers graves still—and that same scarred, vulnerable, triumphant, and earth-shattering love is ours to cherish and ours to give away.

So why are we frightened? Why do we doubt? It is Jesus himself who is among us. Touch him and see.

# But We Had Hoped

## Luke 24:13–35

*Now on that same day two of them were going to a village called Emmaus, about seven miles from Jerusalem, and talking with each other about all these things that had happened. While they were talking and discussing, Jesus himself came near and went with them, but their eyes were kept from recognizing him. (Luke 24:13–15)*

I n this post-resurrection story, Luke has us traveling a road that's uncomfortably familiar. Every one of us, regardless of identity or circumstance, knows this road. We've walked it. We've lost our way on it. We've left it and returned to it. The road is the road to Emmaus, and we recognize it by the words we speak when our feet hit its rough and winding way one more time: *"But we had hoped"* (v. 21).

How many times and in how many varied circumstances have you said these words? "But we had hoped the tumor wasn't malignant. We had hoped our marriage would get easier. We had hoped our son would come home. We had hoped the depression would lift. We had hoped to keep our jobs. We had hoped to carry the baby to term. We had hoped the pandemic would spare our family. We had hoped for a peaceful death. We had hoped for racial justice. We had hoped for a different election result. We had hoped our faith would survive."

The words we speak on the road to Emmaus are words of pain. They are the words we say when we've come to the end of our hopes—when our expectations have been dashed, and there's nothing left to do but walk away, defeated and done. *But we had hoped.*

In Luke's narrative, Cleopas and his unnamed companion say these words to the stranger who appears alongside them as they walk to Emmaus on Easter evening: "But we had hoped that he was the one to redeem Israel."

Jesus—as far as they know—is dead. The Lord they staked their lives on, the Messiah they thought would change the world, has died the most humiliating and godless death imaginable, and his promises of a new kingdom have come to nothing. Worse, Jesus's tomb is empty, his body is missing, and the women who loved and followed him appear to have gone mad, what with their bizarre reports of angels, gardeners, and talking ghosts. How completely things have fallen apart. But we had hoped for so much.

It always startles me to remember that the Emmaus story is an Easter story. According to Luke's Gospel, it happens on Resurrection Sunday. On the very day we pack our churches, flower our crosses, and sing our "Alleluias," the road to Emmaus stretches out ahead of us, offering bewilderment, disillusionment, and misrecognition. Which is to say, sometimes resurrection takes longer than three days. Sometimes new life comes in fits and starts. Sometimes, seeing and recognizing the risen Christ is hard.

I for one am grateful for the honest witness of this post-resurrection story. I'm grateful that the journey continues into Easter evening, when hope is possible but not yet realized. I'm grateful that even the road to Emmaus—the road of brokenness, the road of failure—is a sacred road. A road that Jesus walks. A road that honors our deep disappointment, even as it holds out possibilities of nourishment and revelation.

As I reflect on this story, what strikes me is how much the Emmaus narrative reveals about the heart and character of Jesus. Once again, I am reminded that Jesus is not who I think he is, and not who I necessarily want him to be. Who is the would-be stranger on the broken road? How does he respond when all appears lost? What does he do for the weary and the defeated? Here is what I notice:

*I notice a quiet resurrection.* One would think that a God who suffers a torturous and wholly unjust death would come back with a vengeance, determined to shout his triumph from the rooftops. But Jesus does no such thing. As far as we know, he doesn't enter the Temple and make a scene. He doesn't appear to the Sanhedrin, or show up at Pilate's house, or set the sky ablaze with fireworks. He makes absolutely no effort to vindicate himself or to avenge his cruel death.

Instead, on the evening of his greatest victory, the risen Christ takes a walk. He takes a leisurely walk on a quiet, out-of-the-way road. When he notices two of his followers walking ahead of him, he approaches them in a guise so gentle, so understated, so mundane, they don't recognize him.

This is not, I'll admit, what I always want from the resurrected Christ. "But we had hoped" he'd be more dramatic. More convincing. More unmistakably divine. We had hoped he'd make post-Easter faith easier.

Part of the disappointment we face on the Emmaus road is the disappointment of the quiet resurrection. The disappointment of God's maddening subtlety and hiddenness. The disappointment of a Jesus who prefers the quiet, hidden encounter to the theatrics we expect and crave.

*I notice healing through story.* As soon as Jesus falls into step with the companions on the road, he invites them to tell their story: "What are you discussing with each other while you walk along?" (v. 17). Astonished by the question, Cleopas and his co-traveler tell Jesus everything. They share the story of their faith—its rise and its fall. They explain how high their expectations had been for their now-crucified leader, "a prophet mighty in deed and word before God and all the people" (v. 19). They describe their devastation at his death.

Jesus listens. He hears them out, allowing them the balm of articulation. And then—when they're done—he tells the story back to them, and as he does so, the story changes. In his retelling, it becomes bigger, deeper, older, wiser, and richer than the travelers on the Emmaus road understood. "Here's what you're leaving out," Jesus seems to say. "Here's what you're missing."

When Jesus tells the story, he restores both its context and its glory. He grounds the story in memory, tradition, history, and Scripture. He helps the travelers comprehend their place in the narrative that long precedes them, a narrative big enough to hold and transcend their disappointment. When Jesus tells the story, the death of the Messiah finds its place in a sweeping, cosmic arc of redemption, hope, and divine love that spans the centuries. When Jesus tells the story, the hearts of his listeners burn.

For me, the experience of the Emmaus road begins with a narrowing of my story. My lens becomes very small, very myopic. I lose all sense of the big picture and neglect to place my life in the broader, more expansive context of God's all-encompassing Story. Like Cleopas and his companion, I need Jesus to meet me on the Emmaus road. I need him to weave memory, context, pattern, purpose, and history back into the tiny narratives I cling to. I need the eternal Word to enliven my words.

"But we had hoped the story was bigger. We had hoped it would have a better ending." Well, it is. And it does.

*I notice the freedom to leave.* When the travelers reach Emmaus, Jesus gives them the option to continue on without him. In fact, he makes as if he's leaving, placing them in a position where they have to be intentional and definitive regarding him. Do they want him to stay? Are they willing to host a stranger in their home? Do they wish to go deeper with this man who makes their hearts burn, or are they content to return to their ordinary lives without learning more?

I always shudder a little bit when I get to this part of the story. What would have happened if Cleopas and his companion said goodbye to Jesus when they reached their house? How would their story have ended if Jesus walked away? The companions would have missed so much. The Messiah they thought they knew and loved would have remained a stranger. They would not have experienced the intimate knowing of the broken bread, the shared cup. The joy of resurrection would have eluded them.

I'm perpetually surprised by Jesus's commitment to my freedom. He will not impose. He will not overpower. He will not coerce. He'll make as if he's moving on, giving me space, time, and freedom to decide what I want. Do I desire to go deeper? Am I ready to get off the road of my failures and defeats? Am I willing to let the guest become host? Do I really want to know who the stranger is?

"Stay with us" (v. 29). That's what Cleopas and his companion say to Jesus. Stay with us. An invitation. A welcome. The words Jesus waits to hear.

*I notice the smallness of things.* Once Jesus and his companions are seated around the table, Jesus takes bread. He takes, blesses, breaks, and gives. So small a thing. So small a thing that changes everything.

Sometimes, it's hard for us to trust in the transformative power of small things. A bit of bread. A sip of wine. A common table. A shared meal. But the Emmaus story speaks to this power—the power of the small and commonplace to reveal the divine. God shows up during a quiet evening walk on a backwater road. God is made known around our dinner tables. God reveals God's self when we take, bless, break, and give. God is present in the rhythms and rituals of our ordinary days.

What does this mean right now? It means God is in the text you send to a lonely neighbor. God is in the phone call, the greeting card, the bouquet of flowers near the bed in the hospital room. Jesus is the stranger you see across the street when you walk your dog. The sacred is in the conversation you have with your stir-crazy child, the silence of the church sanctuary before the first organ chord, the loved one who challenges you to reframe the story of these days in the light of God's inexplicable provision. If the Emmaus story tells us anything, it tells us that the risen Christ is not confined in any way by the seeming smallness of our lives. Wherever and whenever we make room, Jesus comes.

"But we had hoped." Yes, we had. Of course we had. So very many things are different than we hoped they'd be. And yet. The stranger who is the Savior still meets us on the lonely road to Emmaus. The guest who becomes our host still nourishes us with Presence, Word, and Bread.

So keep walking. Tell the story, honor the stranger, and attend to your burning heart. Christ is risen. He is no less risen on the road to Emmaus than he is amidst trumpet fanfares and flowered crosses. Look for him. Listen for him. Welcome him. When he lingers at your door, honoring your freedom, but yearning to feed you, say what he longs to hear: "Stay."

# You Know Everything

John 21:1–19

*He said to him the third time, "Simon son of John, do you love me?" Peter felt hurt because he said to him the third time, "Do you love me?" And he said to him, "Lord, you know everything; you know that I love you." Jesus said to him, "Feed my sheep." (John 21:17)*

Here's a composite memory: I am five, eight, twelve, sixteen years old. I've sassed my mother or lied to my father. I've ruined a new dress, stayed out too late, misbehaved in church, or ignored my chores. I've failed in some way, trivial or terrible, and I've been caught. But the most painful part of the memory is not the discovery. It's what happens after I'm caught, after I apologize, after I'm punished and sent to my room. The darkest part is the shame.

I didn't grow up in a home or culture that practiced restoration. Despite my family's best intentions, we never found our way to the language of grace. We didn't say, "I forgive you," or, "It's okay," or "Let's talk things out." Instead, we abandoned each other to silence. We withdrew affection to re-establish honor. We avoided eye contact, shut down conversation, and rendered both offense and offender invisible.

Eventually, after hours, days, or weeks—depending on the severity of the sin—the ice thawed, and life returned to a bruised normal. But wounds still festered beneath the surface.

The story of Peter's "reinstatement" begins with a shame so thick, it makes me cringe. It begins with the disciple Peter battling his humiliation on a fishing boat in the Sea of Tiberias. This is Peter the Rock. Peter who fell to his knees after a miraculous catch of fish. Peter who proclaimed Jesus the Son of God before any other disciple dared. Peter whose mother-in-law Jesus healed. Peter who walked on water. Peter who saw Jesus transfigured on a mountaintop. Peter who promised to stay by Jesus, no matter what. Peter whose courage failed so catastrophically around a charcoal fire one

198

night that he likely expected to spend the rest of his life fleeing that searing memory: "Hey! I saw you with Jesus! You must be one of his followers."

"No. No, I am not! I swear, I don't even know the man."

In John's Gospel account, a wounded Peter returns to his fishing boat after he abandons Jesus. Isn't that what we all do when we're ashamed? Retreat to whatever is safe, comfortable, and familiar? Run headlong towards anything that will help us feel competent and worthy? Peter flees to his boat, his nets, his vocation before Jesus. As if there is some time or place in his life where shame is not. Where his wound is not. Where Jesus is not.

But of course, there is no time or place in our stories where Jesus isn't. He is just as present in our fleeing as he is everywhere else. It's not Jesus who draws out our humiliation and maximizes our penance; that stuff is on us. It's on our flawed theologies. Our voyeuristic obsession with other people's failures. Our need to shame wrongdoers in order to feel pure ourselves. Jesus doesn't have those flaws, obsessions, or needs; his will is reconciliation, and his pleasure is grace.

But Peter doesn't know this, so he spends a long night trying to catch fish without Jesus, and he fails. Dawn breaks, Jesus shows up, a miraculous catch follows a night of futility, and Peter finds himself, breathless and soaked, sitting by a charcoal fire. Again. Looking into the eyes of the Lord he thrice denied. Again. Facing three costly questions. Again.

What I find both searing and instructive in this story is the way Jesus saves Peter by returning him to the source of his shame. He doesn't wrap the humiliated disciple in gauze. He doesn't avoid the hard conversation. He doesn't pretend that Peter's denials didn't happen and didn't wound. But neither does Jesus preach, condemn, accuse, or retaliate. He *feeds*. He feeds Peter's body and then he feeds Peter's soul. He surrounds the self-loathing disciple with tenderness and safety, inviting him to revisit his shame for the sake of healing, restoration, and commissioning: "Do you love me? Do you love me? Do you love me? Feed my sheep" (v. 17).

As I meditate on Peter's story, I wonder what our failures would feel like if we offered each other the safety Jesus offers his disciple. The safety to return to the heart of our wrongdoing and despair. The safety to wrap fresh language around our failures. The safety to experience unconditional love in the midst of our shame, so that we can try again. What would our witness look like if the church epitomized Jesus's version of reconciliation? What would the world be like if Christians were known as the people to run to in times of humiliation? If we offered ourselves as sanctuaries for the shamed?

Around the fire Jesus builds, Peter's fear and denial ("I don't know the man!") evolves into trust and worship: "Lord, you know everything. You know that I love you" (v. 17). In the end, Peter realizes that it's what *Jesus* knows that matters. Jesus knows that we're more than our worst failures and betrayals. He knows that we're prone to shame and self-hatred. He knows that we flee when we're afraid. And he knows how to build the fire and prepare the meal that will bring us back to our true selves.

Jesus's appearance to Peter—like all of the post-resurrection appearances the Gospels record—speaks volumes about God's priorities. In the days following the resurrection, Jesus feeds, restores, and strengthens his friends. He calls Mary Magdalene by name as she cries. He offers a testimony of scars to the skeptical Thomas. He grills bread and fish for his hungry disciples. He faces what's festering between his heart and Peter's.

Jesus focuses on relationship. On reconciliation. On love. He spends the last days before his ascension delivering his children from despair, self-hatred, and paralysis. He lingers on a lonely beach till dawn, waiting for his hungry children to realize how much they need him. He feeds and tends his sheep. He restores both dignity and possibility.

Peter's shame meets Jesus's grace, and Jesus's grace wins. That's the Gospel story at its core. As writer and research professor Brené Brown puts it, "Shame cannot survive being spoken."[1] Shame cannot survive the living Word. Shame cannot tolerate the resurrection. When shame encounters the God who is Love, it burns down to ash and scatters.

1. Brown, in Okura, "Brené Brown On Shame," para. 7.

# Bibliography

Bass, Diana Butler. *Christianity after Religion: The End of Church and the Birth of a New Spiritual Awakening.* New York: HarperOne, 2013.

Bolz-Weber, Nadia. *Pastrix.* New York: Jericho, 2013.

Borg, Marcus J., and John Dominic Crossan. *The Last Week: What the Gospels Really Teach about Jesus's Final Days in Jerusalem.* New York: HarperOne, 2007.

Boyle, Gregory. *Tattoos on the Heart: The Power of Boundless Compassion.* New York: Free, 2010.

Buechner, Frederick. *The Magnificent Defeat.* New York: HarperCollins, 1966.

———. *A Room Called Remember.* New York: HarperCollins, 1984.

Dillard, Annie. *Three by Annie Dillard.* New York: HarperPerennial, 1990.

Eliot, T.S. *The Four Quartets.* New York: Houghton Mifflin, 1943.

Evans, Rachel Held. *Inspired: Slaying Giants, Walking on Water, and Loving the Bible Again.* Nashville: Nelson, 2018.

Gordon, Mary. *Reading Jesus.* New York: Pantheon, 2009.

Lawton, Kim. "Frederick Buechner Extended Interview." *PBS*, April 18, 2003. https://www.pbs.org/wnet/religionandethics/2003/04/18/april-18-2003-frederick-buechner-extended-interview/8658/.

Levine, Amy-Jill. *Short Stories by Jesus: The Enigmatic Parables of a Controversial Rabbi.* New York: HarperOne, 2015.

Mohn, Bent. "Talk with Isak Dinesen." *New York Times*, November 3, 1957.

Norris, Kathleen. *The Cloister Walk.* New York: Riverhead, 1996.

Okura, Lynn. "Brené Brown On Shame: 'It Cannot Survive Empathy.'" *HuffPost*, August 26, 2013. Brown, Brené. "Huffpost Interview." https://www.huffpost.com/entry/brene-brown-shame_n_3807115.

Palmer, Parker. "The Soul in Depression." *On Being with Krista Tippett*, February 4, 2021. https://onbeing.org/programs/the-soul-in-depression/#transcript.

Rilke, Rainer Maria. *Letters to a Young Poet.* New York: Dover, 2012.

Rohr, Richard. *The Universal Christ: How a Forgotten Reality Can Change Everything We See, Hope For, and Believe.* New York: Convergent, 2019.

Stern, Chaim. "'Tis a Fearful Thing." In *Mishkan T'fillah for a House of Mourning*, edited by Hara E. Person and Elaine Zecher, 16b. Philadephia: CCAR, 2007.

Stevenson, Bryan. *Just Mercy: A Story of Justice and Redemption.* New York: Spiegel and Grau, 2015.

Taylor, Barbara Brown. *An Altar in the World.* New York: HarperOne, 2009.

TED Blog Video. "Two Monkeys Were Paid Unequally: Excerpt from Frans de Waal's TED Talk." YouTube video, 2:43. April 4, 2013. https://www.youtube.com/watch?v=meiU6TxysCg.

Teresa of Avila. *The Life of St. Teresa.* Translated by Alice Lady Lovat. California: Herbert and Daniel, 1912.

Vuong, Lily C. *The Protoevangelium of James.* Eugene, OR: Cascade, 2019.

Williams, Rowan. *Tokens of Trust: An Introduction to Christian Belief.* Louisville: Westminster John Knox, 2007.

Wiman, Christian. *My Bright Abyss: Meditation of a Modern Believer.* New York: Farrar, Straus and Giroux, 2013.

Wren, Brian. "Good Is the Flesh." In *Good Is the Flesh: Body, Soul and Christian Faith,* edited by Jean Denton, 6. Harrisonburg: Morehouse, 2005.

# Scripture Index

Made in the USA
Columbia, SC
05 November 2024

45708204R00133